EMPIRE BETWEEN THE LINES

EMPIRE
BETWEEN THE LINES

IMPERIAL CULTURE IN BRITISH AND FRENCH
TRENCH NEWSPAPERS OF THE GREAT WAR

ELIZABETH STICE

University of Nebraska Press

Lincoln

A previous version of "The Imperial Periscope: Germany through the Lens of Empire in British and French Great War Trench Newspapers" was originally published in *Angermion*, Vol. 7, Issue 1, December 2014, pp. 91–104.

A previous version of "Men on the Margins: Representations of Colonial Troops in British and French Trench Newspapers" was originally published in *Journal of Military History*, April 2019, Vol. 82, No. 2, pp. 435–54.

The University of Nebraska Press is part of a land-grant institution with campuses and programs on the past, present, and future homelands of the Pawnee, Ponca, Otoe-Missouria, Omaha, Dakota, Lakota, Kaw, Cheyenne, and Arapaho Peoples, as well as those of the relocated Ho-Chunk, Sac and Fox, and Iowa Peoples.

Library of Congress Cataloging-in-Publication Data
Names: Stice, Elizabeth, author.
Title: Empire between the lines: imperial culture in British and French trench newspapers of the Great War / Elizabeth Stice.
Description: Lincoln: University of Nebraska Press, [2023] |
Series: Studies in war, society, and the military |
Includes bibliographical references and index.
Identifiers: LCCN 2022034429
ISBN 9781496234070 (hardback)
ISBN 9781496235954 (epub)
ISBN 9781496235961 (pdf)
Subjects: LCSH: World War, 1914–1918—Journalism,
Military—Great Britain. | World War, 1914–1918—Journalism,
Military—France. | Soldiers' writings, English—
History and criticism. | Soldiers' writings, French—History
and criticism. | Imperialism. | BISAC: HISTORY /
Europe / Great Britain / 20th Century |
HISTORY / Wars & Conflicts / World War I
Classification: LCC D633 .S75 2023 |
DDC 940.3/41—dc23/eng/20230110
LC record available at https://lccn.loc.gov/2022034429

Set in Vesper.

In memory of Allison Lee, 1982–1997

CONTENTS

ACKNOWLEDGMENTS

This book is the product of research and writing made possible by access to archives, supervision by excellent scholars, and the encouragement of friends and family. Much credit goes to Walter Adamson, Kathryn Amdur, and Brian Vick at Emory University. During my time at Emory, I also benefited greatly from the friendship of Erica Bruchko, Sean Byrnes, Husseina Dinani, and Sergio Gutiérrez-Negrón. At the University Hawai'i, I grew under the guidance of Jerry Bentley, Peter Hoffenberg, and Louise McReynolds. I am grateful to the many people over the years who inspired me to pursue history as a profession, especially Bernardo Michael. I am thankful for all the people I know in West Palm Beach, Florida, who live with my historical observations and have supported my professional development. My parents and sisters were my first companions in learning about history, and my family remains my greatest source of support. Most of all, I am humbled and inspired by the courage and creativity of the Great War trench authors, some of whose words are found in this book.

EMPIRE BETWEEN THE LINES

Introduction

Fog of war is a term used to describe the confusion of the experience of war and the limitations of awareness and memory, even for participants. A soldier may be haunted by a battle for the rest of his life but forget seemingly crucial details or misremember the order of events. The practice of history, too, has its own fog. Though over a century has passed since the Great War—with a century's worth of books—there remain aspects of soldiers' experiences and the nature of the war that deserve a closer look. This book is fundamentally concerned with British and French soldiers' discourses of empire during the war.

Though the Great War was sparked and fueled by nationalism, it was ultimately a struggle between empires. The shots fired in Sarajevo echoed around the globe, mobilizing citizens and subjects across continents and within European empires. During and immediately after the Great War, a number of books examined the extranational context of the war or the involvement of colonial troops. Several of those books were produced by governments, with the use of official documents, or by men who had some direct relationship to the war.[1] And then, for nearly a century, empire mostly disappeared into the fog. Nearing the centenary of the conflict, scholarship reaffirmed the centrality of empire to the Great War. Historians explored the ways in which the war contributed to nationalism in the colonies and Dominions within the British Empire and looked anew to the war outside Europe.[2] Some historians have also attempted to present an overarching view of the war with attention to empire. Hew Strachan's *The First World War: Volume I: To Arms* is a particularly rich example.[3] Even more exciting have been the informative histories that significantly enrich our understanding of the colonial experience of the war. Among the works that stand out are Joe Lunn's *Memoirs of the Maelstrom: A Senegalese Oral History of the First World War* (1999) and David Omissi's *Indian Voices of the Great War, Soldiers' Letters, 1914–1918* (1999).[4] This trend continued into the new century, with works like Richard Fogarty's *Race & War in France: Colonial Subjects in the French Army, 1914–1918* (2008); *The World in World Wars: Experiences, Perceptions and Perspectives from Africa and Asia*, edited by Heike Liebau, Katrin Bromber, Katharina Lange, Dyala Hamzah, and Ravi Ahuja (2010); and *Race, Empire and First World War Writing*, edited by Santanu Das (2011), among others. The British public school boys, whose memoirs once dominated the telling of the war, are facing increasing competition. The imperial side of the Great War is now one of the richest areas of war scholarship.

The dominant trend in recent scholarship on the Great War and empire has been to supplement or decenter (or both) the European narratives with the war experiences of citizens and subjects from outside Europe. Just as Dipesh Chakrabarty called for scholars to "provincialize Europe," historians have turned to previously neglected voices and stories from the war.[5] But few, if any, works have considered the ways in which the Great War was an imperial experience for metropolitan soldiers. In fact, soldiers' own wartime words and writings were very revealing on the matter. Though empire was not the dominant theme of soldiers' writings during the war, it was a persistent narrative thread. This book seeks to decenter Europe by refusing to consider the experiences of the British and French in the Great War as separable from empire. In this way, this project is in keeping with some of the essays in *Race, Empire and First World War Writing* and the work of Tyler Stovall.[6] It "brings empire home" in a way that the war itself did. By interrogating the relationship between European soldiers and empire during the war, this book brings together the study of the war's relationship to empire with the study of imperial culture.

More than any other conflict, soldiers' writings have played a central role in the image and understanding of the Great War. In the March 20, 1916, issue of the trench newspaper *Wipers Times*, a "Notice" read, "We regret to announce that an insidious disease is affecting the Division, and the result is a hurricane of poetry. Subalterns have been seen with a notebook in one hand, and bombs in the other absently walking near the wire in deep communion with the muse. Even Quartermasters with books, note, one, and pencil, copying, break into song while arguing the point re boots gum, thigh."[7] The hurricane of soldier poetry was accompanied by a monsoon of prose. And it has been followed by a century of scholarship about war authors. From the "war boom" of 1929–30 and its bestselling books to Paul Fussell's monumental work, *The Great War and Modern Memory*, soldiers' voices, through literature, have seemingly always shaped the memory and understanding of the Great War.[8] Samuel Hynes even called the war a great "imaginative event." Much of the focus on European soldiers' imagination has been devoted to the horrors of war and the production of poetry and memoirs. This book turns to a less-studied phenomenon of war literature—trench newspapers, also known as trench magazines, or *journaux des tranchées*. In 1915 *Le Temps* informed its readers about the amusing "*journaux du front*" that soldiers had begun to circulate, which should be considered "precious documents on the morale and spirit" of French troops during the "war of 1914–1915."[9] Characterized by "imagination" and "mischief," trench newspapers were a public discourse of the trenches, produced during the war, by and for soldiers. As Graham Seal wrote in *The Soldiers' Press*, trench newspapers reveal the "communal response of those in the trenches to their experience of war."[10] They offer insight about attitudes toward empire that works by individual authors cannot.

This book seeks to add to existing scholarship on trench newspapers and war literature through analysis of imperial culture in wartime writing. The foundational works on British and French trench papers are J. G. Fuller's *Troop Morale and Popular Culture in the British and Dominion Armies 1914–1918* (1990) and Stéphane Audoin-Rouzeau's *Men at War 1914–1918: National Sentiment and Trench Journalism in France during the First World War* (1992, English). Both books established trench newspapers as a significant wartime phenomenon and looked at the role of morale during the war, with Audoin-Rouzeau specifically investigating the role of national sentiment in sustaining the will to fight. More recently, additional scholars have drawn attention to trench papers and relations between them. In 2011 Robert Nelson's *German Soldier Newspapers of the First World War* described German papers. And Graham Seal's 2013 *The Soldiers' Press: Trench Journals in the First World War*, looked at papers in British, Canadian, Australian, New Zealand, and American archives for evidence of what allowed soldiers to endure the war.

This book breaks new ground in the study of trench newspapers by analyzing British and French trench newspapers together. Despite all the wartime collaboration and kinship of experience, historical analysis of Great War literature has often been limited to either the British or the French case. As far back as 1916, Edward B. Osborn suggested in the *Times Literary Supplement* that "there is a family likeness between all trench journals, whether they be of British or of French origin. One and all of them convey a vivid impression of humour and high spirits."[11] Not only were their papers similar and widely read, but Britain and France also fought alongside each other through the duration of the war, with assistance from their empires. British and French trench newspapers relate to each other in the same way that Jay Winter suggested capital cities were comparable in *Capital Cities at War*: "Comparisons are rarely possible on the basis of identical sources, and metropolitan history ran along similar lines in wartime. Finding enough coal for Parisians in the winter of 1916–17 was not very different from the same task faced by administrators in London and Berlin. Who had the responsibility to do so varied, as did the degree to which they succeeded. But the choices they faced were much the same."[12] The British and the French faced many of the same challenges and choices in the war. As Susan Grayzel wrote in *Women's Identities at War*, England and France were "two of the most significant participant nations," and whereas Grayzel wanted to "chart more effectively the resilience of Western gender systems," this book seeks to look at Western imperial culture.[13] Examining Britain and France separately does not do justice to the idea of "civilization" that they saw themselves jointly defending against German aggression and kultur.

British and French trench newspapers pair together not only suitably but also interestingly. The British and French empires both saw themselves as bearers of civilization, but there were significant differences between them. As Timothy Baycroft has noted, "France's position as a republic, and Republican attitudes towards the Enlightenment permeate French colonial discourse in such a way as to distinguish it from other European nations."[14] Rivalry also existed between the empires and, as Hew Strachan has shown, remained active during the war.[15] This book doesn't search trench newspapers for evidence that one empire was more or less oppressive or inclusive. Ann Stoler's warning in *Car-*

nal Knowledge and Imperial Power is crucial: "What could be more reassuring than the argument on which comparative studies of colonialism have thrived; namely, that differences in colonial policies derive from European distinctions of national character. In such a model, some country's legacy was always more benevolent, another's violences were truly atrocious, and yet another's integrative efforts were more effective or more benign."[16] Soldiers' constructions of empire in trench newspapers were more than reflections of national character or constitutional traditions, and Western Front trench papers are hardly empirical evidence of life in the colonies. This book is interested in the ways that empire provided a lens for metropolitan soldiers' views of the war and, in so doing, shaped their war experiences.

The investigation of the imperial experience of the Great War is necessary because empire is irreducible to a set of policies or a structure of rule. Empire was not a reified organization, but a shifting set of relations. As such, empire was a series of constraints and possibilities that influenced lives and perceptions in Europe and in the colonies; empire was experienced. This work follows in the footsteps of authors like Frederick Cooper and Ann Stoler, whose *Tensions of Empire* examines broader *imperial cultures* and considers the histories of *metropole* and *periphery* to be mutually influential and shaped by the structures of imperialism.[17] Scholars have drawn attention to how writing helped Great War soldiers to define and process their experiences and changing selves.[18] But the attention to empire in wartime writings, and how empire shaped soldiers' experiences, is a new angle that will further illuminate European soldiers' experiences of the war.

This book is indebted to the work of previous scholars to define and describe many terms and practices. It draws on the work of Jane Burbank and Frederick Cooper for their definition of *empires* as "large political units, expansionist or with a memory of power extended over space, polities that maintain distinction and hierarchy as they incorporate new people."[19] Both nation-state and empire rule through institutions, but a nation-state "is based on the idea of a single people in a single territory constituting itself as a unique political community."[20] Empires were geopolitical units identifiable to British and French soldiers and civilians, with discrete components, including colonies. Empires were existing political units to Europeans, but imperialism represented expansion, which was a significant distinction. As highlighted by Mira Matikkala in *Empire and Imperial Ambition*, even among anti-imperialists there was essentially little opposition to the settler colonies or the existing empire.[21] But imperialism represented conquest and could be viewed as inherently undemocratic in its expansion. While many Europeans viewed their empires as humanitarian (and even republican) endeavors, *imperialism* and *imperial* as methods or practices did not always refer to existing empires.

In looking at imperial culture, this book is aligned with David Cannadine's view in *Ornamentalism* that "Britain was very much a part of the empire, just as the rest of the empire was very much part of Britain" and the same was true for France.[22] This book, too, is interested in the social structures and perceptions within the respective British and French empires. It follows the orientation of books like Jonathan Schneer's *London 1900: The Imperial Metropolis*, which traced "imperial themes and messages" in daily London life.[23] Like other books on imperial culture, it is interested in the way that colonial practices and events shaped life in the metropole.[24] In this case, it is also interested in how colonial practices and events shaped life for soldiers during the Great War. Yet this book is also indebted to Bernard Porter, and his works like *Absent-Minded Imperialists*, and does not seek to overemphasize the presence of colonial content or overassume the importance of empire to

Entente soldiers from the metropole. In looking to decenter some of the traditional scholarly narratives of the soldiers' experience, *Empire between the Lines* does not want to decenter soldiers' own testimonies.

This book looks to the fraternity of the trenches for its views on empire. But who were the soldiers in the trenches? This book uses the definition given by Leonard Smith in *Between Mutiny and Obedience* that identifies a soldier as "someone receiving an order at the time he receives it."[25] This definition can include junior officers and is less strict than the division between officers and enlisted. But it emphasizes the community that is at the heart of this study, the men who went directly into harm's way and were primarily responding to, rather than giving, orders. This definition captures the men who spent nights in the trenches and could be ordered to go "over the top." This definition of soldier also correlates with the authorship of trench newspapers, as will be explored in chapter 2.

This project makes use of British and French trench newspapers and other sources in collections at the University of Pennsylvania; the Imperial War Museum in London; the Cambridge University Library; the Historial de la Grande Guerre in Péronne, France; and the trench newspaper collections at the Bibliothèque de Documentation Internationale Contemporaine (BDIC) in Nanterre and the Bibliothèque Nationale de France (BNF) in Paris, now hosted online through the BDIC. *Empire Between the Lines* centers on the discourses of British and French soldiers, from and within Europe, about empire during the war. Trench newspapers are the dominant sources, supplemented by some personal accounts of the war, both archival and published. In every possible case, priority has been given to accounts written during the war. Colonial and Dominion trench newspapers have been largely omitted from this project, in order to control its scope. British and French trench newspapers from non-European campaigns receive some attention in one chapter but are not the primary focus of this book.

Like a puzzle, each piece of a book bears its own image and shape, but the pieces must fit together to create a larger image. Each chapter of this book has its own role and its own investigation of the past. Some of the chapters have, in some form, been published before as articles. But together the chapters of this book work to explore the role of empire in shaping the wartime experience for metropolitan soldiers from Britain and France. This book has six main chapters, in addition to the introduction and the conclusion.

The first chapter, "The Great War in Imperial Context," uses mostly secondary sources to give an overview of the ways in which the First World War was an imperial struggle. This chapter addresses the fighting on non-European fronts, the use of colonial troops, the necessity of supplies from outside of Europe, and the role of the British Dominions in the war effort. This chapter explains how the British and French empires mobilized resources during the war and created new wartime networks of exchange and interaction. It also establishes the context of imperial culture in Britain and France at the time of the war and demonstrates, through analysis of trench slang, that the war reshaped imperial culture for Europeans in a way that affected wide numbers of soldiers.

The second chapter, "Who *Is* Christopher of Whisky Fame?," is a detailed look at trench newspapers. This chapter explains their significance, establishing why they are an important hidden transcript of soldiers' collective wartime opinion and distinct from postwar works or literature by individual authors. This chapter describes the format and nature of trench newspapers and their unique satirical approach to the war, highlighting why their humor makes them especially valuable sources. This chapter also explains the advantages of considering British and French trench newspapers together, by clearly identifying the shared traits between the papers, in contrast to some others (such as Germany's trench journals).

The third chapter, "Men on the Margins," examines representations of colonial troops within British and French trench newspapers. According to Alphonse Séché's book about colonial troops, *Les Noirs*, seemingly every small village hospital eventually had a Senegalese soldier, and his arrival was inevitably a sensation.[26] This chapter looks at the narratives and depictions of colonial troops in British and French trench papers, making the argument that while old narratives persisted, the war also created new narratives about colonial peoples that challenged existing imperial culture in Europe. Colonial troops, in particular, prompted thinking about empires and the geographies of their populations because the involvement of colonial troops brought colonial subjects to the heart of Europe, initiating new contact and consideration. Just as notes in the margins highlight a text, depictions of the men from the margins of empire in trench newspapers relate to larger issues. These included the influence of the prewar media on understanding empires, the ways in which soldiers established the "us" and "them" of the trenches, and soldiers' justifications for fighting in the war. "Men on the Margins" also highlights significant differences between the British and the French in the use of colonial troops. A slightly modified version of this chapter has been previously published in the *Journal of Military History* (2019).

The fourth chapter, "Other Fronts, Other Wars?," analyzes depictions of the fighting outside Europe, particularly in the African and the Ottoman campaigns. This chapter looks primarily at Western Front trench papers to explore the contrasts in how different Great War campaigns were portrayed, illuminating a wartime hierarchy of people and places. The chapter demonstrates that even while soldiers continued to place priority on fighting in and for European territory, there was interest in news about the other fronts and some awareness of the fighting elsewhere. This chapter documents the persistence of orientalist themes and a Eurocentric bias during the war. Unlike other chapters, "Other Fronts, Other Wars?" also examines some British and French papers from non-European campaigns, arguing that the cross-cultural contact created by the war challenged existing orientalist expectations for many of the European soldiers who served in Mesopotamia. Papers demonstrate an awareness of the gap between the tropes that soldiers knew and used and the world they encountered through the war, along with their actual experiences in the Near East.

The fifth chapter, "Why War?," outlines the justifications that British and French soldiers gave for war, in their respective trench newspapers. British and French soldiers argued that they fought for their countries and for civilization. Trench discourses surrounding home and nations indicate an important boundary for understanding the importance of empire to the men in the trenches. Entente soldiers from the metropole did not see themselves as fighting for empire. At the same time, the civilization that Entente soldiers sought to defend, and that they contrasted with kultur, had largely been defined in the context of European imperialism. The implicit relationship between civilization and empire is explored in this chapter.

The sixth chapter, "The Imperial Enemy?," takes a close look at descriptions of Germany in British and French trench newspapers. Always blamed for the war, Germany was alternately portrayed as an "imperial aggressor" and described comparably with so-called inferior races in overseas territories. Denigration of Germany in trench newspapers relied on similar tropes to justification for pre-war British and French colonization, such as dismissing kultur in contrast to Anglo-French civilization and suggesting German racial inferiority. Accusations of German imperialism repackaged images from the prewar media and scandals like Leopold's Congo. This chapter argues that descriptions of Germany demonstrate that empire had become a significant lens for interpreting and understanding the war and that while many Entente soldiers did not much question their own empires, the use of *imperialism* as an accusation of the enemy suggests cracks in the façade of imperial culture. A fairly different version of this chapter was published in *Angermion* (2014).

Together, the chapters of this book seek to illuminate the intertwining threads of war and empire. The book looks at the wartime constructions of *us* and *them* with regard to allies and enemies, while looking at the explicit and implicit constructions of empire within trench newspapers. The conclusion of this book provides some preliminary thoughts on the ways in which this study can be relevant to scholars of various fields and the future areas of research suggested by the findings.

This study contributes to a richer understanding of the ways in which the Great War was grounded in empire. Yet this project also breaks new ground. It explores the ways in which the war was an imperial experience for British and French soldiers, decentering the national European experience while remaining grounded in European history. This study also examines ways in which empire provided an interpretive lens for viewing the war, demonstrating that what has often been described as a "European civil war" was often seen by soldiers through the images and tropes of colonial warfare. This book also advances the study of trench newspapers, by considering British and French sources together and by exploring the role of empire within them. This is a necessary step to begin to understand, from within, the wartime cultures of imperialism and the visions of European empire and "civilization" that emerged from and survived the war, especially as they were understood by the public.

ONE

The Great War in Imperial Context

For almost a hundred years, the history of the Great War was like an old photo album full of evocative images. The first pages had the familiar black-and-white photographs of trench warfare in Europe. Pale faces peered out of the French mud and stared bleakly into the camera. Then there were photos of machine guns, tanks, poison gas, and aerial combat. In the margins beside the photos were poems and scraps of novels, and the occasional pasted news clipping. Yet a great many photos hidden away in shoe boxes were never included in the photo album. These photos showed the training and combat of colonial troops. There are also images of Africa, Palestine, and Mesopotamia. There are sands, jungles, the Tigris River, and a notable lack of trenches. For all its power to evoke memories and thought, until very recently the Great War rarely evoked the grip of empire for scholars in the West. For nearly a century, the voices imagined in the trenches were nearly all speaking European languages.

The centenary of the war marked an explosion of new scholarship. Much like Peter Jackson's documentary *They Shall Not Grow Old* (2018) colorized World War I film reels, scholars illuminated the war and focused in on almost forgotten aspects of the conflict. Empire received new attention by war historians, especially the experiences of colonial troops. There are now many excellent studies of colonial contributions and the experiences of non-European soldiers. Those books appropriately center the colonial experience.

Meanwhile, works that center the European experience often neglect imperial context. Few works consider that even for Europeans, the Great War was an experience of empire. One of the chief arguments of this book is that empire shaped the experience of the Great War for Entente soldiers from Europe.

This chapter briefly covers the imperial context of the Great War. The British and the French both utilized their colonies, Dominions, and protectorates for men and material to strengthen their war efforts. These soldiers and supplies played distinct roles in the fighting of the war that affected the functioning of empires after the war. Not only did soldiers and supplies come to Europe from all corners of the globe, but also a significant amount of fighting took place outside Europe. The nature and aims of the African and Ottoman campaigns reveal aspects of the war's meaning and significance often forgotten. This chapter outlines the ways in which the British and the French armed forces, and many of their aims in the war, were imperially constituted, to enable better evaluation of the place of empire in trench newspapers and in soldiers' perspectives on the war in the chapters to follow.

The Reach of Empire: Men and Material from Outside Europe

The Great War flexed the tendons of empires and affected the lives of millions of people around the world. To fight the Central Powers, the British and the French relied on their allies and drew on global resources. Colonial soldiers and supplies helped shape the course of the war and created their own legacies. Entente fighting forces were sustained by men and material from around the world.

India quickly joined the imperial war effort at the outbreak of war in 1914. Bhupendra Nath Basu, president of the Indian National Congress, suggested that for Indians the war was "an opportunity of showing that, as equal subjects of His Majesty, they are prepared to fight shoulder to shoulder with the people of the other parts of the Empire in defence of rights and justice, and the cause of the Empire, we must present to the World the spectacle of a united Empire."[1] That spectacle was significant; by the war's end India contributed 1,362,394 soldiers and noncombatants, 172,815 animals, and 3,691,836 tons of stores and supplies. Exactly 132,496 Indian troops were sent to France, 46,906 to East Africa, 588,717 to Mesopotamia, 116,159 to Egypt, 9,366 to Gallipoli and Salonika, and 49,700 to Aden and the Persian Gulf.[2] Lord Hardinge, viceroy of India, said, "The fact that the Government of India are in a position to help the mother country by the despatch of such a large proportion of our armed forces is a supreme mark of my absolute confidence in the fidelity of our troops and in the loyalty of the Indian people. I trust that this may be fully recognised in England and abroad."[3]

The Indian Army quickly proved itself useful in the war. At the start of the conflict, the reliable troops of the Indian Army numbered 155,423 men, including about 15,000 British officers and 45,660 noncombatants.[4] These Indian troops were recruited according to the theory of martial races, which suggested some people groups were naturally more suited to war, hence the prominent imagery of Sikhs and Gurkhas.[5] Though some Indians served as officers, most officers were European. During the war, the need for troops exceeded the old numbers and the old theories and brought the end of recruiting according to martial races. Yet expanding the army was a struggle against general reluctance to enlist for war among Indians. Recruiting measures became extremely coercive, especially in rural areas, and the Labour Corps met quotas by recruiting as many as fifteen thousand convicts through sentence completion in exchange for wartime service.[6] Within the Indian Army, many of those who served outside India gained a sense of empowerment, and Indians who served in Europe often returned with anti-British sentiments after experiencing better treatment at the hands of the French.[7]

A primary motivation for India's participation in the global war effort was the hope for greater rights within the empire. Many Indian officials expected to reach dominion status as a result of India's wartime support.[8] *India's Contribution to the Great War*, published in 1923, pointed out that following the war, India's Red Cross was "brought within the International League of Red Cross Societies and [now] enjoys the same status as has been granted to British Dominions."[9] The same was hoped to happen soon for the colony itself. Yet despite the prospect of gains, the war had its costs. India's financial contributions to the war effort caused the population to suffer under price and tax increases. India had shortages of all types, food riots, and forty cases of looting in the final year of the war.[10] Unsurprisingly, the war provoked a spike in the home rule movement and more extreme nationalist groups.

Even if India had not contributed men and material on a significant level, India would still have been a significant chess piece in global war strategies. Many suspected that the seizure of India was a German objective. At the very least, the Germans hoped to provoke trouble for the British Empire through Indian dissent. In addition to promoting the jihad against the British, Germany connected with and supported some of the growing Indian nationalist movements. The German Union of Friendly India trained and armed Indian nationals abroad and took propaganda to Indian POWs.[11] According to Mancherjee Bhownaggree, the second Asian to serve in the House of Commons, India had become the jury hearing the case for empire by Germany or Britain.[12] Even the military engagements in German East Africa were partially motivated by the need to protect the route to India. As the jewel in the imperial crown, India and its fate were on many minds during the course of the war.

While India's contribution to the Great War may be largely unfamiliar in the West, the participation of the Dominions of Canada, Australia, and New Zealand has long been the stuff of legend. The parliaments of these Dominions responded immediately to the outbreak of war by placing their navies under British command. They also "recruited and financed large expeditionary forces to ease the burden of the main British war effort in France," which was hardly new because "Australia and New Zealand both had an expeditionary military culture of war service for the British empire" and had sent troops to the Boer War, as had Canada.[13] For many in these Dominions, the sound of war was synonymous with the call of empire.

In the war from the beginning, Canadians experienced it in full. "In Flanders Fields," possibly the most famous English-language poem of the war, was written by a Canadian—Lt. Col. John McCrae. Canadians assumed their place in the war as participants in the British Empire. An anonymous contributor to the *Dead Horse Corner Gazette*, a Canadian trench newspaper, explained in 1915 that "imperialism is at last beginning to be understood. It is not a mere incident engendered by excessive flag-flapping, but is born of national exigencies demanding sacrifices by and for the people. True imperialism is too broad a thing to be hurt by petty jealousies and intrigues, too vital a state to allow the incursion of politics. Imperialism has ceased to be an empty phrase; it has become an actuality revitalised by national sacrifice."[14] That national sacrifice included sending 485,000 men and women overseas and losing 60,000 to war wounds, from a population of a mere eight million. In terms of supplies, in the final two years of the war, Canada manufactured one third of the British Expeditionary Force's munitions. Canada also supplied wheat, oats, beef, and draft animals to the

Entente forces and in 1915 alone spent "half a million dollars per day on the war."[15]

For many in Canada, the Great War was a defining moment. The heroism at Vimy Ridge was associated with stereotyped Western lumberjacks, men of great strength, valor, and rural ways.[16] The shock troops of the empire, these men were also the shock troops of the nation. For participants and historians, the Great War has been viewed as a turning point in Canadian nationalism—ushering in a sense of identity independent of the empire. Even skeptical historians cannot deny the actions of the Imperial War Cabinet in 1917, "classifying Canada and the other self-governing Dominions as autonomous members of the Empire with a right to ongoing consultation."[17]

The role of the Australia and New Zealand Army Corps (ANZAC) in the Great War was even more closely associated with nation building. Though Australia and New Zealand also worked with Japan to take the German colonies in the Pacific and sent men to the Western Front, stories of ANZAC participation in the war typically center on the fighting against the Ottomans, specifically in the Dardanelles campaign. This campaign has its own canon of film and literature in Australia and New Zealand. The film *Gallipoli* (1981), which tells the tale of the ANZAC troops in the failed campaign, even helped launch Mel Gibson's career. Heavily deployed to non-European campaigns and experiencing high losses, ANZAC troops made a name for themselves, and their experiences were seen as distinctive, in terms of battles and military culture. ANZAC soldiers were portrayed as "successful because their civilian, primarily bush, background fitted them for their role as soldiers."[18] Though soldiers for empire, ANZAC troops fit least with the authoritarian structure of the British military system and had high rates of disciplinary issues as well as more camaraderie between officers and the lower ranks.[19]

Great War in Imperial Context

ANZAC soldiers were portrayed as successful in terms of military service ideals but were also portrayed as youth wasted in battle by foolhardy, old generals. The massive bloodshed sustained in the campaigns against the Ottomans bred resentment toward the British Empire. The dramatic losses of ANZAC troops were not forgotten. In 1928 Australia celebrated its first Anzac Day, with a service of remembrance at 4:30 a.m., "the time when the first troops landed at Gallipoli," and by 1939 there were thirty thousand participants.[20] It was the beginning of a new tradition. Not only did ANZAC participation in the war directly lead to greater legal autonomy for the Dominions in the empire, but also the traditions that emerged around commemoration of ANZAC troops fostered nationalism in Australia and New Zealand.

Compared to the other British Dominions, South Africa's government was perhaps the most reluctant to participate in the First World War. The embrace of the British Empire was none too warm for those South Africans who had opposed the British in the Boer War. However, at the outbreak of war, South Africa immediately released six thousand imperial troops and promised to provide for its own defense.[21] Soon South Africa became more involved in the war efforts in Africa and Europe, despite the 1914–1915 Afrikaner Rebellion.

South African involvement was by no means negligible. By the end of the war, 146,000 white men and 400 white nurses volunteered, 45,000 Africans served as labor auxiliaries, 15,000 "Coloured" troops and noncombatants served, and 12,500 South Africans were killed in action or "died as a direct consequence of active service."[22] Those who served were recruited for specific campaigns: to German Southwest Africa, German East Africa, and Europe (with some diverted to Mesopotamia). Due to the 1912 Defence Act, the South African military was limited to white South Africans, and Africans were never welcomed as combatants. "Coloured" troops, however, were able to serve in the Cape Corps, and some were combatants. Not only did they serve in Mesopotamia, but also the Cape Corps was viewed by many as a means of achieving greater rights within the empire, and within South Africa specifically.[23]

Though most South African soldiers and noncombatants were active in Africa, they also made an impact in Europe. Approximately twenty-one thousand Africans in the South African Native Labour Contingent went to France between 1916 and 1918.[24] White South African soldiers in Europe were a trench spectacle, imitating Zulu war cries and intriguing British journalists, who regarded them as a "colonial ace in the pack."[25] Black South Africans also occasionally performed for the public.[26] Though South African soldiers were ultimately unprepared for trench warfare and by no means exceptional combatants, to some European observers these veterans of colonial policing and warfare were living characters from a Rider Haggard novel.

Smaller numbers of men from other places in the British Empire also served, or attempted to serve. A handful of soldiers were from Fiji, for example. Some men from Bermuda and the Caribbean also joined the British Army. Ray Costello's book *Black Tommies* highlights the experiences of British soldiers of African descent who faced a color line when they answered the call of empire. Nonwhite men from the Caribbean were often only able to serve as British officers if they were able to pass as white.[27] Anna Maguire's *Contact Zones of the First World War* explores the wartime interactions of men from the colonial periphery and includes the experiences of men in the British West Indies Regiment, who had distinct experiences in the metropole compared to men from Australia and New Zealand, including the Māori, on account of race.

Like the British, the French had considerable overseas resources to draw upon when the war began. The French

Empire was the second largest in the world, with a population of 44 million that spanned the globe.[28] Unlike the British, the French did not have white Dominions and had more limited European settlement in their colonies. However, the French Empire had a long tradition of recruiting colonial subjects for military and labor services. The French colonies and protectorates were a natural source of support when the Great War began.

The French began recruiting indigenous troops, known as *troupes indigènes*, as early as the seventeenth century in India. In the nineteenth century, African recruits were used in the conquest of French West Africa, and Algerians were also deployed in Crimea, Italy, and France.[29] Recruiting *troupes indigènes*, before and during the Great War, included conscription and coercion.[30] The French took over earlier conscription services in conquered territories and often instituted their own, with quotas for regions and people groups, which were often locally understood as a "blood tax." As with British colonial soldiers, distinctions were made regarding martial races—*races guerrières* and *races nonguerrières*. The famous *tirailleurs sénégalais*, in reality from all of French West Africa, were considered natural warriors, while others, such as the Indochinese, were considered better suited to labor and supply work. Colonial troops had some of their own officers but were largely under the direction of French officers, and during the Great War their battalions would often be mixed with the metropolitan French. This was due to belief in their need for European intellect and guidance in Western combat. When the war began, already approximately ninety thousand *troupes indigènes* were ready for deployment.[31] In the course of the war an additional five hundred thousand were recruited, from West Africa, Madagascar, Indochina (Vietnam, Cambodia, Laos), Algeria, Tunisia, and Morocco.[32]

French overseas possessions also made substantial material contributions to the war effort. To fight the war, France had to import much of the material needed to fuel its battle technology, including coal and oil, as well as cotton and raffia, most of it coming from the colonies. Many of the statistics regarding colonial supplies were not kept until 1916; from then until the end of the war, metropolitan France imported millions of tons of supplies of all sorts from its colonies. These contributions included 200,000 tons of rice from Indochina, 560,000 tons of oil from Senegal, and 240,000 tons of sugar from the Antilles and Réunion. North Africa provided 1.5 million tons of cereal, 3.5 million tons of mutton, and 27.5 million hectoliters of wine and also helped supply campaigns outside Europe.[33] The availability of these overseas resources and the sacrifices of colonial subjects and citizens helped France to endure invasion and made possible a struggle against Germany that might otherwise have been undersupplied.

Though in many ways the British and the French both hoped to use the colonies to offset costs of the war to Europe, the French had a somewhat different relationship with their colonial troops. In a 1904–1905 French military publication regarding the role of officers in colonial armies, it was suggested that while the English avoided the indigenous populations of their colonies, sipping cocktails in the most comfortable hotels in the European quarter, the French mingled with their subjects, enjoying the native quarters and throwing the idea of European prestige to the wind.[34] That was as it should be for the authors, who advised officers to respect their indigenous charges and learn their ways in a mission of love; indigenous troops were excellent when understood and well commanded.[35] Though colonial troops were often coerced to serve, believers in the French policy of assimilation suggested that soldiers were benefiting from the civilizing mission of the French and making cultural advances through service. Military service was considered part of the adoption of French culture.[36] It was a tradition launched in France with the Revolution itself, during the *levée en masse*.

French colonial troops were more directly tied to France proper than their British counterparts were. In 1910 the French general Charles Mangin published a famous book, *La force noire*, that advocated African soldiers as a remedy for France's demographic problems and military needs. This suggests somewhat permeable boundaries within empire, with populations able to substitute for each other. In contrast, the British were reluctant to use Africans as combatants of any kind and unwilling to assign Black soldiers to combat in Europe. Even the Indian Army was removed from Europe in 1916. In France during the war, Senator Henry Bérenger claimed that European France was no longer separated from colonial France.[37] This was an exaggeration, but the competing colonial ideals of assimilation and association gave French colonial troops more opportunity to participate widely in empire. While everyone in the British Empire was a subject, as many as 875,000 colonial French, of non-European descent, were citizens like their metropolitan counterparts.[38] Through the efforts of Blaise Diagne, a parliamentary representative from Senegal, Senegalese participation in the war became effectively a war for rights within empire—especially citizenship.[39] The contributions of colonies brought their people closer to the status of metropolitan French.

The experiences of *troupes indigènes* in the Great War were varied. Colonial troops were deployed to Europe, the Dardanelles and Macedonia. Those who were believed to lack the martial spirit saw little combat, while more "martial" recruits were often used as shock troops—the tirailleurs sénégalais were two-and-a-half times more likely to be killed than their metropolitan French counterparts.[40] Considerations of race and climate also affected wartime experiences. Those believed to be especially vulnerable to the cold were removed from the front lines to spend the winters in southern France.[41] Colonial troops, especially Muslims, were also subjected to more direct German propaganda—appealing to their faith and decrying French imperialism in their homelands. While most colonial troops remained loyal, the war considerably changed colonial expectations of empire, and *troupes indigènes* returned home consistently more resistant to arbitrary rule and seeking more tangible benefits from French presence, including citizenship.[42]

Many members of the French *troupes indigènes* and the Indian Expeditionary Forces entered the Great War with military experience. These colonial armies not only predated the war but also had been used in previous conflicts and "small wars." The Indian Army played a meaningful role in border conflicts on the subcontinent and had been sent to the Boxer Rebellion. African soldiers for France, like the tirailleurs sénégalais, had served in Madagascar, the Congo, Chad, and Morocco. An example of that continuity is the service of Bakary Diallo, who joined tirailleurs sénégalais in 1911 and was one of few African wartime combatant writers. His recently translated memoir, *Force-bonté* (*White War, Black Soldiers*), ties together his time in Morocco before the Great War with his time in France during it. It was all part of his military service to France, and, though not all colonial troops would have agreed, he considered that service and the empire noble. Even years later, he wrote, about his deployment to Morocco, that "the soldiers all stand together, ready to emphasize even more vigorously, if possible, how they respond to the call for the ultimate sacrifice from their adopted homeland, France."[43] For some colonial troops, the Great War was a continuation of military service to empire that began years before.

The participation of colonies, Dominions, and protectorates in the Entente war efforts ranged the spectrum from voluntary to coerced. Yet almost no part of the British and the French empires remained completely untouched by the Great War. The contributions of British and French imperial subjects and citizens were laden with symbolism but by no means primarily symbolic and often came at great cost to the giver. Aiding the war effort was seen as confirming and strengthening the bonds within empire, but political advocacy accompanied troops going to and returning from fronts abroad. Colonies and Dominions leveraged their participation with their place in empires, assuming greater responsibility within and independence from their empires. Respect shown to the empire could sometimes translate to respect gained within the empire.

The War beyond Europe: The African and Ottoman Campaigns

The fronts outside Europe are often obscured by grainy images of the trenches in France. Though significantly different from European fighting, the campaigns in Africa and against the Ottomans were allocated significant imperial resources and indicated the colonial ambitions of the Great War. While not the center of historical imagination, these fronts were not peripheral to the Entente aims in the war. In fact, the first and last shots fired in the Great War took place in Africa.

The aims of the African campaigns were relatively simple. Entente forces wanted to take the German colonies. German forces hoped to use fighting in Africa to distract from fighting in Europe and to drain resources from the British and French empires. From 1914 to 1915 the British and French together captured the German colonies of Togo and Cameroon, with the help of the Belgians in Cameroon, and with the French providing the bulk of the troops and receiving the bulk of the partitioned colonies.[44] During the same years German Southwest Africa was taken, primarily by troops from South Africa, accompanied by over thirty-five thousand African auxiliaries.[45] From 1915 to 1918, fighting in German East Africa took place between German and British forces, with the British taking significant territory but unable to capture elusive German forces, who surrendered only after the armistice in Europe.

One of the most significant differences between the campaigns in Europe and Africa was the composition of the military forces. According to Hew Strachan, "somewhere over 2 million Africans served in the First World War as soldiers or labourers, and upwards of 200,000 of them died or were killed in action."[46] The majority of these soldiers and laborers served in Africa, where they sometimes provided the majority of combatants and always the entirety of noncombatants. In the West African campaigns, the French utilized African soldiers and porters, drawing on their long tradition of *troupes indigènes*. The government of India was given the primary responsibility for conquering German East Africa, and the Indian Expeditionary Force (IEF) provided the bulk of British soldiers there.[47] Otherwise, the British campaigns in Africa were staffed by South African soldiers and African auxiliaries—unlike the French, the British used African combatants reluctantly, even in Africa. German forces were directed by German officers but consisted primarily of African soldiers, known as *askaris*. The campaigns in Africa utilized vast numbers of men, with the British using as many as 160,000 soldiers and one million porters in German East Africa alone.[48]

The nature of fighting in Africa was as different from the fighting in Europe as the composition of its forces. Artillery was limited, and armies kept tremendous numbers of porters and auxiliaries to carry and move supplies. In the case of the German Army, entire families sometimes accompanied African soldiers.[49] Terrain was difficult, and in at least one case, an attack was foiled by bees.[50] Disease and injury were significant hazards and created a near constant turn-over among soldiers and porters. The legendary Paul von Lettow-Vorbeck also contributed to differences in fighting style. Commander of the German troops in East Africa, von Lettow-Vorbeck fought with guerrilla tactics and eluded capture by the British when they were as many as seventeen times his force's number. Always one step ahead of the British, he even led his men into Portuguese East Africa. He finally surrendered on November 12, 1918, the day after the armistice in Europe.[51] Von Lettow-Vorbeck "had had experience of native and bush warfare gained in the Herero and Hottentot Campaigns of 1904–1906" in which he was a company and detachment commander and was wounded.[52] Histories of the campaigns in East Africa often read like narratives of his personal exploits.

The fighting in Africa was also shaped by the imperial ambitions of the Entente forces. The French were eager to expand their holdings in West Africa and prepared to engage in fighting in East Africa, as well. The British declined this assistance and gave the French the lion's share of the partitioned German colonies in the west in the hope of gaining a free hand in the east.[53] The prospect of gaining German East Africa revived "Cape to Cairo" dreams for the British. Further, some British officials thought that German East Africa provided a perfect opportunity for Indian colonization. As early as 1916, a secret letter from the Government of India suggested that "no other territory is so suitable for Indian colonization, none other so convenient of access, and there is already a considerable Indian population settled in the vicinity."[54] Others saw the opportunity, as well. In von Lettow-Vorbeck's memoirs, he recorded that "an Englishman captured during the war at Mahenge remarked that it would be possible to make East Africa into a second India, and I think he was right."[55] Throughout the fighting in Africa, Entente forces measured collaboration against colonial competition, seeking to limit the territorial gains of their allies while harming their enemy. Entente forces also had to balance war aims with management of their colonial possessions, like India and South Africa and French West Africa.

Apart from the futility of Gallipoli, the campaigns against the Ottomans often seem shrouded in Lawrence of Arabia's robes. Entente fighting against the Ottoman Empire was more extensive than many realize. The Russians met the Ottomans in the Caucasus. Together, the British and French suffered through the Dardanelles and Gallipoli campaign. The British, with some help from the French, also defended their interests in Egypt and launched offensive campaigns into Mesopotamia and Palestine. Simultaneously, the British worked to encourage Arab revolt against Ottoman rule. By the end of the war, the Ottoman Empire was effectively being dismantled.

Objectives in the Ottoman campaigns were very similar to the war aims in Africa. The Ottomans and Germans hoped that having another front would divert troops and resources from Europe, giving the Germans relief in France and against the Russians.[56] Initially, the Ottomans hoped to retake Egypt but soon "focused on maintaining control of the imperial provinces of Palestine and Syria as an integral part of the empire."[57] While the British and French began merely intending to protect the Suez Canal and India, their campaigns became more offensive and imperial-minded.[58] Planners of the Dardanelles campaign hoped to take Constantinople. The British also hoped to secure their interests in the Middle East, which included oil, by marching to Baghdad ahead of the Russians and taking Jerusalem. Though the Entente was partially thwarted by the League of Nations after the war, the Sykes-Picot Agreement demonstrates the extent of French and British territorial lust: "The Agreement gave Britain direct control over Lower Mesopotamia and the western/southern Persian Gulf littoral, and 'influ-

Great War in Imperial Context

ence' over a swathe of territory to the west (but not as far as the Mediterranean coast save at the ports of Haifa and Acre), while the French got direct control over the southern coast of Anatolia and the coastal region of Syria, including the Lebanon, and of a large portion of south-eastern Anatolia, and 'influence' over the remainder of Syria and northern Mesopotamia."[59]

The composition of troops in the Ottoman campaigns was significantly different from that of the Western Front. Most of the Entente fighting in Mesopotamia and Palestine utilized the Indian Expeditionary Force. As in East Africa, India was responsible for the administration of the Mesopotamian campaign. The French contributed ships and air support to various campaigns but were primarily a ground force in the Dardanelles. At Gallipoli, too, troops were often from the reaches of the empire—with significant Indian and ANZAC presence and French *troupes indigènes*. Though Gallipoli is an almost exclusively ANZAC narrative in popular historical memory, in reality, it involved a very diverse Entente fighting force.

Indian soldiers had an especially prominent role in Mesopotamia, during and after the war. In 1914 Indian Expeditionary Force A went to Europe, B and C were sent to Africa, but D, E, F, and G all were sent to face the Ottomans. By the end of the Mesopotamian campaign, "there were 113,000 Indian combatants in Mesopotamia and 183,000 followers, the latter including twenty-six Indian Labour and Porter Corps and a large number in the Inland Water Transport and Railways."[60] So significant was the involvement of India in this region, some in the British Empire considered it a potential location for Indian colonization.[61] And even after the war was over, Indian soldiers and laborers remained for some time. Radhika Singha has reminded scholars that "the segueing of global conflict into imperial geopolitics over 1919–1921 meant that 'the end of the war' was a very protracted event for Indian soldiers and followers."[62] That was especially true in Mesopotamia.

The fighting on the Ottoman fronts differed from that in Europe in many ways. Although Gallipoli had trenches, most fighting against the Ottomans took place without trenches. Navies and armies worked together in Egypt and in Mesopotamia. Weather extremes ranged from over 100 degrees Fahrenheit to below freezing. Irregular troops, such as Arab groups, were a feature of fighting in the Ottoman territories. The Ottoman campaigns also featured some of the most memorable British defeats. The Mesopotamian campaign experienced a massive defeat in a siege at Kut-al-Amara and a sad march to Baghdad which "cost 40,000 casualties, including nearly 12,000 captured at Kut, 4,000 of whom then died in captivity."[63] The Mesopotamia Commission, created later, found that the advance toward Baghdad lacked sufficient preparation and stated of the campaign in general that "no overall strategy or definite goals were ever formulated."[64] The Dardanelles campaign was such a spectacular failure that it led to a lull in Winston Churchill's political career. All told, in the Dardanelles campaign the British lost 37,000 dead and 83,000 wounded: 25,200 from Great Britain and Ireland, 7,300 from Australia, 2,400 from New Zealand, 1,700 from India, and 22 from Newfoundland.[65] Though their participation is often overshadowed in the English-speaking world, the French lost 47,000 killed and wounded.[66] The failures of the Dardanelles and Mesopotamian campaigns led to investigation by British commissions.

Despite the costs and poor administration, the Entente forces still triumphed against the Ottomans. Turkey surrendered on October 31, 1918.[67] Though often depicted as a sideshow to the fighting in Europe, the Ottoman campaigns set the tone for the twentieth century for many of the nations involved. In addition to playing a role in the birth of Australian and New Zealand nationalism, the campaigns against the Ottomans changed the power structure of the Middle East. When the smoke cleared from the war, much of the Ottoman Empire was on the path to independence, the Balfour Declaration was issued, and Wahhabi political forces were on the rise in Saudi Arabia.

Imperial Armies? Military Experience within Empire Prior to 1914

Whereas colonial soldiers and the African and Ottoman fronts were substantial parts of the Great War efforts, the focus of the war was in Europe, and the vast majority of its soldiers were European. Yet even these forces were in many ways imperially constituted. When the war began, the first troops to respond were expeditionary forces, organized for use in imperial campaigns. Within military leadership, many generals had risen to power and to prominence in imperial contexts. For example, the French general Joseph Joffre made his career in the colonies before the war.[68] So had Philippe Pétain. In Britain, General Herbert Kitchener entered World War I already famous for his activities in Egypt, Sudan, and the Boer War.

Many European soldiers had military experience outside Europe prior to the Great War. Like many other young men of his generation, Paul Pireaud, the subject of Martha Hanna's book on communication between the front lines and home front, *Your Death Would Be Mine*, had served in Morocco during his mandatory years of military service before the war.[69] Under French military service requirements, at least 60 percent of each age cohort was deemed fit to serve.[70] Considering early-twentieth-century French involvement in Morocco, Madagascar, Tunisia, Algeria, and French West Africa, in addition to the Far East, a sizeable percentage of French soldiers in Europe had imperial military training and experiences to draw on in European combat. The soldiers' first taste of warfare and of the military was closely connected to the colonies and protectorates. Robert Gildea confirms that "officers who saw action in the colonies and indigenous troops recruited into French units played a significant role in the war effort of 1914–1918."[71]

Trench newspapers make clear the prior military service and colonial experiences many soldiers had. Two of the killed officers mentioned in the June 1917 *Fifth Glo'ster Gazette* had imperial experience. Second Lt. H. E. Hawkins was "a rubber planter in the Malay Straits" who "immediately came to England and enlisted in the London regiment" when the war began. Major George Ward "served throughout the South African war as an expert on machine guns" and later settled in Johannesburg.[72] He came to London on holiday and joined up when war broke out. The Gloucestershire Regiment itself was part of the British Expeditionary Force, was associated with non-European combat, and had battle honors in the nineteenth and twentieth centuries from Egypt, Italy, India, Crimea, and South Africa. Even trench newspapers not connected to the British Expeditionary Force indicate that many soldiers had imperial military experiences. The Christmas 1915 *Lead-Swinger* included a memoriam for Colonel Wright, which featured this poem:

Fearless and without reproach, his life;
Gallant and without a stain, his death.
A noble English gentleman, whose breath
Was drawn from childhood 'mid the sound of strife
In India, with the Pathans, first he came
To know the "zipp" of bullets, and the need
Of courage, manliness and simple creed;
To give English rule a noble name.
Worshipped by all the men in his care,
Well-loved by every officer apart.
Brave to the point of folly, in his heart.
With every hero—honour be his share.[73]

According to the poem, Colonel Wright was a "noble English gentleman" but he was knowledgeable about the "zipp" of bullets from his time fighting in India, while striving "to give English rule a noble name." In the poem, Wright's Englishness and nobility are intrinsically related to his time in colonial military service. Wright was one of many in the British military with experience of the empire. The *Wipers Times*, the most famous trench newspaper of the First World War, was edited by Lt. Col. F. J. Roberts. Before he returned to England and volunteered for the war, the lieutenant colonel was Fred Roberts, a mining engineer and prospector in Kimberley, South Africa.[74] In a UK hospital paper, the *Stretcher Bearer*, a Lt. Mowbray Taylor praised the camp magazine and planned to send copies to the men at the front, "many of whom I knew years ago, and some were out with me in South Africa."[75] Even among men who did not live in South Africa, a number of British soldiers had experienced the Boer War, as had troops from other Dominions, including McCrae, the author of "In Flanders Fields."

Even those with no experience of the colonies or the military before the war would have been familiar with a connection between empire and military service. Between 1896 and 1914, British officers read *Small Wars*, a best-selling book about colonial campaigns.[76] More significantly, British and French civilians were widely exposed to colonial narratives involving military heroes. Apart from the Crimean War, all British wars between 1815 and 1914 were colonial.[77] The idea of the imperial soldier dominated the soldierly ideal at the outbreak of war. Edward Berenson's recent book, *Heroes of Empire*, looks at the media attention given to charismatic men in the conquest of Africa, covering the careers and fame of Jean-Baptiste Marchand, Charles Gordon, Henry Morton Stanley, Pierre Savorgnan de Brazza, and Hubert Lyautey. Stories about these men appeared in the penny press, boys' magazines, and illustrated periodicals.[78] Men like Brazza were the inspiration for memorabilia and kitsch including papers, pens, medals, and books. He also had a bust in the Musée Grevin.[79] Marchand, who went on to be a general in the First World War, was used by the media to attempt to unify France after the divisions created by the Dreyfus affair.[80] As Berenson writes, the French army was "a colonial army, an army of imperial heroes like Marchand, Gallieni, and Lyautey. The leaders of this more activist army, one that worked for the prestige and glory of France, had all cut their teeth fighting the endless and often brutal colonial war of the past decade and a half. They would lead French forces in the Great War to come."[81] Civilians and soldiers alike connected the colonial exploits with the Great War as it began. Tensions existed between Germany and France over Morocco from 1911 until the eve of the war, and, according to Berenson, many believed that "if Lyautey could defeat Moroccan barbarism with the promise of a humane, French peace, there was reason for confidence that other French generals—or perhaps Lyautey himself—would overcome German barbarism as well."[82] British and French civilians and soldiers alike had long been conditioned to understand their military in terms of imperial exploits. From music halls to magazines, the soldier of the imagination fought in colonial struggles. As men enlisted and were drafted for the Great War, their entry to the military was shaped by this imperial context, even if they fought only within Europe.

It can be argued that the armed forces in general were in many ways imperially constituted, even if many wartime soldiers came from Europe and fought there exclusively. The armies that began the war, particularly the expeditionary forces, were shaped by earlier imperial action. Much of their leadership had risen to prominence through overseas action. Soldiers with prior military experience were likely to have gained it within their empires. Those with no prior military experience were still influenced by the ideal of the colonial soldier and their knowledge of the imperial context of the army. Whether or not British and French soldiers envisioned the Great War taking them to the colonies, the colonies were the context behind their understanding of military life and traditions.

Conclusion

The scale of colonial contributions, the non-defensive aims of the non-European fronts, and the imperial experiences of European troops force us to recognize that empire was not a footnote in the Great War. Though the Great War has been understood as causing a spike in nationalism, recognizing the fundamental role of imperialism in the war compels us to reevaluate the relationship between nation and empire, especially as it functioned during the war. Gary Wilder has "tried to approach France as an imperial nation-state in which a parliamentary republic is articulated with its administrative empire to compose a single, albeit fractured, political formation that has exceeded supposedly national boundaries since its inception."[83] This type of approach to Britain and to France, especially during the war, can be helpful.

The Great War brought a significant number of colonial subjects and citizens to Europe in a variety of roles, initiating new contacts among populations and representing a short-term immigration challenge. It also moved colonial subjects and citizens within empires. These population movements took place within a context of imperial hierarchies and citizenship potentialities. The non-European fronts, and perceptions of their significance, were also connected to geographic hierarchies within empires. The valuation of Europe relative to other locales was not disconnected from the sacrifice of soldiers' lives and the perceived benefits of colonial possessions. A broader view of the constitution of armies and the locations of fighting will expand our evaluation of the war's effects beyond the impact of the Treaty of Versailles on Germany.

Soldiers' own language suggests that empire played a role in shaping their war experience. Trench slang was a mélange of languages, with many words borrowed from the colonies. The British Expeditionary Force entered the war with "its own language, a polyglot mix of words and phrases collected from decades of service around the empire, particularly in India and the Middle East."[84] That lexicon expanded during the conflict. For example, the term *chit*, for a piece of paper, came from Hindi, and the term *wallah* described relationships between men and assignments—like a "base wallah" or "mongey wallah" (for a cook or cook's assistant).[85] Soldiers from the United Kingdom also adopted terms from Australia, like *dinkum* for "good," and the habit of calling a shovel a *banjo*.[86] As more parts of the British Empire came into contact, imperial slang spread further. Australian trench slang also adopted and adapted words from Arabic and Hindi. For example, Australian soldiers referred to something genuine as *pukka*, from Hindi, and transformed the Arabic for "a damned fool" into *Andy McNoon*.[87] All of the troops involved in the war traded terms.

French war slang was also a product of imperial exchange. In his 1915 *L'argot des tranchées*, researched from soldiers' letters and trench newspapers, Lazare Sainéan identified "colonial terms" as one of the chief sources of trench slang. Sainéan observed that since the conquest of Algeria, colonial terms had made their way into French slang, sometimes only within the military and sometimes as far as Parisian streets. That process of adoption continued during the war. Among trench terms shaped by empire, Sainéan identified *bardin*, which referred to military baggage; *gourbi*, for a type of Arab hut; and *toubib*, adopted from the Arabic for doctor.[88] The celebrated *débrouillard* of the French trenches, an expert in the arts of *le système débrouille* (*Système D*), was one who could make do and get by on very little, who was creative and resourceful and a master at improvising on the fly. The famous term itself, *la débrouille*, like the now defunct *le débrouillage*, had been coined by the French Army in North Africa in the mid-1850s.[89] During World War I, it assumed a much wider circulation and came to represent the resilience of all French soldiers.

In his recent book, *War beyond Words*, Jay Winter argued that "language forms memory."[90] If it has formed memory, it certainly shaped experience. It is significant that the language of the trenches was the product of the languages of empires. For the French, two words for shelter even came from the colonies. *Cagna* was a colonial import from Tonkin, where it referred to huts.[91] *Guitoune*, which came from the Arabic for tent, referred to "a makeshift shack that was half dugout, half hut."[92] The very terms used for safer spaces at the front came from colonial corners of the globe. Soldiers' own language clearly demonstrates that empire shaped, in some ways, how they viewed the war and the world.

To some extent, that language gathered from empire may have reshaped how soldiers viewed their own homes. In a 1915 letter to his wife, A. J. Sansom, with the Fifth Royal Sussex Regiment, wrote about "Blighty," the soldiers' nickname for England. According to Sansom, Blighty "they say is really a corruption of a Hindustani word, 'Balati,' meaning the 'beautiful country.'"[93] Even those wanting to be invalided home to England were aware, to some extent, of the wider context of the war and the relationship of England to empire. The "they say" in Sansom's letter is where this study begins, by exploring soldiers' public discourse within the pages of trench newspapers. What was it they said regarding empire? Though it may not have been their primary focus, many soldiers wrote about their relationship with empire in trench newspapers. Those papers provide a location to explore soldiers' shifting perceptions of empire and hierarchies within and among empires during and through the prism of the war. Looking at British and French soldiers' constructions of empires and the people and places that comprised them during the war will help us understand the lived experience of European empires during the war and the two allied, yet competing, visions of European empire that survived the war.

TWO

"Who *Is* Christopher of Whisky Fame?"

"Who *is* Christopher of whisky fame?" This cheeky question was posed in a Things We Want to Know column of the April 1917 *Fifth Glo'ster Gazette*, a trench publication of the Fifth Battalion of the Gloucestershire Regiment. Things We Want to Know columns featured questions that needed answers and that highlighted the community of the trenches. The inquiries were typically gossipy, teasing, and lighthearted. On February 12, 1916, the *Wipers Times* asked, "Why the dug-out of a certain Big Man is so much affected by subalterns of tender years, and if this has anything to do with the decorations on his walls."[1] On September 18, 1915, the *Lead-Swinger* wanted to know "Why Sgt C . . . s looks so pale, and if unreciprocated affection is the cause."[2]

The *Glo'ster*, the *Wipers Times* and the *Lead-Swinger* were among many British and French trench newspapers created by and for soldiers during the Great War and circulated at the front. They were also sometimes known as trench magazines or trench journals. Headquarters may have encouraged some trench newspapers, but almost all British and French papers were initiated from below and were the result of writing and editing by officers and enlisted men during downtime.[3] The papers circulated on the level of the company, battalion, brigade, and sometimes division and could last merely a few issues or nearly the length of the war.[4] Trench newspapers solicited contributions from all readers, and issues appeared from weekly to monthly. Though soldiers had regular access to a variety of reading material, including letters, civilian periodicals, and books, soldiers still created their own publications for circulation. Though Things We Want to Know columns never provided answers, the *Glo'ster* and other trench newspapers of the Western Front can tell us a great many things we want to know about the experiences of men like Christopher and the ways in which they constructed understandings of themselves and their place in wider political contexts during the war. By investigating the public discourses of the men in the trenches, this chapter, and the book as a whole, contributes to the history of wartime literature, trench culture, and imperial culture, and the experience of the common soldier during the war. This cultural and discursive history of soldiers' ideas and attitudes can be set alongside existing studies of intellectuals, press, and propaganda during the war.

In 1917 *Le poilu* endeavored to explain the phenomenon of trench newspapers in a special English-language "Sammies" edition for the American troops joining the war. The editors wrote the following:

> This life in the trenches is hard. The spirit of sacrifice, the denying oneself all that helps to make life pleasant is one's daily task. Yet out of the surroundings of this fearful drama, which no language can depict, has sprung up a literature which is amusing, humorous and known the world over. We refer to the French Newspapers more familiarly known as the «Canards » or «Ducks » of the trenches. The ducks are not journalistic eagles, and do not try to soar, but if these ducks do not fly very high, they know how to keep going, and exist a long time. At the end of November 1914, there were rarely three or four. Now there are more than hundred [*sic*].
>
> Sammies, «Le Poilu» is contributed to by officers as well as soldiers. It is the work of all who are in the trenches and at the camps. It is a round robin letter where in each who

writes may give his pen full liberty. It is a chronicle of human living and interesting military doings, all in a humorous, jolly and amusing strain, with no allusion to war, religion or politics. Sammies you are part of a great nation which understands and appreciates humor. Why do you not help us to do for you what we have done for our «poilus»? Little by little thus, the bond of understanding and sympathy will be strengthened. We shall print bright and witty stories coming from America and from France. Thus will you boys, far from home, be diverted and amused. Do not think for a minute that laughter or smile is forbidden in this living drama on the front, in these circumstances, laughter is courageous, more than courageous. It is the best way to mock, to despise, to endure this sad war, as it reaps our comrades one by one.[5]

Le poilu had a typical understanding of the purpose of trench papers. In "The Why of Us," the *Pennington Press* explained its mission: "Our aim will be to uphold the honour of the M.T. in all paths; and to promote good feeling and fellowship in every way. Not being bothered with any political principles and with no axe to grind, we shall endeavor at the same time to instruct and amuse."[6] Full of literary references and local gossip, trench newspapers endeavored to bring a smile to war-weary comrades. In *Le poilu du 6–9*, a column about trench newspapers described them as "full of powerful reasons for hope."[7] Trench newspapers helped soldiers endure the conflict and build a supportive community in the trenches.

For a long time, war poetry and postwar memoirs and novels have intrigued scholars and general readers alike, while the trench newspapers of the Great War have been less examined.[8] In the 1990s two important works broke significant ground on the study of hundreds of British and French trench newspapers: J. G. Fuller's *Troop Morale and*

Popular Culture in the British and Dominion Armies 1914–1918 (1991) and Stéphane Audoin-Rouzeau's *Men at War 1914–1918: National Sentiment and Trench Journalism in France during the First World War* (1992, English). Fuller and Audoin-Rouzeau researched and explained the phenomenon of trench newspapers in detail, including authorship, methods of production, circulation figures, and other aspects. Their work helped to identify the value of trench newspapers as historical sources and began the conversation about their meanings. More recently, Graham Seal has taken a broad look at the phenomenon of trench newspapers among the British, Canadians, Australians, New Zealanders, and Americans in his 2013 book, *The Soldiers' Press: Trench Journals in the First World War*. Together, these works consider over five hundred Entente trench newspapers and share a fairly consistent overall understanding of them. All agree that trench newspapers played a significant role in combating despair and motivating soldiers to keep fighting. J. G. Fuller saw trench journals as part of maintaining morale, like sports and other entertainment would. Audoin-Rouzeau's work highlighted national sentiment and found that trench newspapers existed to distract "but also to bring a little beauty to life in the ugliness of war."[9] Graham Seal argues that "these extraordinary periodicals" were "a major reason for the willingness of soldiers to endure the palpable insanity to which they were consigned by forces beyond their control."[10] Audoin-Rouzeau, Fuller, and Seal all identify a significant role for trench papers in maintaining morale and, as a result, sustaining the war effort.

Trench newspapers were, in many cases, also a testament to soldiers' ingenuity. For a time, the *Wipers Times* staff used an abandoned printing press discovered in a barn, and *L'écho du boqueteau*'s editors famously built a rotary press using umbrella handles, while other newspapers used gelatin mixes, Roneo printing, or the services of printers away from

Christopher of Whisky Fame

the fighting to create copy.[11] Papers varied in size and ranged in length from one or two pages per issue to sixteen, and some papers reprinted many issues together in book form during or soon after the war.[12] Some papers looked very like their civilian journalistic counterparts, and others resembled homemade newsletters—some were even handwritten. Nearly all papers contained some drawings, but French papers often had more drawings than British papers. The physical papers relate to soldiers' sometimes limited access to materials as well as the scope of their imaginations and their literary awareness.

In *The Great War and Modern Memory*, Fussell commented on the "unparalleled literariness of all ranks who fought the Great War."[13] The literariness of the soldiers may surprise us now, but we should remember that in 1914, "except for sex and drinking, amusement was largely found in language formally arranged, either in books or periodicals or at the theater and music hall, or in one's own or one's friends' anecdotes, rumors, or clever structuring of words."[14] Trench journalism reflected understanding of existing literary conventions and cultural discourses. Whereas trench newspaper contributors displayed their own styles and poetic aspirations, British poems and plays often imitated well-known works and authors, such as the *Rubaiyat*, the Old Testament, and works by Kipling and Shakespeare. Serialized stories were modeled on Sherlock Holmes and other famous narratives. The French produced feuilletons of the trenches and imitated Voltaire and Rabelais. Trench papers elevated the literary efforts of soldiers. *Rigolboche* even invited "members of the Académie française to contribute pieces to run alongside work produced in the trenches," which led to "publishing the responses of famous intellectuals alongside the work of ordinary *poilus*."[15] Trench journalism offered soldiers an opportunity to see their words in print and appreciate them, which would not have otherwise existed.

Trench newspapers were a distinct product of trench culture across various dividing lines. British trench newspapers were edited by both officers and enlisted men, separately and together.[16] One-third of the French journalists came from the ranks, lower ranks such as corporals were half the staff, and noncommissioned officers and subalterns each supplied only a quarter of the editorial teams.[17] Higher-ranking officers represent less than 2 percent of the identified editorial staff.[18] Trench newspapers are especially but not exclusively reflective of the efforts of lower-ranking officers, but even when officers comprised the editorial board, papers accepted submissions from soldiers of all stripes. One issue of *Thumbs-Up* even advertised, "We want more contributors from the Rank and File."[19] According to Graham Seal, the trench press was "effectively a democratic cultural republic amidst a hierarchical martial regime, a militocracy engaged in the largest mass conflict humanity had known."[20] Both in contributors and in content, trench newspapers rested on republican ideals. Scholar Nichole Gleisner has found that "the trenches were a place where radically different aesthetics could sit side by side in the same newspaper columns, reflecting an utterly democratic notion of what constituted a writer."[21] Trench newspapers are uniquely reflective of the wide swath of soldiers at the front lines.

German trench newspapers have also attracted the attention of more scholars in recent years. Two books that stand out are Robert Nelson's 2011 work, *German Soldier Newspapers of the First World War*, and Jason Crouthamel's 2014 *An Intimate History of the Front: Masculinity, Sexuality, and German Soldiers in the First World War*, which uses trench newspapers in its analysis. Nelson's work is explicitly informed by Fuller and Audoin-Rouzeau and provides useful insight into German trench newspapers. Nelson also attempts some comparative insights regarding British and French trench newspapers in relation to German papers. There was a considerable difference between German and Entente trench papers. As Crouthamel points out, the Germans had more official army newspapers, which were more top-down than bottom-up.[22] Nelson suggests that German papers had less of a focus on entertainment and that the Germans had less shared popular culture to make use of than the British or the French.[23] British and French papers certainly referenced popular culture and resembled many aspects of the popular press.

Laughter Is Courageous

According to *Le poilu*, "in these circumstances, laughter is courageous, more than courageous. It is the best way to mock, to despise, to endure this sad war, as it reaps our comrades one by one."[24] In their own words, trench newspapers were humorous, literary, and diversionary. *Les boyaux* was certain that its readership had "enough idiots" to make it "*le journal le plus abracadabrant, le plus hilarant, le plus funambulesque du front.*"[25] *La marmita* was a literary review that was "*anecdotique, humoristoque, fantaisiste.*"[26] *Le mouchoir* advertised itself as "*artistique, litteraire, humoristique*" and the "*seul remède contre le cafard.*"[27] On its anniversary, *The Dump* told readers that immediately after its birth it had given "proof of its powers of eloquence and humor."[28] Some titles were themselves humorous, such as the *Lead-Swinger*, which took its title from a slang term for an exaggerator. Unlike official gazettes, trench newspapers were committed to a sacred union of literary aspiration and humorous content to fight the dreaded *cafard*.[29] Papers were always interested in witty contributions.[30]

In 1916 Edward B. Osborn suggested in the *Times Literary Supplement* that "there is a family likeness between all trench journals, whether they be of British or of French origin. One and all of them convey a vivid impression of humour and high spirits."[31] British and French trench newspapers shared a template, based partially on civilian satirical journals like *Le rire* and *Punch*.[32] Like civilian satirical papers, many trench newspapers included poetry, play parodies, serialized stories, illustrations, humorous correspondence, sporting columns, alphabets and dictionaries, and outlets for gossip. The references to satirical papers were implicit in format and often explicit in the writing, as well. For example, British papers often referenced the highly popular *Tit-Bits*, which "marketed short, miscellaneous, entertaining snippets of information and opinion" to a working class audience at a penny an issue.[33] The *"P.P."* referenced *Tit-Bits* as "our famous contemporary" and used its format in its column Tales That Are Told/Bagged Bits from Everywhere.[34] The *Lead-Swinger* regularly featured a section titled Tit-Bits Culled from the Stew.[35] The *Fifth Glo'ster Gazette* used the same format in its regular Bricks from the Editor's Pack section.[36] Other papers were also specifically referenced. Every issue of *Trot-Talk* offered "apologies to 'Punch' and 'Dicky' Doyle."[37] *Brise d'entonnoirs* echoed *Le rire* by even spoofing its regular advertisements.[38] The trench journal *Le klaxon* featured a column titled À la Manière de . . . , like the French parody book *À la manière de*, with pieces imitating Racine, Gabriele d'Annunzio, Chateaubriand, Stéphane Mallarmé, Paul Verlaine, Rudyard Kipling, and Charles Péguy, among others.[39] Humor was at the center of literary expression in British and French trench newspapers of the Western Front and shaped the format of trench papers to mimic the satirical civilian press.

Humor may seem to stand in contrast to the context of wartime violence, but laughter and violence are physiologically intertwined. Philosopher Anthony Ludovici pointed out that "when you have listed the significant aspects of the act of laughing (elevation of the head, baring of the teeth, emission of harsh guttural sounds), you have given the symptoms of an animal enraged."[40] Laughter is one way for the body to excise the symptoms of anger and rage. Laughter can also allow the release of tears. According to Havelock Ellis, the "most ticklish regions [of the body] correspond to the spots most vulnerable in a fight."[41] Thus the humor in trench newspapers should be seen in direct relationship with the violence soldiers were exposed to and committing. Humor helped soldiers to address the dangers of their situation while excising physical symptoms of violence and fear to curb excesses.

Humor was not just a product of the violent context but also a strategy for survival in that context. In his work on humor during the Holocaust, Steve Lipman explained that humor "means more than jokes or funny dialogue"; it is "a liberating sense of perspective" that includes "irony, parody, sardonic exaggeration, situation reversals, morbid twists on reality."[42] All of those characteristics were common in trench newspapers, which used humor to resist the deleterious effects of the war. Though there are very significant differences between the violence of the trenches and the violence of an extermination camp, in both places persistent violence threatened the body and the mind.

The humor in trench newspapers provided a type of relief from circumstances. The *Wipers Times* asked its readers in the Wednesday, August 15, 1917, edition, "Can you sketch?" The advertisement for drawing lessons included a testimonial: "The other day by mischance I was left out in No Man's Land. I rapidly drew a picture with a piece of chalk of a tank going into action, and while the Huns were firing at this I succeeded in returning to the trenches unobserved. Could You Have Done This?"[43] Though soldiers were unable to escape the violence of the trenches bodily, the jokes in the *Wipers Times* sometimes allowed them to escape mentally. Writing about his personal Holocaust experience, Viktor Frankl suggested humor was one "of the soul's weapons in the fight for self-preservation. It is well known that humor, more than anything else in the human make-up, can afford an aloofness and an ability to rise above any situation, even if only for a few seconds."[44] Frankl even remembered fellow prisoners so desperate for a laugh that they went to a camp cabaret, despite the fact it would cost them their daily food ration.[45]

Laughter also allowed soldiers during the Great War to acknowledge their situation without falling into despair. They faced the kind of "structural ambivalence" that sociologist Gary Alan Fine described in amateur mushroomers. "The desire to eat and the desire to be safe conflict with each other and must be repressed and dealt with through humor. Just as risk is a social construction, its resolution and control are created by people, who establish new meanings and rituals to deal with fear."[46] Eating wild mushrooms makes finding them worthwhile, but it also creates the risk of death. Individuals share jokes to acknowledge the risks and ambivalence, and when others laugh there "is a communal recognition that others have noticed the same dilemma—and that they haven't resolved the issue either. They respond through gallows humor directed at the potential of real danger."[47] Real danger was ever present during the Great War. In trench newspapers, soldiers commonly joked, and truly dreamed, of getting the injury grave enough to send them home permanently but without causing death or serious disfigurement. The prospect of a viable peace was inseparable from the continuation of violence until victory, especially for the French who were committed to regaining lost territory. There was also ambivalence about the military hierarchy, as Leonard Smith so well portrayed in his work on the French mutinies, *Between Mutiny and Obedience*. In his examination of the French Fifth Infantry Division, Smith found that authority was often negotiated more than military policy would indicate.[48] Humor helped soldiers to

Christopher of Whisky Fame

approach the structural ambivalence and absurdity of their situation in a socially acceptable way while developing "new meanings to deal with fear."

Military authorities tolerated, and sometimes encouraged, trench newspapers partially because they recognized the value of "grousing."[49] As Freud observed in *Jokes and Their Relation to the Unconscious*, jokes can offer the "protection of sequences of words and thoughts from criticism."[50] Trench newspaper questions not only teasingly identified individuals who might be failing in their duties but also often indirectly questioned military policies and represented a challenge to the methods of battalion headquarters. Humor helped trench authors avoid catching military discipline by cloaking rage and by sidestepping censors with satirical references. In his era, Erasmus argued that "if there is any way of mending men's faults without offence to anyone, by far the easiest way is to publish no names."[51] Many times trench newspapers took a similar approach. For example, the November 6, 1915, *Lead-Swinger* asked, "If the new 'position of attention' as exemplified by the hospital staff, necessitates retention of the hands in the pockets, and if certain N.C.O.'s do not set an excellent example."[52] This was a direct critique of certain NCOs and their treatment of the wounded that might not have been uttered in person or by name without risk of reprisal. Of course, not only did trench newspapers offer critiques of unnamed individuals, but also the critiques typically came from unnamed individuals. Anonymity and humor worked together to make observations and criticisms acceptable.

In his defense of his satirical masterpiece, *In Praise of Folly*, Erasmus suggested criticisms were best delivered by leaving out what is "repugnant to the ears of decent men"; one should "put everything into the mouth of a comic character so it will amuse and divert, and the humor of the spoken word will remove any offensiveness."[53] Likewise, trench newspapers typically used humor to avoid offensiveness even in criticism. One author in the *H.C.B. Gazette* ended a poem teasing various members of the battalion with the following lines:

> Your humble
> Resembles a bumble
> Bee, as the sort of thing
> That buzzes but doesn't mean to sting![54]

Humor in trench papers was an acceptable form of "friendly fire" used to make criticisms and complaints more tolerable for authorities and other readers. The British soldiers' paper *Thumbs-Up* suggested it was an opportunity for "various anonymous contributors" to "hurl 'bombs of satire' and 'shells of criticism' at their particular foes" and be answered in turn.[55] Humor in trench newspapers helped protect authors from sensitive readers and authorities.

Perhaps most obviously, soldiers used humor in trench newspapers to build and sustain community. Jokes were more than individual expressions; they linked readers together. As Freud perceptively noted, a joke must be shared; it is necessarily social.[56] A successful joke requires an audience, and shared jokes further social bonds. In July 1918 the *Glo'ster* asked, "Whether a certain Editor and Self-Advertiser now knows what under fire means? Whether he enjoyed the experience? And whether he now knows the meaning of 'Somewhere in Hell'?"[57] This comment separated the readers, who already shared the experience of being under fire, from someone who, presumably, had not. With limited circulations and coded references, the shared laughs of trench newspapers affirmed a shared experience. "Getting" the jokes in the trench newspapers indicated belonging in, sometimes specific, trench communities. The *Staff Herald*, a newspaper read by signalers, wondered "if our first issue was really a 'signal' success."[58] Other papers had more cryptic jokes and

Christopher of Whisky Fame

references to shared knowledge. The *H.C.B. Gazette* reminded readers that much of its contents would be "inscrutable to the wider circle of our readers, and inevitably not understandable to them"—it was intended "primarily for the amusement of the Battalion."[59] After all, a magazine like it would be "almost of necessity personal in tone" and full of "allusions to idiosyncrasies and eccentricities of individuals," however, not "a channel of spite" but meant to share a "spirit of friendliness and good feeling."[60]

Humor reinforced the boundaries of trench communities as well as the value of those within them. *Embusqués* were a constant target of wit in French trench newspapers. Meaning "shirker" or "slacker," the term *embusqué* was also occasionally used by the English. Attacks on embusqués gave the readers categories for "us" and "them" identities. At times humor helped delineate group boundaries in terms of nation, race, or gender, among other characteristics. *Le poilu* sometimes featured jokes about Englishmen. Jokes about the Germans were in British and French papers, which further distinguished already identified enemies. *Le bochofage* advertised itself as an organ "Anticafardeux, Kaisericide et Embuscophobe" (against cafard, the kaiser, and embusqués), clearly identifying its three main enemies.[61] Shared humor forged social bonds, and jokes were used to police the boundaries of the social unit.

Humor is a window into trench community, helpful for analysis of trench culture and soldiers' wartime beliefs. As writer Rudolph Herzog explained in *Dead Funny*, his book about humor during the Third Reich, through jokes "we get unusual access to what people really thought . . . what annoyed them and what made them laugh, and also what they knew and otherwise took pains to repress from their conscious minds."[62] Inside jokes and gossip and teasing show us how soldiers in the trenches related to one another and what were considered acceptable or outlandish behaviors.

Poetry and stories demonstrate the shared cultural references and accepted means of expression. Wit and satire show what could not be expressed openly, for a variety of reasons. Humor in trench newspapers shows us the means of escapism and, often, through implication, what needed to be escaped. The use of humor to solidify social bonds and form boundaries around communities can also help to identify imperial culture in trench newspapers and the ways it changed during the war. Very specifically, trench newspapers can show understandings of the place of different ethnic groups and colonial soldiers within the British and French armies and empires.

Discourses from the Front

If any opinion was shared across national lines by all combatants in the Great War, it was a dislike of the civilian press, the alleged sources of news and information.[63] The less than accurate war news in the civilian press was known as "eye-wash" by the British and "skull-stuffing" by the French. Like soldiers' letters and memoirs, trench newspapers bemoaned eye-wash and skull-stuffing, which they faulted for misleading the public and making it difficult for civilians to understand their soldiers.[64] A November 6, 1915, *Lead-Swinger* Natural History column related, "I myself have seen a Flemish cow attempt to eat a copy of the 'Daily Mail'; it managed the advertisement columns quite well, but when it came to the page of war news, the poor thing choked. There were statements there that even a Flemish cow couldn't swallow."[65] Under its masthead, the French trench journal *Le Filon* promised it did not practice skull-stuffing.[66] For many combatants, the civilian papers rendered their true struggles and identities invisible. At the outset of the war, Captain Edward Devonport Ridley of the Grenadier Guards told his mother, "You will not get the true story of each action, step by step, the moment they occur.

You must absolutely disregard all news not published as official. The vast majority of official news will probably be all right, but it is very likely that even official news will be untrue in many important details, such as *place*, numbers engaged and even units engaged. You see such news *must never* reach the *enemy* even a week old."[67] Ridley himself regularly received the *Daily Mail*, the *Morning Post*, and *Land and Water* in the trenches. Though he initially did not put the blame on journalists, as the war progressed, he became more strident in his criticism. In a later letter he suggested that "if those damned fool newspaper men knew what we thought of them, they would hang themselves quick."[68] Trench newspapers demonstrate the lost faith in civilian periodicals. In an anecdote from *Le rire aux eclats*, one soldier received a daily newspaper while saying, "Here is the news," and then another soldier sarcastically responded, "The news is what we make it."[69]

The trench press did not compete with the civilian press as much as they mocked it. In a 1986 interview for the Imperial War Museum, Col. Harold Essex Lewis was asked about the *Wipers Times*, "Was it a good source of news and information?" Lewis responded, "No, it was quite lighthearted—parodies and that sort of thing. Very original stuff in there."[70] Real news could be dangerous in the hands of the enemy, so it rarely appeared. But commentary on newspapers was common. A July 1916 *Glo'ster* article entitled "Startling Truth Discovery; From Phillip Fibs—Revelations of a Journalist" mocked Philip Gibbs and informed readers that "journalism is the stepping stone which leads across the flood of current affairs to Sensationalism. Sensationalism is Fame." For one interested in journalistic sensationalism there were five items of advice:

1. Never stir from safety. An O.P. in Fleet Street is best.
2. Write most of what you know least. This is an unfailing

maxim. It appeals to the general public who will believe you implicitly.

3. Remember there are only four kinds of soldiers in the British Army—Scotchmen, Londoners, Lads and Fellows.

4. Cultivate the use of adjectives. 'Brawny' is particularly popular. On an average at least every third word should be an adjective.

5. WRITE FOR FULL PARTICULARS OF MY SCHEME TO-DAY.[71]

At other times, civilian periodicals served as humorous inspiration. A French trench paper was called *La guerre joviale* after Gustave Hervé's paper *La guerre sociale*. Many French papers' titles began *L'écho de*, which was a riff on *L'écho de Paris*, the well-known paper with an almost-daily column by the nationalist Maurice Barrès. Puns on the names of famous war correspondents were common in British and French trench papers.

Trench publications were a distinct alternative to all civilian press, including the satirical press. Trench papers were explicitly intended for a military, and not civilian, audience. Even some of their humorous pricing schemes demonstrated this. *Face aux Boches* was allegedly five centimes for military readers and ten for civilians, *L'écho des guitounes* charged civilians a package of provisions per issue, and *Le Bochofage* was free to soldiers but charged 12 francs and 95 centimes for civilians and 2,000 francs in gold for embusqués.[72] Trench papers were intimately linked to their context. Some newspaper titles, such as *Poison Gas*, *The Salient*, and *Le schrapnell*, reinforced the relationship between readers and the struggles at the front. Readers were distinguished from other patrons of the civilian press and from the loathed embusqués.[73]

Even within the military, trench journals were intended for very specific audiences, with shared experiences. The

Fifth Glo'ster Gazette billed itself as "a chronicle, serious and humorous, of the battalion."[74] Trench newspapers were created on the company, battalion, regiment, and division level. Many papers were named after their readership, such as the *79th News*, *Pulham Patrol*, and *Pennington Press* among the British and *Le 120 court*, *La voix du 75*, and *Les boyaux du 95ème* among the French. Unlike the civilian press, trench papers invited contributions of all kinds, from all kinds. *Poil . . . et plume* welcomed writing in Occitan, Provençal, langue d'oc, and Catalan.[75]

Trench newspapers bear a resemblance to what James C. Scott termed a "hidden transcript." In his works *Domination and the Arts of Resistance* and *Weapons of the Weak*, Scott focused his attention on subordinate groups and their discourses and strategies of resistance and empowerment. Though the soldiers in the trenches should not be compared to slaves or an oppressed working class, Great War soldiers at the front lines were in a vulnerable position and subject to orders, with little recourse, and had little control over their daily activities and, in some sense, their fate. They certainly employed strategies for empowerment and survival, as shown in Alexander Watson's work *Enduring the Great War*, but they were officially and unofficially subordinate to others and subject to external control. The political climate was such that open resistance to orders or the conflict was not a viable option for most soldiers. Scott described the hidden transcript as "produced for a different audience and under different constraints of power than the public transcript."[76] If we consider that the civilian press resembled a public transcript, the trench press resembled a hidden transcript. A hidden transcript is significant because it is a "critique of power spoken behind the back of the dominant," and it is "not just behind the scenes griping and grumbling, it is enacted in a host of down-to-earth, low-profile stratagems designed to minimize appropriation."[77] It often relies on anonymity and questions the status quo. In so many ways, trench newspapers did just this. While they may not have challenged the authority of generals and governments, trench newspapers questioned the status quo of the trenches and provided soldiers an alternative to the public transcript, which they often found false with regard to experience and ideology. Though trench newspapers were not the voice of the oppressed, they were the voice of ordinary men subject to orders with life-altering consequences. Despite some exceptions, amateur soldiers were also amateur authors in most trench journals.

If trench newspapers were a hidden transcript to the civilian population, they were still the public discourse of the soldiers in the trenches. In 1916 Alfred John Sansom, then a lieutenant with the Fifth Royal Sussex Regiment, wrote to his wife, "We are going to start a magazine. They are becoming fashionable for Battalions at the front, and some of them are awfully good."[78] As indicated by Sansom's use of *we*, trench newspapers were never individual endeavors; they were the product of a group experience and shared among men who had not only a war in common but also shared assignments and associations. In their collective nature, they differed from other wartime and postwar writings. Wartime letters were often written to a civilian audience. Wartime diaries were often dominated by accounts of the day's events, listing the wounded or sick among the men and keeping track of supplies, but lacking personal reflections or responses. Both letters and diaries were individual efforts, unlike trench newspapers. Many of the best-known memoirs and books about the war were written after the conflict and for the public. Trench newspapers were written by and for soldiers themselves, *during* the war. Trench newspapers were also distinctive in their use of anonymity. Though some trench authors and artists are known, such as Jean Galtier-Boissière and Gilbert Frankau, most of the prose, poetry, and art of trench newspapers went unsigned or acknowledged only by pseudonym. Trench papers went beyond the identity of individual authors and became the voice of the community that produced them.

Due to their purpose and design, British and French trench newspapers provide a unique access point to soldiers' wartime public discourse and what others have called "war culture." In a 1973 audio interview with the Imperial War Museum, Patrick Beaver, editor of the complete *Wipers Times*, asserted that *Wipers* had historical significance "because it is spontaneous and it preserved for us the thing itself, the very nature of life in the trenches, the slang, the jargon, the character of the conversation, and all the depressing surroundings and above all it gives us the resolution and the humanity shown by these men in the face of violent death."[79] Audoin-Rouzeau defined *war culture* as "a certain number of mental attitudes, of reflexes born of the harshness of their living conditions, of immersion in battle and confrontation with death" shared by the men at the front lines.[80] Audoin-Rouzeau thought that trench newspapers reflected that culture. J. G. Fuller agreed that trench newspapers "deliberately set out, in many cases, to capture the spirit of the army" and "addressed themselves directly and continuously to a task which letters and diaries tackle only peripherally and randomly."[81] Considering that at least one trench newspaper sold more than twenty thousand copies and several as many as five thousand, they must have captured "the spirit of the army" to some degree.[82] In his work on the French mutinies, Leonard Smith incorporated Maurice Agulhon's idea of sociability into the notion of the culture of the trenches. Smith brought out the "'horizontal' links among men of varying ranks who shared common hardships and dangers" and emphasized the "constant and informal interaction between social classes."[83] Trench newspapers were an important part of that wartime sociability, across class and rank and reflecting shared hardships and time.

Reading and Writing the Self

Reading, especially of newspapers, played a major role in the lives of the men who participated in the Great War. Male literacy was high in the Entente Powers—98 percent in France at the outbreak of the war—and some individual newspapers had circulations of over a million copies.[84] Increases in literacy and trends in educational practices had prepared readers for close reading, and texts were part of growing into adulthood and sexual and professional maturation.[85] Newspapers defined the contours not only of opinion but also, increasingly, of life. In England, they were part of the lives of all classes.[86] Fussell suggests that "with all this reading going on and with all this consciousness of the world of letters adjacent to the actual world—even louse-hunting was called 'reading one's shirt'—it is to be expected that one's reports on experience will to an extraordinary degree lean on literature or recognize its presence and authority."[87] Reading and writing in trench newspapers provided context for interpreting the war experience and the new selves emerging from it. In *Reading Berlin 1900*, Peter Fritzsche compares newspapers to maps for urban settings, suggesting that the "word city" taught readers how to read the "lived city." Fritzsche asserts that "the city as place and the city as text defined each other in mutually constitutive ways" and reading and writing "constructed a second-hand metropolis which gave a narrative to the concrete one and choreographed its encounters."[88] Urban dwellers especially were accustomed to utilizing the paper to navigate their city by locating events of interest, safe and unsafe areas, and job opportunities. Soldiers in the city of trenches likewise utilized trench newspapers to find their way.

As their lives entered new chapters, soldiers relied on

reading and writing to create new narratives. In his research, Martyn Lyons found First World War soldiers who were "writing to stay alive"; writing was an act of survival and "synonymous with existence itself."[89] According to Nichole Gleisner's study of French soldiers, in many cases, "to be a soldier was to write, not just fight. It became another facet of a soldier's duty—culturally, morally, and aesthetically—to capture his experiences in written word."[90] The *H.C.B. Gazette* encouraged more submissions from readers, telling them that if writing "accomplished no other object than that of your own improvement and the production of a keener edge to your own education, it will at least do that, and you will be all the better for it."[91] Not all of that war writing was done in isolation. Soldiers often expected their letters home to be read within the community.[92] Within the trenches, they also wrote for each other. As Leonard Smith pointed out, soldiers had "time on their hands to think and to exchange their thoughts with their comrades."[93] Trench newspapers were part of that exchange. Soldiers used trench newspapers to explore and define their emerging military identities. A special issue Canadian trench magazine, *Another Garland from the Front*, featured a poem called "The Disc Identity" that exemplifies the situation of a newly formed military identity, divorced from civilian life. (Identity discs were precursors of military dog tags.) It begins:

> When I was born I got the name
> Of Smith, Augustus John,
> And when a soldier I became
> And put my khaki on,
> I felt as proud as Punch could be
> When some old Sergeant said to me,
> "You're now a separate entity,
> And here's your DISC-identity."

When on a list he entered me,
My bosom swelled with pride.
"You're twenty-two, six, seven three,"
"Yes, Sergeant," I replied.[94]

The subject's civilian identity has been swallowed up in the army. The poem ends in a striking fashion, pitying the "chaps at home" and reminding readers that "A fellow's a nonentity / Without a DISC-identity." Trench newspapers allowed soldiers to narrate their transformations and simultaneously provided a script for transformation. Reading trench newspapers was not just recreation, but also re-creation.

In *Creative Writing: Translation, Bookkeeping, and the Work of Imagination in Colonial Kenya*, Derek Peterson found that people in colonial Kenya used all types of writing to construct identities and, in a sense, to write scripts for the future. Identity cards, plays, and record books all provided ways of being in the world. In the same way, trench newspaper stories about subjects like romantic relationships, the fraternity of the trenches, and alcohol provided scripts that readers could recognize and choose among. The themes and morals of serialized stories, poetry, and cartoons also provided ways for soldiers to sort out meaning in their experiences of war. Soldiers were not just reading and writing trench newspapers; soldiers were being written by the newspapers.

British and French trench newspapers were explicit about how soldiers' discourse was redefining existence. Trench newspapers commonly redefined terms and experiences with "dictionaries" and "alphabets." Although often written very tongue in cheek and sometimes clearly intended to explain trench slang, dictionaries and alphabets also suggested new meanings. Words like *peace* and *home* appeared with definitions radically different from those of an official (or civilian) dictionary. Soldiers' slang evolved throughout the war and was even published in books.[95] The obvious uniqueness of soldiers' language further emphasizes the value of soldiers' discourse for revealing wartime beliefs in the trenches. Within trench newspapers, the redefined words and alphabets could be informative about trench culture. A Mesopotamian Alphabet from the *Wipers Times*, on January 20, 1917, referenced not just *quinine* and *rations* but also *harems* and suggests "I is the Indian Government but / About this I'm told I must keep my mouth shut, / For it's all due to them that we failed to reach Kut- / El-Amara in Mesopotamia."[96] This alphabet reflects on censorship, evaluates the Indian Government and the situation on the Mesopotamian front in contrast to the government position, all the while constructing an image of Mesopotamia for other soldiers to internalize.

In the foreword to a published collection of the *Wipers Times*, Henry Williamson, a Great War veteran, who was only seventeen at the outbreak of hostilities, related that when he went home on leave he would spend much of his time crying alone in his bedroom. The questions people asked him were too much for him to handle. A trench newspaper was his solace, and "even fifty years later, I can feel myself to be surrounded by the spirit of the Western Front in the pages of *Wipers Times, accepted* as part of myself, for every item is gentle and kindly in attitude to what was hellish—and this attitude, its virtue, was extended towards the enemy. It is a charity which links those who have passed through the estranging remoteness of battle . . . men who were not broken, but reborn."[97] Trench newspapers catalogued and empowered these rebirths. They sustained the men in the trenches with humor, linked readers together, provided a forum for expression and criticism, and warded off boredom. Most significant, trench newspapers linked together the parts of men that could not leave the trenches and the parts that could never be confined to them.

Conclusion

As an imperfect mirror, trench newspapers reflected the men who read and wrote them. In its first issue, *Brise d'entonnoirs* described a trench newspaper as an organ that permitted all the *poilus* of a regiment to communicate with each other, "rubbing elbows" about shared views via the paper.[98] Recurring themes ran across British and French trench newspapers of the Western Front, largely born of shared experiences. Almost every paper provided some commentary on shirkers, mud, alcohol, orders, loss, and the Germans. On many topics, there seemed to be some consensus in the trenches. The views of individual authors may be difficult to disentangle from their pages, but the jokes, stories, and opinions circulating among the readers are apparent. Precisely because trench newspapers reflect the collective culture of the trenches, there is no better place to explore imperial culture in the trenches.

Though empire was not the primary focus of Entente trench newspapers on the Western Front, significant content was related to it. As explored in chapter 1, the Great War was a struggle between empires. It was also an experience of empire for many soldiers. Many British and French soldiers from the metropole served near or alongside colonial troops for the first time. Soldiers came in contact with the people and realities of empire in new ways, which shaped their experience of war.

Trench newspapers are an excellent source to explore imperial culture within the trenches. An alternative to the civilian press for their readers, trench newspapers also represent an alternative point of entry for historians into soldiers' wartime discourses and provide unique insights into soldiers' thoughts about empire during the war. In their writing about empire-related things, in what ways did soldiers stick to existing literary conventions and in what ways did they depart from them? How did soldiers write about non-western fronts? In what ways did empire-related language shape discourses about the war more generally? Or about the Germans? Santanu Das writes that "if the First World War is usually understood as a military conflict between European empires . . . it can equally be reconceptualised as a turning point in the history of cultural encounter and entanglement."[99] To what extent did soldiers, among themselves, see the war as a matter of conflict between empires, and how did they process the cultural encounters within and between empires? In the identities and communities that they created and carried through the war, when and how did empire matter?

THREE

Men on the Margins

Though the Entente Powers were centered in Europe, the Great War was an imperial effort. With the outbreak of war in 1914, the British and French relied on their empires in new and profound ways. Colonial troops were among the most notable and visible imperial contribution to the war effort; just over two million Africans served in the First World War in some capacity, and India alone sent over a million men as soldiers and laborers.[1] Over one hundred thousand Indians and five hundred thousand Africans served on the Western Front, near or with British and French soldiers.[2] Once overlooked, the contributions of colonies and Dominions have been more fully recognized of late, and numerous works have explored the realities surrounding the service of colonial troops and the significance of their contributions.[3] This unprecedented influx of colonial troops to Europe occurred simultaneously with massive wartime conscription by the British and French, meaning more soldiers of all types would have exposure to each other than ever before. What did British and French soldiers from Europe make of colonial troops? Did the imperial cooperation in the Great War challenge or change their understandings of the peoples within their empires?

The Great War brought empire home in many ways, by bringing men and material from the edges of empire into the heart of Europe and initiating a new arena of reliance and exchange. That the British soldier's word for home could be connected to colonial peoples reflects how influence could travel in multiple directions within empires. This chapter looks at European soldiers' writings about colonial troops, particularly in British and French trench newspapers of the Western Front, to demonstrate how the war challenged existing imperial culture. As Jane Burbank and Frederick Cooper have pointed out, empire was "a variable political form" and there were "multiple ways in which incorporation and difference were conjugated."[4] The Great War was a moment in which the political form of European empires took on a new shape. Though the war did not dramatically overturn preexisting understandings of race and hierarchy for all soldiers, the shared imperial war effort created new and competing narratives about colonial peoples and the possibilities of empire.

In trench newspapers, as in the Entente fighting forces, colonial troops did not make up the majority of the subject matter but, as in the fighting, that did not prevent them from having a presence and an impact. Colonial troops appear in articles, stories, poems, cartoons, and plays, both centrally and peripherally. Colonial troops, like the Indian sepoy, were already a "recognisable type" by the time of the war.[5] Metropolitan soldiers were very much interested in their colonial counterparts. In one French paper, a cartoonist added that he had made a character black in order to sustain readers' curiosity.[6] That curiosity was built on ideas and opinions about colonized peoples and empires that already existed, influenced by the print culture and popular opinions of the day. But the experience of the war created an opportunity for new perspectives and more opportunity for interaction than ever before. A consistent presence in the margins of British and French Western Front narratives, soldiers' wartime writings reveal an awareness of colonial troops, demonstrate the strength of prewar stereotypes, and indicate that there was an ambivalence about colonial troops as new, positive narratives emerged about them in the context of the Great War.

Awareness of Imperial Cooperation

European soldiers' wartime public discourse reflected an awareness, and typically appreciation, of imperial cooperation. In 1916 the British *"P.P."* reminded readers about the diversity of the Entente fighting forces:

> A contemporary obligingly reminds us that fully seventy-five separate races and peoples are now fighting in the greatest war of the world's history.
>
> Fighting under the British Flag are eleven distinct races— English, Scots, Irish, Welsh, Hindus, Australians, Canadians, New Zealanders, Boers, native Africans of various shades of colour, Red Indians, and in addition several indefinable small peoples from the South Sea Islands and elsewhere.
>
> Included in the French armies are no fewer than seventeen races, amongst them being Moors, Kabyles, Anamites, Senegal Negroes, Arabs, Turkos, Hovas, Dahomey Negroes, Congo Negroes, Cambodians, and Tunisians.
>
> On the side of Russia are fourteen races, the principal being Finns, Poles, Lithuanians, Kirghese, Kalmuks, Tungueses, Tartars, Turcomen, and Mongols.
>
> In addition are Japanese, Portuguese, Belgians, Serbs, Montenegrins, Rumanians, and Albanians.[7]

The readership of the *"P.P."* most likely did not include colonial troops, but the readers were familiar enough to only need a reminder of them. This list of "seventy-five separate races" demonstrates that soldiers were aware of the imperial nature of the fighting forces in the war and the involvement of non-Europeans. In "the greatest war in the world's history," the English were only one of eleven perceived races under the British flag, the French one of seventeen. Now people from seemingly far-flung reaches of empires, even "several indefinable small peoples," were engaged in a struggle centered on Europe. Most of the military conflicts of the late nineteenth century had been colonial, but the Great War brought parts of the empire home to Europe, a fact not lost on the authors and readers of trench papers.

The breadth and variety of imperial cooperation is clear in British and French soldiers' writings.[8] Non-European laborers also appeared occasionally in trench papers. Many British and French soldiers had exposure to, and contact with, colonial subjects serving in labor positions with the military. France alone brought three hundred thousand men from the colonies to help with fields and factories.[9] Although colonial soldiers had a generally positive image, Tyler Stovall has found that foreign factory workers were perceived and portrayed as a threat by French unions and the working class and were at times subject to racially based physical violence.[10] Some of the foreign laborers in Europe for the war were not colonial subjects at all. China sent 140,000 men to France as contract workers for the British and the French, and their experiences have been well described in Xu Guoqi's *Strangers on the Western Front: Chinese Workers in the Great War*.[11] Though much less prominent than colonial troops, Chinese laborers were also noted in trench journals.[12] An issue of the French paper *Le dernier bateau* reflected awareness of the Chinese with a joke about Alsatian soldiers speaking patois and their general mistakenly thinking they had learned Chinese in two days.[13] British and French soldiers were very much aware of non-European help, combatant and noncombatant, on the Western Front. Though the majority of the British and French armies were still from the metropole, there was a recognition of the impact of empire on the struggle for Europe.

Trench newspapers demonstrated that soldiers were members of imperial cultures. British trench papers sometimes had real or satirical advertisements for all kinds of

Men on the Margins

products that might be wanted in the trenches or on leave. Common advertisements for genuine products were for luminous watches or trench coats or tailoring. The British paper *Trot-Talk* regularly featured advertisements, some for products tied to empire. *Trot-Talk* routinely advertised "Belle of the Orient, Egyptian Blend Cigarettes."[14] The AAC *Journal* included advertisements for Lipton's tea, with a plantation scene and Ceylonese pickers. These images in trench newspapers were like advertisements in the civilian press, which tied labor to racial hierarchy, as described in Anandi Ramamurthy's examination of illustrated newspapers in *Imperial Persuaders*.[15] Whereas these advertisements may have appeared in civilian papers before, they now appeared in papers designed for soldiers at the front lines, demonstrating the extent to which the goods of empire promised the comforts of home.

Old Ideas and New Contexts

British and French soldiers entered the war already exposed to ideas about empire, which were embedded in various hierarchies. Before they began trench newspapers, they were members of empires, and their cultures reflected that. British and French children's literature often contained colonial imagery.[16] Adult periodicals also featured news and stories from the empires. From the 1890s, articles and images related to Africa abounded in the popular press, particularly in France, and the Boer War was international news.[17] Before the war, most juvenile and adult reading material reflected widespread notions of European superiority. A belief in a fixed hierarchy of civilizations, with Europeans at the top, had permeated society and published news, and opinion, scientific, and historical perspectives of the time typically reinforced this position.[18] Africans tended to be at the bottom of the hierarchy, and images of Africans shifted between representing them as savages and as overgrown children.[19] Within the colonies, racial hierarchies were supposed to be strictly observed.[20]

The Entente armies of the Great War were shaped by the racial thinking of the time. The British and French wanted few nonwhite colonial officers, and those who existed were intended to serve only with colonial troops. European officers were often encouraged to be especially paternalistic with colonial troops. French officers sometimes referred to their colonial troops as their children.[21] A similar race-tinted paternalism was at work in the British Army. The 1919 work *The Indian Corps in France*, intended to be a narrative of the Indian Army in France, compared the typical officer of Indian troops to a mother and her children and suggested that "it is unnecessary to point out—for everyone knows it—how much the Indian troops owed to their British officers, and to the British regiments with which they were brigaded."[22] Although Germans accepted the use of colonial troops "if they remained in their proper geographical (and cultural) context," they strongly and publicly protested the use of colonial troops in Europe, especially Africans.[23] The French deployed soldiers from Africa to Europe and kept their colonial troops in Europe until the end of the war, and even after. The British resisted the use of Black combatants in Europe but found the Indian Army essential as a prepared army during the first two years of the war.[24] As more European soldiers became available, Indian soldiers were rerouted back to the margins of empire. Significant differences existed between the British and the French armies. Whereas everyone in the British Empire was a subject, as many as 875,000 colonial French of non-European descent were citizens like their metropolitan counterparts, and French colonial troops were less segregated than the British.[25] However, in neither army were colonial troops on equal footing with their European counterparts.

Did trench newspapers simply perpetuate the racial hierarchies of the time and mimic the images of colonial peoples in the prewar civilian press? Trench newspapers and soldiers' diary and epistolary accounts do sometimes show a continuation of prewar depictions of, and themes regarding, non-Europeans in literature and the press. A 1917 issue of the *"P.P."* offered tongue-in-cheek advice on writing letters to various types of women. A woman fond of fruit could be called "apple of my eye" or even "perfect little prune," but "a negress" could be "My Dusky Darling" or "Brunette o' Mine" or "C— of my soul."[26] Though intended to amuse rather than offend, the language reflected the terminology of the times and a limit of inclusion. A later issue described a night of music that included Rachmaninoff, Sinding, and "a n— sketch."[27] British occasional use of terms like *S—* and *n—* was paralleled in French papers, where Africans, including soldiers, were variously referred to as *noirs* and *nègres*, with the latter having more negative connotations and pejorative uses. Certainly, trench newspapers sought to brave the world and its dangers by confronting it with humor and jest. Few subjects were safe from mockery. But language like this relied on tropes that represented non-white members of society as socially inferior.

Specific stereotypes also crossed into trench newspapers from the civilian press; an issue of *Le mouchoir* featured a caricatured *tirailleur*, with the phrase "Y a bon," like the famous marketing image for the chocolate drink Banania created during the war.[28] Banania as a brand combined the appeals of exoticism and patriotism in its tirailleur image.[29] Before the war, images of Africans typically shifted between savages and overgrown children, like Kipling's "half devil and half child" in "The White Man's Burden."[30] The most persistent stereotype of non-European people was to see them as childlike.[31] A British veteran recalled the men of the Chinese labor corps as "very simple, very strong, and very entertaining people."[32] René Prud'homme served briefly near soldiers from Martinique, whom he described in his memoir as "the most beautiful black children."[33] *Les boyaux du 95e* once claimed its editor-in-chief was "M. Bamboula," who was perfect for the job primarily because he was illiterate.[34] Using familiar tropes, a story in *Le poilu*, intended to be humorous, described a Chinese man selling a crate of oranges to a Black man (and cheating him) while they were being engulfed by a flood and certain to perish.[35] The Black man was assumed to be foolish or childlike, and the Chinese man was depicted as intent on making money whatever the circumstance. Other groups were also occasionally the target of race-based humor, such as Jewish people, in British trench papers. Soldiers' wartime writings do reveal the tremendous gravitational pull of prewar stereotypes and hierarchies. Some stories and cartoons certainly perpetuated existing negative images of non-Europeans. But depictions of colonial troops were not simply and exclusively racialized tropes, and those tropes were contested by new images created during the war.

Representations of colonial peoples in trench papers and wartime writings must be evaluated with attention to the context of the Great War. Some generalizations about colonial troops functioned differently and with additional meaning in the wartime context. For example, the British and the French recruited colonial troops according to the theory of martial races, which suggested that some tribes or groups were more naturally suited for warfare than others.[36] Groups like the Gurkhas or the tirailleurs sénégalais were often reputed to be particularly fearsome fighters, characterized by both bravery and bloodthirstiness.[37] This could be a demeaning indication of savagery, but this "natural" suitability for warfare was considered useful to the Entente, which used colonial soldiers as shock troops. Consistent with stereotype and use, colonial troops became associated with the violence of battle for their fellow combatants. The main

Men on the Margins

character in Henri Barbusse's famous *Under Fire* knows an attack is imminent when he sees the tirailleurs sénégalais moving toward the front line.[38] In "Sketches of the Poilu's World," James P. Daughton suggests that in French trench newspaper cartoons "black soldiers from the French colonies are portrayed much like the enemy, as stupid and even savage."[39] However, representations of colonial troops were more varied than this. Daughton's article overlooks the positive representations of nonwhite soldiers and the alteration, within the context of war, of the meaning of *savagery*. What was previously a threat to colonizers sometimes became a virtue in the trenches because it now represented a threat to the German enemy. The negative traits of the stereotype were now in demand and perceived as positive.

Within British and French soldiers' writings, excessive violence was exclusively assigned to the enemy. The violence of the Entente, even seeming bloodthirstiness by colonial troops and others, was valued. During the war, British Lieutenant F. B. Turner wrote to his father about "slaughtering Huns . . . I revel in it, every Hun I see I generally fire a salvo at him and if it doesn't kill or wound him probably gives him shell shock and makes him windy. The Major seems rather pleased with my bloodthirsty nature."[40] In the trenches, many individual soldiers accepted the martial races theory and thought that colonial troops were vicious fighters but were not dismayed by that. When Frenchman Louis Barthas saw the "Hindus" in the trenches, he noticed their famous knives.[41] English officer Edward D. Ridley served near the Indian Army for a time during the war and commented one night in his diary, "Hear the Indians have taken a trench and some prisoners. More trench than prisoners I expect."[42] However, he was not entirely upset. Troops from outside the metropole were imagined terrorizing the enemy, as seen in an issue of *Le ver luisant*, where above the lyrics of a song, "My Bayonet," was a cartoon image of a Zouave threatening a German.[43] The song celebrated the moment when "my bayonet" would be all red with German blood. The singer was not encouraged to see himself as a savage. German propaganda set forth "a deeply racist campaign that represented the non-white colonial soldiers as beasts."[44] But not all Entente soldiers equated the rumored passions and fearsome fighting abilities of colonial troops with barbarism. When British general Sir James Willcocks reflected on the few Indian officers, he described them as mostly "men who had earned their commissions by brave and loyal service, of fighting stock, with martial traditions, ready to give their lives for their King Emperor, proud of the profession of arms."[45] Here the "natural" martial ability of Indians is comparable to the heritage of the English aristocracy. Rather than seeing the violence associated with colonial troops as savagery, British and French soldiers could see it as an indication that colonial troops were valued members of the Entente forces. Although some might perceive depictions of bloodthirstiness in colonial troops as perpetuating a prewar stereotype, understanding the context of the war makes it clear that such a depiction is, in fact, more complicated.

While the colonial troops used their "natural" fighting abilities for good—the purposes of the Entente—the Germans were actually portrayed as warlike and evil. The contrast between images of colonial troops and negative depictions of Germans are instructive. The illustrations that associated Germans with barbarism were, at times, quite extreme. A drawing in *Le mouchoir* depicted Wilhelm II at the Cathedral d'Angers, a murdered baby with missing hands and feet on the ground before him, while three handless children reach for him beside a retinue of skeletons and he recoils in horror.[46] An illustration in *Le dernier bateau* showed a blindfolded woman before a German firing squad.[47] Nothing similar appeared depicting colonial troops. The most recent

Men on the Margins

prior European military conflicts had been colonial, but in the Great War the Germans replaced non-European peoples as the military enemy and were now perceived as barbarians.[48] Though there were also more lighthearted references to the Germans, in British and French soldiers' wartime discourses Germans were frequently described as primitive and barbaric, by use of terms like *Huns* and *Boches*. Germans were even occasionally described as subhuman. Some trench papers defined them as animals or even apes.[49] Though not all depictions of Germans were so stark, such representations of Germans are in marked contrast to even the stereotyped depictions of colonial troops. For many Entente soldiers, Germans were the embodiment of barbarism, not colonial troops. This was precisely what the Germans feared about the use of colonial troops in Europe, that it had the potential to challenge the prewar racial hierarchy that kept all Europeans together at the top.

If the Germans had become the primary "them," how did colonial troops fit into the "us" of the Entente? Colonial troops were included, but not fully assimilated into the "us" present in Western Front trench newspapers.[50] Though clearly on the side of the Entente, they were nonetheless distinguishable from European soldiers, mainly on the basis of language and race. Language was a chief marker of difference between European and colonial troops identified in trench newspapers. Colonial troops were often represented as ill-versed in English or French. The Europeans were in the position to "speak to" colonial peoples, but the reverse was not often true. Two articles in a single issue of a French trench paper demonstrate the contrast well. *L'horizon* noted the death of General Baratier, a "hero in Africa," and suggested that he got large smiles from African soldiers when he spoke to them in their language, clearly and strongly. He was remembered as well loved by both his white and his Black soldiers.[51] A different article in the same issue,

"Gri-Gri," related that the strong, childlike "Senegalese" soldiers did not speak French well, but did have interesting and musical accents.[52] Within *L'horizon*, the linguistic gap was bridged by the Europeans, like General Baratier, who speak "clearly and strongly" in foreign languages, while the Africans utilize interesting and "musical" accents. This was a common perspective. The war letters of British soldier S. H. Steven, who served near the Indian Army, show many similar themes. Relating an incident in the trenches, Steven wrote the following:

> We were held up by a party of about 300 Indians going up with spades and sandbags over their shoulders. They are a funny looking lot of little beggars. They creep along, each one looking like the next and they are always smiling. They whisper away to each other in their own musical tongue and occasionally come out with 'Teek, Johnnie, teek' to us which means I believe, that everything is fine, aright, good and going well. We shout to them 'Chell-on' or something like that and they put a spurt on and get going smartly. Physically they are a wonderful crew.[53]

The sounds of colonial soldiers are again "musical," and their mastery of English is nonexistent while they smile away. Race was a continuing marker of difference, but language was frequently represented as a significant barrier between colonial and European troops in many trench newspapers, diaries, and letters. An issue of the *Lead-Swinger* described a hospital full French colonial troops after a battle as "crowded with dark-skinned, curly-headed sons of the South, who one and all avowed a blissful ignorance of either French or English."[54] Colonial troops did frequently have limited knowledge of English and French. Ironically, joining the military was little help. Language instruction was minimal. In fact, the pidgin French that tirailleurs were sometimes mocked for speaking was officially recommended for instruction due to belief in their limited linguistic capacity.[55] Colonial troops were not the only ones with language problems. Language was also a divide between the British and the French in trench newspapers. Many British papers contained stories about the woes of British soldiers trying to communicate well with French women. And a 1917 issue of *Le poilu* jokingly advertised for "20,000 *nègres* who speak a little bit of French to serve as interpreters for the first contingents of Americans."[56] Americans were also considered unprepared for more than "a little bit of French." Language was a consistent marker of difference within and between empires.

Race was still a factor in how European soldiers constructed their identities in the trenches and one that prevented colonial troops from completely blending into the larger armies. The masthead of an issue of *La première ligne* featured two soldiers pointing at the newspaper's title, one a typical white poilu, the other a caricatured tirailleur.[57] The presumably Senegalese soldier is across from the prototypical poilu, and both are shown representing the military. The inclusive gesture is minimized by the caricatured depiction of the tirailleur. Although trench newspapers frequently employed caricature for a variety of subjects, there is a difference between a caricatured individual, such as an officer, and an anonymous figure caricatured by race and meant to stand in for that race. However, despite the caricature, *La première ligne*, named after the front line, associates colonial troops with the front line and even with its paper. This journal, which saw itself as a "pure emanation of the French spirit" in the face of death and the enemy, chose to use a colonial soldier in its imagery.[58] Colonial troops were definitely *with* the readers of the paper, even if they were not always *of* them.

Frederick Cooper posits that empire is "a terrain where concepts were not only interposed but also engaged and contested."[59] The Great War was an event in which imperial concepts and ideas were put to the test and wartime experiences could lead European soldiers to question stereotypes. Soldiers' trench writings show the emergence of new narratives about colonial peoples. In his war notebooks, Louis Barthas recorded numerous times when he observed colonial troops and he mused on the diversity of the Entente fighting forces. In quarantine with many men, Barthas observed that "all the parties of the world, all races, and all colors were represented. Moroccans, Annamites, white and black Americans, Italians, etc., and five or six French."[60] The ensuing conversations he described as a "pretty cacophony." Though not all soldiers felt that way, some did see the diverse fighting forces as in some way beautiful.

In many cases, colonial troops were praised in soldiers' accounts. Gurkhas and Sikhs were prominent and celebrated among British colonial troops. An article titled "Boots, Unlimited" in the *"P.P."* described the incredible variety of military boots produced at a single factory and noted that "some of the most remarkable boots turned out in this most gigantic factory are the tiny boots of the gallant Gurkhas and the enormous ones of the Russians."[61] The "gallant" Gurkhas nearly always stood out in trench narratives, British and French. In the special Sammies edition of the French trench journal *Le poilu*, published in English for American soldiers, a poem, "The Road to France," included the lines "To France—the trail the Gurkhas found / To France—old England's rallying-ground!"[62] Here the French encouraged the Americans to follow the same trail the Gurkhas had; the Gurkhas could serve as pathfinders for new Entente forces. Whether because they were famous before the war or seemed recognizable in the trenches, Sikhs and Gurkhas consistently made a big, and typically favorable, impression on Entente soldiers. In an oral interview kept at the Imperial War Museum, former soldier Eric Wolton, when asked about colonial troops, remembered seeing the "Sikhs and Gurkhas—lovely people; especially the Gurkhas. Sikhs very tall and dignified. I loved the Gurkhas."[63] Wolton had not served in close quarters with Indian troops, but he was full of admiration for them. In this case, the fascination was also true for civilians. In his book about his war experience, General Sir James Willcocks, who served with the Indian Army, wrote that "a great part of the public appeared to think that Indian brigades and divisions were composed of Sikhs and Gurkhas alone."[64] Government media contributed to that tendency. For example, in the 1916 official government film *With the Indian Troops at the Front*, Sikhs and Gurkhas featured prominently and almost exclusively.[65] Soldiers and civilians did not need personal, close contact with colonial troops from India to be interested in and appreciative of them.

French trench newspapers best illuminate the ways in which the war expanded understanding and appreciation of some colonial peoples. An article in *Le poilu* titled "Memory of Africa" described a French officer serving with Arab cavalry and observing Ramadan with troops.[66] The article was not humorous but portrayed an aspect of the war and the connection between officers and their men. Even apart from stories of interaction, French papers presented colonial troops as friendly allies. The trench journal *Face aux Boches*, which published a "Petit Dictionnaire," intended to explain terms in ways relevant to the war, defined *Sénégalais* as "l'ami noir."[67] The Senegalese were defined as friends. Tirailleurs actually became popular figures during the war, even among civilians, due largely to "tales of steadfastness."[68]

The French Army used colonial troops more extensively

and French trench newspapers contain more evidence of new understanding and appreciation of colonial troops. In 1917 a long article about "L'armée noire" appeared in *Le crapouillot*, written by a former legionnaire. This article was intended to inform Frenchmen who had less experience with colonial troops. Sgt. Maj. Raoul Bouchir went beyond stereotype, explaining that not all tirailleurs sénégalais were actually Senegalese and describing the various types of troops coming from Africa, distinguishing between spahis, tirailleurs, and so forth. He praised the discipline of the spahis and celebrated the tirailleurs sénégalais as "elite soldiers" of "infinite courage." Most significant, the author suggested that wartime cooperation could lead to a more intimate connection with overseas subjects and should reassure Africans of their place in a more united France.[69] The new possibilities for colonial troops are well represented in a song from *L'artilleur déchaîné*. The song described a review of troops in Paris. Each stanza featured a different type of soldier marching by the encouraging crowd. Here is one of the stanzas:

> Then our blacks (*noirs*)
> All these valiant heroes
> Marching through the echoes (cries)
> Of the Marseillaise . . .
> Under the sacred flame
> The public was inspired
> Acclaiming: Long live the French Republic![70]

In the song, the colonial troops are still distinguished from the Europeans; however, these colonial heroes marched to the Marseillaise just like their brethren born in Europe. For the author, colonial troops fought for the French Republic, and for liberty, equality, and fraternity. Reality may have differed from the author's perception; however, the poem demonstrates that colonial troops could be closely associated with the French Republic, not just the empire. In the song, colonial troops were considered "valiant heroes."

For many trench authors, personal experience with colonial troops especially seemed to create a new level of respect and connection. Santanu Das has argued that war writings show "preconceptions were challenged and altered during the actual encounters."[71] Trench newspapers bear that out. A 1915 issue of *Le poilu* took the time to inform readers about "our Spahis," in an article by that title. The author was a wounded lieutenant who had served with the spahis and shared amusing anecdotes and serious stories about these "admirable soldiers" whose "warrior spirit" and "incomparable vigor" were of great benefit to France.[72] The author marveled at the contributions of North Africans to the war cause, on behalf of a France they had never previously seen. For the lieutenant who wrote the article, the experience of serving with colonial soldiers caused him to value North Africans in a new way. This transcendence was not always achieved, but it was more likely in the context of the war. According to Richard Fogarty, colonial troops in Europe challenged white superiority and "opened up many possibilities for the destabilization of hierarchies that were virtually immutable back in the colonies."[73] Soldiers' testimonies indicate the possibility of bridges between groups created by service together. English soldier Joseph Murray remembered that when his division was briefly attached to some tirailleurs sénégalais during a battle, they were "greeted as pals" and given red wine and black bread.[74] While serving near the Egyptian Labour Corps, British Private Frank Lindley shared meals with Egyptians and formed friendships.[75] In a 1915 letter Lt. Col. H. F. Bateman-Champain of the Indian Corps reflected on the distance between the image of the corps and what it had achieved. He wrote that the Indians made a significant contribution and that "they held their own (in spite of many rumours to the contrary)."[76]

Bateman-Champain resented the gap between the perceptions of Indian soldiers and the reality of their worth that he knew from experience.

Trench newspapers did not merely reiterate existing understandings and images of colonial peoples. Many representations of colonial troops reflect a profound ambivalence that evolved during the war, as old ideas about race and empire began to compete with new ideas and actual exposure. In an issue of *L'horizon*, the article "Gri-Gri" described the sad state of African soldiers in winter, suggesting they looked like large, very sweet and slightly timid children in their nightgowns while they stayed in bed to avoid the cold.[77] Indeed, the French Army was concerned that African troops would be unable to handle European winters and practiced *hivernage*, sending them to southern France and north Africa during the colder months. However, the same article that infantilized the colonial soldiers as large, timid children in winter also described them as "magnificent men, with long legs, strong torsos" and impressive muscles who were valuable in the trenches when the weather was warmer.[78] And while the article suggested they had limited ability to speak French, it relayed happily that the Senegalese had adopted many French customs in their time of living with poilus, such as smoking pipes and drinking *pinard*, the French wine of the trenches. The bond of the trenches transcended language. Not free of racialized thinking, the article nonetheless expresses an appreciation for colonial troops and a familiarity, along with sympathy for their misery. The French soldiers did not enjoy being exposed in the cold during winter either.

Another topic that reveals the ambivalence and competing understandings of colonial troops has to do with representations of their sexuality. The Great War made relationships between European women and colonial men more likely—an unsettling reality for Entente governments. French censors checked mail for content about sexual relations between French women and non-Europeans, as explained by Fogarty in *Race & War*, because "injuries to Frenchwomen and their prestige were equally injuries to France and to the white prestige that justified and supported European rule."[79] And when Chinese laborers married French women, the government tried to keep those stories quiet.[80] Yet the content of censored mail, as well as historians' findings, suggest that many women were willing and interested partners in relationships with Chinese laborers and colonial troops. What the government found undesirable, many individuals found desirable. Similarly, the British government took care to isolate Indian wounded not only from white wounded, but even from white nurses.[81] However, among European nurses who worked with colonial wounded for a long time, Alison Fell has found their diaries "sometimes suggest that their experiences led them to question racist and imperialist assumptions."[82] Again, the old narratives about colonial peoples were challenged by the realities of the Great War.

Were colonial troops a source of sexual anxiety in trench newspapers, in soldiers' public discourses? Within British trench newspapers, colonial troops do not appear to be a source of sexual anxieties at all. In French trench newspapers, stories of tirailleurs in love with their Red Cross nurses typically revolve around tirailleurs' inability to win back affection or understand French romantic relationships. In a 1915 issue of *Rigolboche* was a humorous poem about a certain Mamadou, an African soldier who had comically fallen in love with Madame Croix Rouzé.[83] In trench newspapers, the tirailleur never gets the girl, sometimes because he doesn't speak French well or because he offers to exchange livestock to secure a marriage. Another issue of *Rigolboche* had an illustration of a wounded tirailleur in a hospital bed with two nurses worrying over him, asking, "Don't you think Mohammed is a bit pale?"[84] The emphasis on race and different customs creates a distance between the tirailleur and other soldiers in these jokes. This could be read as an attempt to defuse anxiety about colonial troops as sexual rivals, and certainly race is used to distinguish those troops. But hopeful encounters with women nearly always ended in disappointment in trench newspapers, regardless of race. The wounded soldier never gets the nurse. Sexual frustration and a lack of female understanding of the soldier's position were very much a shared experience. For example, *Le klaxon* featured a story about a white soldier going home to his family on leave. He began his leave with "joy" and "happiness" but found himself unable to spend quality time with his wife because his friends and family wanted time with him and pestered him with questions.[85] In this case, even the married soldier doesn't get the girl. This reality does not erase the distance created by a focus on race, but it does suggest a recognized commonality of experience among European and colonial troops.

Though colonial troops were not consistently "valiant heroes" in the pages of trench papers, they were consistently soldiers. Even if race and language were still factors in their representations within European soldiers' writings, colonial troops now had meaningful identities tied to combat against the Germans. The British and French colonial troops were consistently part of the broader fraternity of the trenches. A 1916 cover of *Rigolboche* showed two tirailleurs casually sitting and smoking, with a caption of "Embarking for . . . hush."[86] In this illustration by P. J. Poitevin, the tirailleurs sénégalais are not caricatured, and their pause en route to some point at the front is treated like that of anyone else. They are natural in this European, wartime setting. Acknowledgement of colonial sacrifices and effort, if at times reluctant, tempered negative stereotypes of colonial troops. According to *The Indian Corps in France*, Europeans and Indians "were coadventurers and gallant comrades. They trod together the Valley of the Shadow of Death."[87] Colonial troops were not interchangeable with their European counterparts, but they had a shared wartime experience and an identity as comrades. That was a powerful narrative even where stereotypes persisted.

Conclusion

The Great War called into question the status quo of the Entente empires while they played a critical role in the war. The loyalty of British and French colonies and Dominions reached its apogee in their wartime contributions, even while the conflict sparked and strengthened nationalist movements. At the level of the government, imperial cooperation led to shifts within the structures of empire as colonies and Dominions pushed for greater autonomy and rights within empire as compensation for their wartime contributions. In France, Blaise Diagne, a parliamentary representative from Senegal, pushed for more rights within empire—especially citizenship for African soldiers.[88] Within the Raj, Edwin Samuel Montagu, secretary of state for India, promised the "development of responsible government by gradual stages" as early as 1917.[89] Hew Strachan writes, "This was a great war because it was a war fought over big ideas."[90] The ideas behind empires may not have caused the conflict, but the identities of and relationships between peoples within the British and the French empires were in flux during the Great War.

Within the trenches, many men saw the Great War as transformative of empire. The Canadian trench newspaper *Dead Horse Corner Gazette* suggested that because of the Great War, "imperialism is at last beginning to be understood."[91] Reflecting on their own service and sacrifice, the soldiers who wrote for *Dead Horse* saw imperialism as more than "excessive flag-flapping" and beyond politics. It had "ceased to be an empty phrase; it has become an actuality revitalised by national sacrifice."[92] According to *Dead Horse*, imperialism was not fully understood before the conflict, with its demand for "national sacrifice" from all kinds of people all around the world. Trench newspapers reveal the ways in which the Great War had the power to change imperial culture for men in the British and French armies. Men from various parts of empires heard rumors of each other and interacted more closely for the first time. The war did not reverse stereotypes, but it challenged many, including the myth of European superiority. British and French soldiers were aware of imperial cooperation and, in many cases, appreciative of colonial troops. Trench newspapers demonstrate the presence of new, positive narratives about colonial troops that emerged in the context of the war. Though not always noble heroes in trench newspapers, colonial troops gained an identity as Entente soldiers in a struggle for civilization. Against the *them* of the Germans, they joined the *us* of the trenches.

Though colonial troops had not earned total equality, they had earned respect in the eyes of many other British and French soldiers. Just after the war, in 1919, Alphonse Séché published *Les noirs*, meant to be a historical account of colonial troops and compiled largely from official documents. In it, Séché suggests that indigenous colonial troops earned the admiration of their metropolitan brothers in arms and that they also played a role in ending the war when it ended, diminishing losses and modifying the conditions of victory.[93] What did the metropolitan men from the trenches think? The French trench journal *Le poilu*, still being published after the war, noted Séché's publication in a 1919 edition. The editors of *Le poilu* were pleased that there was "finally" a book on this subject, because the tirailleurs sénégalais "merited" their own historian.[94]

Men on the Margins

FOUR

Other Fronts, Other Wars?

Though the "guns of August" fired in Western Europe, the Great War involved campaigns and battles as far away as the Pacific Ocean. Away from Europe, the Ottoman and African campaigns, in particular, spanned a vast geography and engaged a diverse group of soldiers and noncombatants.[1] Fighting in Africa relied heavily on African soldiers and the mobilization of hundreds of thousands of porters.[2] The British Indian Army played a dominant role in the East African campaigns and in the Ottoman campaigns. The Indian Army had been involved in prewar East African campaigns and was also utilized because threats in the regions were considered by the British to be threats to India.[3] At the start of the war, India's Expeditionary Force A went to Europe, B and C went to East Africa, D went to Mesopotamia, E and F were sent to Egypt, and G went to Gallipoli.[4] Though soldiers of European descent served in the African and Ottoman campaigns, especially as officers, the composition of the fighting forces outside Europe was much more diverse than, and quite distinct from, the armies within western Europe. The battles and objectives were also distinct from the Western Front. As discussed in the earlier chapter "The Great War in Imperial Context," the fronts in Africa and Mesopotamia became largely struggles for colonial possessions. The Entente sought to take away German colonies and, at minimum, wrest control away from the Ottoman Empire in much of the Middle East.[5] For its part, Germany sought

to incite colonial rebellions in British and French possessions, which would distract their leaders, reroute Entente
soldiers from Europe, and affect Entente supplies.[6] Entente
soldiers starting from Thessaloniki were also sometimes
involved in fighting against the Bulgarians. For soldiers
back in Europe, the African and Ottoman campaigns were
distant, and the war outside of Western Europe seemed far
removed, in terms of experience and imagination.

This chapter explores descriptions of the war outside
Europe, especially the African and the Ottoman campaigns,
in British and French trench newspapers, beginning with
papers based in Europe and then examining a small selec-
tion of European papers from the non-European campaigns.
From informative to humorous, references to the Ottoman
campaigns, in particular, displayed an awareness of, and a
desire for, news of other fronts. Descriptions of the war outside Europe in European trench newspapers make apparent a geography of value among Entente soldiers, with the
Ottoman campaigns garnering significantly more attention than the African campaigns. Fighting outside Europe
was valued according to its perceived relevance to the war
in Europe, with Africa largely absent.

Though not all papers frequently commented on the war
outside the Western Front, Entente papers make it clear that
soldiers were aware of the world nature of the war. A 1915
cartoon in *Le dernier bateau* put forward a newly created,
humorous map that would allow all the fronts to be shown
together for the ease of the reader trying to follow the war.[7]
Now Petrograd was just southeast of Paris, and the Eiffel
Tower was northwest of Berlin, which bordered the Sahara,
and was east of Turkish Europe. *Le dernier bateau* assured
its readers that they now had no need to consult multiple
maps to understand the war in its complexity. Even if the
rest of the world was not at the forefront of the imagina-

Other Fronts, Other Wars?

tion of soldiers in Europe, they were not ignorant of the existence of other fronts.

British and French trench newspapers represented the Ottomans and their lands as both familiar and exotic. The images used in trench papers drew on Romantic and travel literature running back centuries, in addition to the stories of The Thousand and One Nights and the poetry of Omar Khayyam. The tropes were well known to soldiers, but the people and places were presumed exotic and romantic, like clichéd perfumed cigarettes and welcoming harems. Within European trench newspapers this thread is stable, but within the papers from the Ottoman campaigns this thread wore thin as soldiers experienced the distance between their representations and the reality of the region. Trench newspapers based outside Europe are considered here in the section "On the Ground."

If trench newspapers demonstrate an awareness of other fronts and the persistence of orientalism, they may also say something about how Entente soldiers in Europe understood the role of empires in the war. In *The Indian Empire at War*, George Morton-Jack argues that "broadly speaking, if the war on Germany was for democracy, the war on Turkey was for imperialism."[8] To what extent did Entente soldiers in Europe comment on, or approve of, the imperial objectives of the African and Mesopotamian campaigns? Trench newspapers can offer us insight into the ways that Entente soldiers understood the relationship between the war and their respective empires.

The terminology utilized within trench newspapers is included in this chapter. In the papers, the terms *Orient*, *Turks*, and *Arabs* are all used, often inaccurately and with sometimes confusing effect. For example, Ottoman soldiers might be referred to broadly as "Turks" or "Arabs" though not all were, in fact, Turkish or Arab. The Ottoman Empire bridged East and West and included Turks and Arabs, but neither exclusively. Including soldiers' descriptions of the people and places they encountered is another way of showing how they understood and represented the Ottoman Empire but is not meant as an acceptance of soldiers' informal ethnographies. By including the perspective of soldiers who served in Mesopotamia, this chapter gives a glimpse into the wartime experience of empire of those whose soldiering most clearly resembled the actions of agents of empire before the war.

News and Opinion

In the March 15, 1916, issue of *The Gasper*, the so-called Cockney Critic asked for information from "noospapers" about the Dardanelles and the situation in Russia.[9] Though trench newspapers were often short of traditional news, they still reflected soldiers' desires to be informed about other fronts involved in the war. Censorship may have prevented more detailed information about fighting in or outside Europe from appearing in the pages, but it did not prevent curiosity, rumor, and speculation on the part of trench authors. In particular, the efforts against the Ottomans often seemed newsworthy in Western Front papers. Though not analyzed here, somewhat common and comic references to the Russians were also in some papers. In contrast, the fighting in Africa was almost never mentioned.

Within trench newspapers, the struggle against the Ottomans seems to have been part of the public consciousness of the trenches. The Ottoman campaigns were referenced in both subtle and explicit ways. The *Wipers Times* used the "Eastern theatre" to mock Hillaire Belloc in a March 6, 1916, article by "Belary Helloc." The article made outlandish claims about who held the front and found "by logical deduction we can prophecy that the Eastern Campaign must end disastrously to the Central Powers."[10] Of course,

Other Fronts, Other Wars?

any prediction of Belloc's was taken to be false by most *Wipers* readers, and the article was published *after* the apparent failures of Gallipoli. The Ottoman campaigns also crept into other subjects. In the poem "The Left Barrel" in the May 1, 1916, *Wipers Times*, Gilbert Frankau describes himself as a poet known by girls "from Camberwell to Kut."[11] "Kut" was a reference to Kut-el-Amara, where the British were surrounded by the Ottoman Army and twelve thousand men were captured by the Ottomans after a period of siege and starvation. Though chosen for the purposes of the rhyme, the reference to Kut demonstrates an awareness of the situation and the assumption that the reference will be understood by readers.

Brief news reports about war events outside Europe were fairly common in trench newspapers. The March 15, 1916, issue of *Le plus-que-torial* featured an article titled "The Situation in the Balkans," which attempted to provide analysis of the political situation in Greece, including King Constantine's decision-making process and the influence of his royal, German relatives.[12] The March 1, 1916, *Le canard poilu* included news from Constantinople about the actions of the Russians in the Caucasus.[13] That issue also had news ostensibly from contributors in Sofia and Vienna. A 1915 *Le poilu St.-Émilionnais* featured a news column that included an update from Athens, discussed the Balkan campaigns, spoke of the Indian troops in the Dardanelles, and asserted that Turkish officials believed their cause to be lost.[14] The existence of these articles suggest that British and French soldiers had some interest in the war outside their own front.

The Ottoman campaigns, in particular, likely figured in soldiers' consciousness because many soldiers from Europe served there. A 1917 issue of *Taca tac teuf teuf* informed readers that "we have dedicated many issues to relating the exploits of the auto machine gunners on our front and in the Orient."[15] In 1916, the editors of *Boum! Voilà!* wrote about the paper's connections with soldiers at other fronts, claiming the paper was not just "a paper of one part of the front, but of all fronts," because it had correspondents and subscribers elsewhere, in Alsace, Champagne, and Salonika.[16] Those correspondents and subscribers outside Europe had been reassigned from the Western Front. And other trench authors seemed to think of reassignment to Mesopotamia as a constant possibility for themselves. In an issue of *Le paix-père*, the third scene of a play includes soldiers sitting around, eating and arguing about where they will move next. Some think they will move closer to the German border; others believe they will move to Salonika, the launching pad for attacking the Ottomans in the Dardanelles (or the Bulgarians); and others predict moving elsewhere.[17] Trench newspapers sometimes continued to publish pieces and information from soldiers reassigned to other divisions.[18] But occasionally the paper itself moved. The *Mudhook* was a British divisional magazine based in France whose predecessor was the *Dardanelles Driveller*, also called *Dardanelles Dug-Out Gossip*.

Within soldiers' discourse, specific campaigns and battles overshadowed others. The Dardanelles campaign was the most written-about non-European campaign within trench newspapers. In a letter to his wife in the autumn of 1915, A. J. Sansom wrote, "I am more anxious about the Dardanelles than any other part of our operations, as I should think it was almost impossible to hang on there through the winter, and the obstacles they have to encounter seem to be almost insurmountable at the present."[19] Sansom's anxiety was shared by many trench authors. An article about the Dardanelles began on the front page of the August 1915 *La guerre joviale*. It suggested that the prize of Constantinople was only a matter of hours away.[20] *La guerre joviale* regularly informed its readers about the other fronts, including those in Russia, Turkey, and Italy. In the September 1915 issue, the paper acknowledged that the Dardanelles was often spoken of, and it provided information about the deployment of English troops to Gallipoli.[21] Whereas after the war the Dardanelles and Gallipoli became central to the national narratives of Australia and New Zealand, trench newspapers remind us of the importance of the Dardanelles campaign to British and French soldiers during the war as well. It was one struggle they tried to follow closely from afar.

Though not as prominent as the Dardanelles, the Battle of Kut-el-Amara unsurprisingly received considerable mention in British trench newspapers. The battle was the result of overextension by the Indian Expeditionary Force, which was meant to defend nearby oil fields but soon became more ambitious about the possibilities of territorial gains in the Ottoman Empire. British troops found themselves chased to Kut-el-Amara, on the Tigris River, in early December 1915 and were under siege there until April of 1916. The siege left soldiers and locals "trapped in an insanitary, disease-ridden enclave plagued by dysentery and diarrhhoea, scurvy, malaria and pneumonia."[22] The result was an unconditional surrender, a "truly humiliating capitulation of around 12,500 British and Indian soldiers."[23] The British had also suffered nearly twice as many men as casualties during relief efforts, and thousands of the prisoners would die during a forced march away from Kut-el-Amara.[24]

Coverage of the events at Kut-el-Amara showcased the various ways in which such references could operate, chiefly humor, practical orientation, or gripping serial account. In *The Gasper*, a small notice titled "Kutting" read as follows:

MINISTER: The Government has nothing further to communicate with reference to Kut.

M.P.: We must assume, then, that it is a case of *cut communications.*[25]

Still in the crisis of the siege, *The Gasper's* "cut communications" shared the gravity of the British soldiers' isolation in Kut with a tongue-in-cheek approach. Like most truly news-related items in trench papers, humor was used to mask content. After the humiliating defeat, *Wipers Times* offered a not-so-veiled critical commentary, which is a good example of the satiric humor in trench newspapers. The *Wipers Times'* "Mesopotamian Alphabet" referenced Kut-el-Amara under I:

> I is for the Indian government, but
> About this I'm told I must keep my mouth shut,
> For it's all due to them that we failed to reach Kut-
> El-Amara in Mesopotamia [26]

The Battle of Kut-el-Amara also provided the material for gripping news accounts similar to the colonial stories of the prewar civilian press. As with Charles "Chinese" Gordon at Khartoum in 1884–1885, the British forces at Kut-el-Amara were surrounded. The siege of Kut-el-Amara lasted 147 days.[27] During the siege, at least a dozen men died per day of starvation.[28] Like Gallipoli, the Battle of Kut-el-Amara was a major defeat outside Europe that drew the attention of both soldiers and civilians.

Although the African campaigns had a few of their own trench newspapers, such as *Doings in East Africa*, the campaigns were essentially absent from European trench newspapers. There are many possible explanations for this absence. It could reflect the lack of available news from the African campaigns. Or it could reflect indifference. Soldiers from Europe certainly had fewer personal connections to the fighting in Africa because relatively few of them were assigned to the African campaigns and many of the white soldiers who served in Africa for the British were from South Africa. European trench authors may also have been uninterested in fighting done primarily by nonwhite soldiers.

Whatever the reason, trench newspapers definitely demonstrate that the war in Africa was perceived as less significant, or less interesting, than the war in Mesopotamia or Europe. In fact, in British trench newspapers more references were to the Boer War than the African fronts of the Great War.

One way to consider the implications of the absence of African-campaign coverage is to look at the discussion of the Eastern Front. The Russian forces were more commonly referenced in both British and French trench newspapers than African forces, quite apart from the Russian Revolution. The July 1917 *Le tord boyau* featured a serious article titled "The Situation in Russia."[29] It outlined Russia's commitment to see the war through, an absence of fraternization with the Germans, and the presence of female fighters on the Eastern Front. In a lighter vein, the September 8, 1917, *Wipers Times* advertised a fictional revue titled "Goodbye-ee-e, We Mos-cow" with the "Bally Russe."[30] In an issue of *Le crapouillot* was a "small Russian story" about a group of Russian soldiers in the trenches. The slice of life story described the Russians as having "clear eyes, red skin, and blonde hair" and presented them as sympathetic and familiar as they sat in the trenches sharing stories.[31] Stories that emphasized the beauty and the strength of the Russians were common in the civilian press at the time of the arrival of the Russian Expeditionary Force in France.[32] Though Russians were not always historically considered white in the West, unlike most of the soldiers fighting against the Central Powers in Africa, the Russian forces could be considered white. The physical description within the *Crapouillot* story certainly suggests whiteness. Though their prominence may have been, in part, tied to perceived whiteness, the Russians were also certainly discussed for other reasons.

For most European soldiers, the Eastern Front was directly related to the Western Front. The Russian threat on the Eastern Front prevented the Central Powers from attacking the Western Front with all of their resources. In fact, the Russians captured more German prisoners in the first two years of the war than did the British and French combined.[33] Many British and French soldiers also pinned their hopes on a Russian advance that would squeeze the Central Powers and defeat the Germans in Europe. There were many fantasies in trench newspapers about Russians marching deep into Germany or about Russian relief troops appearing on the Western Front. Though most British and French soldiers actually had little personal connection to the Russians or the places they fought—the Russian Expeditionary Force in France had only two brigades—their significance was clear.[34]

In contrast, Germany had relatively few forces in Africa, and even the defeat of the Germans in Africa would not have hastened the end of the war. Hew Strachan has written that the African campaigns more closely resembled colonial campaigns than the Great War, even if they were fought for European objectives, and "in relation to the outcome of the war they were, as is too often remarked, sideshows."[35]

When trench newspapers acknowledged the Russians, it was not to suggest that their efforts were sideshows. They were thought to play a valuable role against the Ottomans, in addition to against the Germans. The March 1917 *Le petit echo* included news on the "oriental front" and informed readers that the English troops took Baghdad and were pursuing the Turks without ceasing while the Russians were coming in on the other side.[36] References to Russia in British and French trench newspapers were common throughout the war, and those before the revolution in 1917 far outnumber those about the revolution. They suggest not only that Russia was perceived as a valuable ally but also that the fighting against the Central Powers in Europe was, unsurprisingly, the most significant struggle for most European trench authors.

Other Fronts, Other Wars?

The value of the perceived winnings may also have shaped the attention given to some campaigns over others. Though significant for affecting Germany's war effort, the war at sea was largely absent from trench newspapers. The fighting in Africa and Mesopotamia was driven by empire-related objectives to seize new land and prevent the growth of other empires. The British Empire was 27 percent larger after the war.[37] But between African and Ottoman lands, the Ottoman lands were considered more valuable in trench papers. The Ottoman Empire and its former holdings, especially Baghdad, were also more directly contested with the Germans for control, even before the war. And though Africa had a place in the European literary imagination, through works by H. Rider Haggard and others, there was a much greater legacy of orientalist literature.

Orientalism

Whereas realism may have motivated quite a bit of the interest in the Ottoman campaigns, it did not drive representations of them. For many British and French soldiers, the Ottoman Empire was both exotic and familiar. Orientalism appears in French tales as far back as *The Song of Roland*. The English reading public had been exposed to Turkish histories and travel literature as early as the sixteenth century, and such books were widely disseminated in the seventeenth century.[38] In the nineteenth century, Shelley, Byron, and other Romantics utilized orientalist themes while academic scholarship about the Middle East increased during "the period of unparalleled European expansion, from 1815–1914."[39] The Greek War of Independence and the Balkan Wars brought the Ottoman Empire into the newspapers of Europe. The struggles over the Suez Canal had not only made news but also emphasized the weakness of the Ottoman Empire in resisting European attempts at control and the rivalry of the British and the French in the region. In *The Other Empire*, Filiz Turhan argues that

> during the years in which the British Empire was expanding its holdings in the East and defining its role as a world empire, the Ottoman Empire acted as a provocative counterpoint in a way that differed from other regions in the East or from other European nations. Turkey's position as a disintegrating, medieval empire that was both incredibly familiar (due to the exhaustive writing about it, as well as its physical proximity to Europe) and yet still foreign (unmistakably Muslim and Asiatic), established it for decades as a pliable trope for writers who sought to understand England's evolving policies in the global scene.[40]

Many trench newspaper inclusions about the Ottoman campaigns maintain the sense both of the foreign and of the familiar.

Many trench newspaper articles tried to call up the fantastical "Orient" known to readers from The Thousand and One Nights or the works of the Romantic poets. Poems especially utilized familiar themes and settings. A poem titled "Restrictions" in *The Gasper*, authored by "Twopence," reads as follows:

> In far enchanted Orient lands,
> Where here and there amid the sands
> Are oases of palmy trees,
> And caravans, and nomad bands;
>
> Where Grand Viziers have plotted since
> They first salaamed Caliph or Prince,
> And wise Cadis pronounce degrees,
> Whose stoic victims never wince;
>
> Where great Pasha make amorous raids
> In quest of ever fairer maids,

And gather new if one's untrue,
Or as the earlier Queen-rose fades;

Where in the cities mosques lift high
Their minarets against the sky,
And all men pray at close of day
As peals the Muezzin's pious cry;

Where in bazaars they drink sherbet
And pull the perfumed cigarette,
And talk as men were talking when
The Prophet's beard was bristling jet;

Though spirits of a choicer wit
Have less regard for Holy Writ—
Though wine's taboo it's not na poo
To him who'll risk the burning pit!

They hold a fast in such domains,
A month of penalties and pains:
In Ramadan a greedy man,
His twelve Hours full hardly gains.

From sunrise to the day's eclipse
No bite of food his jawbone grips,
No cigarette in mouth is set,
No sup of liquor wets his lips.

But as the runner crouches low
At the sharp pistol's crack to throw
Him off the mark like spinning spark,
That bellows' breath may lift and blow.

So, while the sun swings slowly down,
A smell of cooking floods the town,
They spread the board, the drinks are poured,
The baccy waits, an odorous brown.

Thus have I watched on sultry days
Before the closed Estaminets
A queue that licks its lips till six—
Then drowns the memory of delays![41]

This poem contains many recurring themes in portrayals of the Orient within trench newspapers and literature. The "Orient lands" are immediately both far away and enchanted, full of sand, palm trees, oases, caravans, and nomads. All of the stock characters have been conjured up in the second stanza: viziers, caliphs, princes, cadis. The Orient in this poem is at once familiar and fantastic to readers. The Ottoman lands are those of fairy tales and adventure stories, with almost no relation to the trenches of Europe.

Many of the common negative tropes about the Ottomans are present in this poem. According to Turhan, there were three "primary ways in which the Ottoman Empire represented despotism: its treatment of the Greeks; the institution of the Harem; and the failure of the empire to modernize itself commercially and industrially."[42] In the third stanza the Pasha's quest for "ever fairer maids" is made known, a reference to the harem. The sherbet and smoking suggest lassitude, and the bazaar hints at a precapitalist society. Soon after, the men drinking sherbet and smoking perfumed cigarettes in bazaars are described as talking "as men were talking when / the Prophet's beard was bristling jet." In effect, the style of conversation and perhaps the language have not altered since the time of Muhammad, in the seventh century, demonstrating a failure to modernize.

The poem also describes the practice of Islam. Readers are introduced to the sound of muezzins, the practice of prayer, and the fasting of Ramadan. The muezzin's cry is "pious" and even the "greedy man" is portrayed as observing the fasting of Ramadan, disdaining to smoke a cigarette. The drinking of alcohol is also discussed. The author, Twopence, suggests that although alcohol is forbidden, those willing to risk eternal damnation can find it. One wonders if Twopence has read Omar Khayyam.[43] Unlike some other poems in trench newspapers, on various topics, "Restrictions" attempts to present an objective account. The author neither mocks nor praises Islam but takes faith practices seriously, if relying on a mythic setting.

The poem also presents an interesting contrast in the opening and closing stanzas. The poem begins in "far enchanted Orient lands," with caravans, nomads, and sands—essentially the open space of the desert. The poem then moves into the city and closes with estaminets and queues, all of which the author claims to have witnessed firsthand. Those "Orient lands" are familiar from legends and stories; their exoticism is expected and anticipated. However, the people within them sound familiar; they observe religious practices, they enjoy food, they have cities and restaurants and even queue like the English. The lands are both far away, as in the first stanza, and up close, personally witnessed, as in the last stanza. This combination of exoticism and familiarity runs through many trench newspaper references to the Ottomans, especially those that relied on Romantic images.

Many trench newspapers utilized shared tropes in portrayals of the Ottoman campaigns. The Mesopotamian Alphabet in the January 20, 1917, *Wipers Times* provides a good example. Of course

> H are the Harems, which it appears
> Have flourished in Baghdad for hundreds of years,
> We propose to annex all the destitute dears—
> When their husbands leave Mesopotamia.[44]

The harem was one of the primary themes in portrayals of the Ottomans before the war, and such references continued to serve the interests of eroticized humor and colonialist

ventures during the conflict, as well. The "Alphabet" conjures up other familiar images. *A* brings a reference to the
apple in the Garden of Eden, which was widely believed to
be in Mesopotamia. *L* is for loot, "wives and wine and bags
of rupees," the soldiers hope to receive in Baghdad.[45] Baghdad itself, then, is portrayed as a place of harems and riches,
much as in the tales of Sinbad the sailor. The "loot" and the
imminent departure and replacement of the harem owners
suggest traces not only of Crusades-era fantasies but also
of colonial practices.

The Mesopotamian Alphabet was sent to the *Wipers Times*
by an "old divisional friend" reattached to the Indian Army,
and it is ultimately more valuable for the ways it presents
the experiences of European soldiers in Mesopotamia. Most
of the letters are defined by the experiences of the soldiers,
such as the "B is the Biscuit," which "breaks your teeth and
bruises your belly, / And grinds your intestines into jelly."[46]
Many of the complaints would be familiar in any wartime
setting; the food, the work, the supplies, the censor. In that
way, the alphabet demonstrates the shared experience of
soldiers on all fronts with the discomforts of war and the
dissatisfaction with supplies. Other letters in the alphabet demonstrate how soldiers felt specifically about serving outside Europe:

> C is the poor old Indian Corps,
> Which went to France and fought in the war,
> Now it gathers the crops and fights no more
> In the land of Mesopotamia.[47]

This entry suggests that some soldiers felt they were out of
the war by being in Mesopotamia, critiquing the move out
of Europe. The alphabet emphasizes the nonfighting aspects
of life in Mesopotamia, but at every front of the war soldiers
experienced breaks in fighting, and even regular removal
from the frontline trenches in France and Belgium. For the

Other Fronts, Other Wars?

"old divisional friend," the important fighting was in Europe or done in the style of the fighting within Europe. Though leadership may also have been suspect on the Western Front, the alphabet indicates almost no confidence in the leadership in Mesopotamia. The author discusses the efforts of the staff and determines, "The net result was the Turks had a laugh."[48] About the orders from Indian Corps, the alphabet concludes, "Thank goodness by now we are perfectly sure / If issued at three they'll be cancelled by four."[49]

The Mesopotamian Alphabet certainly presents a picture of discomfort for seemingly little purpose. However, it is no more extreme than some of the satirical poems about life in the trenches in France. Ultimately, its author has much in common with the British soldiers fighting elsewhere. He would rather be at home, where

> K are the Kisses from lips sweet and fair,
> Waiting for us around Leicester Square,
> When we wend our way home, after wasting a year
> Or two in Mesopotamia.[50]

The perceived difference between the fronts seems to be captured in the "wasting."

French trench newspapers also made references to the Orient that would be familiar to their audience. As in British papers, The Thousand and One Nights was referenced many times. Some trench newspapers occasionally included "Arab proverbs."[51] Like the British, the French had an orientalist tradition within both academia and the arts. A book of "Arab stories" was included on a list of interesting, recently published books in La fusée à retards.[52] A humorous article in Le marteau presented columns with changes in Parisian entertainment from 1913 to 1915, because of the war and a sudden dislike of cultural products drawn from the Central Powers. Though in 1913 the Comédie Française column would have featured "the bourgeois gentleman and the

Turkish ceremony," in 1915 the ceremony would have been replaced with a scene from *Le mariage de Mlle Beulemans*, a Belgian play. Other replaced events were Wagner's German opera *Siegfried* and the quintessential Viennese operetta *The Happy Widow*.[53] The people and lands of the Ottoman Empire had figured within French popular culture long before the war. Another issue of *La fusée à retards* reminded readers that the practice of drinking coffee spread from the Orient.[54] Whether or not soldiers had practical or personal experience with the Ottoman Empire, many ideas and images about the Ottomans were circulating among soldiers and were apparent within trench newspapers.

Many references to the Ottomans in French trench newspapers also reflected the relationship between the Germans and the Ottomans. A cartoon in the March 11, 1917, *Le petit echo* featured a startled Wilhelm waking up suddenly in bed. Beside him is an open copy of a Thousand and One Nights story. From his room he sees a train coming from Baghdad and, looking frightened, he exclaims, "Baghdad to the English, no! I was dreaming."[55] This cartoon accurately depicts the importance of Baghdad in the Mesopotamian struggle and its then, and previous, significance as a railway hub for European imperial designs. Interestingly, it is the Germans who are seen as having control of the region to lose. Within trench newspapers, the words of Edward Said are quite relevant: "The other feature of Oriental-European relations was that Europe was always in a position of strength, not to say domination."[56] Though the Ottomans were, according to Strachan, "a worthy ally of the Central Powers," they were often portrayed as little more than puppets of the Germans. A cartoon from *L'esprit du cor* depicted this relationship.[57] Titled "The Germans in Constantinople," a larger-than-life German cavalry officer holds a small Turkish man, in traditional dress and a fez, on his knee. One of the German's arms is up in the air, and he is loudly singing, while behind him are the domes and minarets of a city under a crescent moon. The song is from the opera *Carmen*, "Et si je t'aime / Prends gaaarde à toi!!" From the crescent moon over the domed buildings to the fez, everything in Constantinople is both clichéd and overshadowed by the German. The image also continues the practice of infantilizing non-Europeans, which was common in French advertising, in which, for example, "African men were depicted as helpless babies."[58] The German here holds "the other" on his knee like a child. The words attributed to the German in the drawing suggest that the alliance may not even be in the best interest of the Turks. In this cartoon, and in other papers, the Germans are shown to overwhelm and to command their allies in an unequal partnership, the result of German will to power and Ottoman weakness and underdevelopment.

The October 1, 1916, *Bleutinet* featured a poem with the following second stanza:

> Y a des copains à Salonique
> Qui cont pour combattre le turc;
> Aux gros obus ils font la nique
> Et logent des call's dans les kul-turc.
> Les autres sont sur la Mer Noire,
> Ils torpillent avec brio.
> Moi, c'est toujours la même histoire,
> Je repére le crapouillot.[59]

The poem refers to friends in Salonika who fight against the Turks. Even here we see the presumed influence of the Germans, in the use of *kul-turc*, yet another in the endless plays on kultur. As discussed in the chapter "Why War?" German kultur was a competing, modern system of values seen in opposition to Anglo-French civilization. This term, *kul-turc*, also appeared in other trench newspapers. While it indicates the involvement of the Ottomans, it reinforces the idea that the Germans were the ones with objectives in the war and possibly suggests that Ottoman involvement was the result of bad influence. As with a cartoon showing Wilhelm losing Baghdad, the Ottomans were sometimes shown to have little at stake even in their own lands. What was gained or lost was gained or lost for Germany. In an issue of *Brise d'entonnoirs* a German offensive in Egypt was discussed, without reference to the non-Germans who fought there for the Central Powers. It was Wilhelm who wanted to take Cairo.[60] In trench papers, the Ottomans were not taken very seriously as an enemy, despite significant Entente military losses against the Ottomans at places like Gallipoli and Kut-el-Amara.

Like the Ottoman Empire, the Austro-Hungarian Empire was typically overshadowed by the Germans within British and French trench newspapers. In a telling example, the first issue of *La musette* published an "Austrian legend" supposedly found among the papers of Austrian prisoners and widespread within their army. In the story, the heads of the Great Powers, fatigued by war, send their ambassadors to heaven to find mediators for peace. They speak to Saint Peter, Moses, even Jesus Christ, but all decline their invitation. Finally, the ambassadors speak to God himself, who says he cannot leave his throne for one moment because Emperor Wilhelm would take possession of it.[61] For the author of this piece in *La musette*, even the Austrians identify Wilhelm as the chief aggressor and consider Germany to be the greatest enemy of peace. Seldom discussed on their own and taken less seriously than the Germans, the Austro-Hungarians were typically shown, like the Ottomans, to be subordinate to the Germans. *Le poilu sans poil* acknowledged that Austrians were often considered negligible adversaries when the paper referenced fighting in Italy.[62] That the Great War began with the affairs of Austria-Hungary was a forgotten aspect of the conflict for

British and French trench authors. Like gas that occluded the trenches, within trench papers, Germany hid the rest of the Central Powers or offered them tutelage in kultur. A reader of Entente trench journals would not be surprised by Article 231 of the Treaty of Versailles, which assigned the blame for the war to Germany.

On the Ground

British and French soldiers who fought in the Ottoman campaigns and elsewhere outside Western Europe also had trench newspapers. Some were founded there, such as *Le bavardar de l'A.O.*, which served the French Army of the Orient, or *The Gnome*, which served the British Royal Flying Corps in Egypt. Other trench newspapers migrated from Western Europe with their soldiers, such as *La bourguignotte*. A look at some of these newspapers can provide further insight into orientalist themes in soldiers' discourses and the extent to which the Ottoman and Central European campaigns were "a sideshow" even for many of those in that particular show.

As in Europe, many trench newspapers for soldiers outside Western Europe provided some kind of minimal news function. In many cases, that was truer outside Western Europe than within. While the first issue of *Le bavardar de l'A.O.* did describe Salonika as a "Babel" because of the diversity of current residents, nearly the entire two-page paper was devoted to the fire that had recently swept through the city.[63] *The Gnome* regularly provided descriptions of recent aerial battles and bombing runs. Its readers included men studying at the School of Military Aeronautics, so it often contained long articles about flying and equipment. Those articles offered practical advice and covered differences in weather conditions, in addition to what was different from flying in Europe. Trench newspapers outside Europe also put forth an effort to inform readers about events in Europe. Though the sample size is quite limited, trench papers outside Europe seem to have had more of a news function than those in Europe and provided more factual information, alongside the humor.

British and French trench newspapers in the "Orient" definitely made use of orientalist tropes in imagery. Based in Egypt, *The Gnome* masthead had a decorative scroll for "editorial notes" framed above with an empty landscape of two pyramids and a small group of palm trees, while a biplane flew beside a single cloud. The last page of the May 1917 *Gnome* included a clichéd drawing of an older Egyptian with a small boy.[64] The older man is sitting cross-legged on the ground and attempting to read *The Gnome* but holds it upside down. The small boy beside him stares up into the sky. For the artist of the cartoon, the contents, like its European authors, seem beyond the limited comprehension of the locals. Such images were not limited to British trench papers in Mesopotamia.

The use of orientalist themes extended beyond images and into the text of Ottoman campaign newspapers. The May 26, 1916, *Le clairon* included a poem set during an Oriental night, complete with perfumed wind, a mosque, and minarets.[65] Nearly every paper included references to a muezzin, as did the September 1917 *Le bavardar de l'A.O.*, in an article about the sun in Salonika.[66] The "oriental sun" was a trope in itself. Depictions of the Ottomans were fairly consistent; the Turks were regularly portrayed as despotic and backward.[67] As Edward Said has written in *Orientalism*, recurring themes within European portrayals of the "Orient" were "backwardness, degeneracy, and inequality with the West."[68] Based in Palestine, the *Chronicles of the White Horse* included articles about the local ethnic groups, which often demonstrated these themes. Writing about the Bedouins, the paper suggests that "the Beduin is thriftless and does not lay by against a bad season and in such a time the Egyptian Government has had to distribute great quantities of Barley to the poor to keep them from starving."[69] Later in the article, the author claims that "their clothes and their wanderings show little change since the days of Abraham. It is a simple life."[70] In addition, "practically all the work is done by the women."[71]

The same kinds of tropes were sometimes applied in southeastern Europe. The soldiers of *La bourguignotte* passed through Greece, Macedonia, Albania, Bulgaria, and Serbia and liked little of what they saw. One author concluded that while perhaps those in Constantinople lived well, the Ottoman subjects in the isolated mountain villages were not well off. They had been closed to progress for centuries, living a simple and rustic existence, indolent by nature, passive slaves to a religion that annihilated all energy and initiative.[72] *La bourguignotte* found the Albanians a "bizarre race" with a "foreign mentality."[73] And, of course, at least one author in *La bourguignotte* blamed the "oriental sun" for apathy and laziness because it annihilated energy and created lethargy.[74] Like orientalist academics in the preceding centuries, the trench authors found unchanging, backward, and despotic traditions wherever they looked.

Personal narratives from Ottoman campaigns yield much the same impression. In his diary, Lt. Col. J. W. Barnett wrote positively of the Indian soldiers he served alongside but very negatively about the Arabs he encountered. He and his men requisitioned supplies from a village, which brought an encounter with locals. Barnett wrote, "Large number of scoundrels in village so glad had big guard. Dislike Arab practice of trying to kiss hand & arm. Arab woman kissed my arm 4 times in vain attempt to save her favourite ram but as ram was very fat was unable to see my way to giving back."[75] A few days later he wrote, "Arabs have no modesty at all. Strip naked at any moment. One Arab captain says he had 20 wives, & only 5 survive. Evidently they take a wife & if she does not produce children after a reasonable interval she is kicked out & another wife taken. They are quite immoral & liars & thieves of the worst description.'"[76] While Barnett clearly had a strong dislike of the men and women he met, he was nonetheless convinced that the area would be a great prize for the British in the war and could be well cultivated. His chief concern was that the Russians might reach Baghdad first.

There is some contrast between these opinions and those in the trench newspapers of the Western Front. The scathing assessments offered by Barnett, *The Chronicles of the White Horse*, and *La bourguignotte* are significantly different from the tone of the poem "The Restrictions" in *The Gasper*, which was based in Europe. Although "The Restrictions" also conjures an image of preindustrial life and leisure-oriented people outside Western Europe, it does not use terms like *thriftless*, which *Chronicles of the White Horse* applied to Arabs, or describe a "bizarre race," as *La bourguignotte* termed the Albanians.

Perhaps the encounter with the other was rendered more difficult outside of Europe for most Europeans. For example, whereas African troops could be celebrated within European trench newspapers, in Africa, white settlers worried that whites fighting each other in Africa and Africans killing whites in Africa for the war effort would threaten white racial supremacy.[77] A certain amount of the disparity in descriptions was also no doubt tied to the surprise of the actual encounter with the "Orient" supposedly well-known from orientalist tropes. Much about the Mesopotamian experience seemed unsettling for Entente troops from Europe. Within the Ottoman Empire, too, the war initiated more diverse interactions. According to Leila Fawaz's study of the Middle East during the Great War, *A Land of Aching Hearts*, those interactions "on occasion . . . led to the growth of prejudice, with some developing stereotypes about the 'other,'" but there was "also a concurrent openness to the new."[78]

Other Fronts, Other Wars?

British and French soldiers in non-European campaigns were very clearly aware of the imagery associated with the East and made use of it within their papers. However, soldiers also became dissatisfied with the very tropes they knew and used. The fifteenth issue of *La bourguignotte*, recently reassigned from Europe, had a large drawing on its front page of a naked woman fanning a heavy-set poilu who was sitting on a carpet and enjoying a hookah. The caption was "The Orient seen from France."[79] The very next page of the paper began with an article titled "The Disenchanted Impression of a Poilu of the Orient," which was chiefly about being misled by "Orientalists." The Orient the author found was not the enchanted garden described by poets and romantics, with white minarets, palaces, and mysterious mosques.[80] No beautiful, lounging women awaited the French. He concludes that the Orient is "an idea so beautiful . . . and so false."[81] The disenchanted author does allow that the French might enjoy the scenery more if they weren't there to play a part in the unfolding drama of the war but maintained that a large distance is between the Orient he found and the one he read about within literature. These sentiments were quite common. An issue of *Chronicles of the White Horse* included a small section titled "Shattered Illusions:"

1. A land flowing with milk and honey.
2. Open warfare is vastly more exciting than trench fighting.
3. Turkey cannot hold out for more than another month. (November 1916)
4. The plague of flies was removed in the reign of one of the Pharaohs.[82]

That same issue included a poem titled "A Sand Grouse" by C.G.B.:

Oh! Sunny Land of Promise
Oh! flowery Palestine!

Oh! Land of corn and olive
The Fig-tree and the Vine.
The fruit we thought to gather
Seems always out of reach,
The flowers we heard so much of
Are only flowers of speech!

Jerusalem the Golden,
With milk and honey blest;
Where is that milk and honey?
It seems to have "gone West."
The honey that I've met here
Is Crosse and Blackwell's brand,
The only milk I've tasted
Has come from Switzerland.

I sometimes sit and wonder
If all we read is true,
And why these ancient S—s[83]
Thought such a lot of you!
Would I were back in London
In a cosy "Private Bar",
With a pint of foaming bitter
And a Sixpenny Cigar.[84]

C.G.B. lamented the lack of milk and honey and the presence of so many people who would be excluded from a "private bar" in London. Here the "land far away" is not exotic and exciting, as in Romantic literature, but repulsive and too proximate.

British and French soldiers entered the war familiar with oriental themes in advertising. In particular, there was an association between "the East" and luxury in marketing campaigns. This marketing ploy sometimes appeared in trench newspapers too. *Trot-Talk*, for example, advertised Belle of the Orient Egyptian-blend cigarettes. But once they actually were in the legendary land of "perfumed cigarettes" and sumptuous tobacco, many soldiers reevaluated the advertisements they had known. Consider the following from *The Gnome*:

> A Cigarette Advertisement culled from an English contemporary reads: "especially such a 'smoke' as Ariston, the delightful cigarette with the full exotic aroma that one associates with the shadow-bound mosques, spice-laden breezes, strange priceless perfumes, and the alluring sweetness of the East."
>
> On the whole, Mr. Muratti, we do *not* think that *such* a cigarette *would* improve the mood, assist thought, or calm disquietude!!![85]

Instead, *The Gnome* advertised Johnnie Walker. Whether or not soldiers altered their biases about people in the Middle East based on their experiences in the Ottoman campaigns, they were made aware of the stereotypes and the fantasies that their culture had conditioned them to believe. Many who wrote in the trench newspapers of the Ottoman campaigns seemed unable to absorb literature and travel narratives about the region in the same way during the war.

The Ottoman campaigns presented European soldiers with new enemies and challenges. However, within their trench newspapers, British and French soldiers continued to emphasize the German threat just as had their counterparts back in Europe. The September 20, 1917, *Le bavardar de l'A.O.* discussed the kaiser and the "boches" rather than any other Central Powers.[86] *Le clairon* was based in Salonika, not fighting directly against the Germans, but on May 26, 1916, it suggested, "We knew boche brutality" and asserted, "Kultur was judged and condemned from Belgium."[87] For most Entente soldiers, the Ottomans had nothing like kultur to oppose.[88] As with the term *kul-turc*, the Ottomans were represented as carrying foreign values and not forming their own. The next issue of *Le clairon* included a review of Guglielmo Ferrero's book, *La guerre européenne.*[89] Books about the Ottoman campaigns were not even suggested. From Egypt, *The Gnome* tried to inform its readers about all the fronts, but when it came to the enemy, the Germans had priority. In March 1917 *The Gnome* told readers that "Germany has put forward some suggestion anent peace."[90] Though it was far from Europe, *The Gnome* was primarily concerned with Germany's involvement in peace talks.

Trench newspapers reinforced the idea of inequality with the West, which Edward Said identified as a dominant theme in representation of the East.[91] Though the Ottoman Empire technically bridged the East and West, in trench newspapers' portrayals it was distinctly Eastern, for the papers written by troops in the theater and for those based in Europe. Trench authors extended that inequality to the partnership between the Germans and the Ottomans and other Central Powers. The sixteenth issue of *La bourguignotte* included a poem about Wilhelm, "emperor of the Boches," which claimed he had promised his people they would rule over a world of slaves and promised his subjects the Orient and mastery over Austria.[92] According to the poet, the Germans viewed their own allies as the spoils of war. Another issue of the same paper had an article claiming all was not well in the house of the Boches. The Turks in Bulgaria were shocked by German mistreatment, and an accompanying drawing showed Germany putting its allies to work at manual labor, running the German war machine.[93] In the illustration, dozens of Turks, some of them sailors and some of them soldiers, manually powered the "Motor Boch" while a bespectacled, bearded, overweight German officer with an Iron Cross laughed and gestured at the laborers with his thumb.

For trench authors in the Ottoman campaigns, equality with the West was not something that could be achieved

Other Fronts, Other Wars?

by their local enemies. British and French soldiers were disappointed by the inaccuracies in the oriental literature they had received, but they were often not impressed by the people they met either. Despite some good fighting, the Ottomans were chronically undersupplied, and the Empire struggled with hunger during the war.[94] Entente papers in the Ottoman campaigns continued to emphasize Germany as almost their only enemy. Articles and drawings that portrayed the alliance between the Germans and the Ottomans suggested the inferior status of the Ottomans and that the Germans made all decisions regarding the war and used the Ottomans for labor. Interestingly, this was mirrored in Indian autobiographies, wherein the war "is remembered pre-eminently as a clash between Britain and Germany, even though the greater proportion of South Asian troops fought in Ottoman domains."[95]

Whether due to a belief in the German threat, a belief in the inferiority of the Ottomans, or the lack of personal imperial ambition, soldiers in the Ottoman campaigns often made it clear within their trench newspapers that they would rather be fighting in Europe. In the second issue of *The Gnome*, the editorial notes reviewed *The First Seven Divisions* by Lord Ernest Hamilton. The trench newspaper editor gave the book a positive review. He also offered thoughts for his readers. After discussing the zeal of new officers and soldiers on the Western Front, he asked, "Are we, living in the Middle East—particularly those who are still in training almost out of range of the echo of war—keenly sharpening our wits, laboriously increasing our knowledge, making ourselves efficient for the action which will come presently to each of us?"[96] The author clearly doubts the severity, and also the value, of the fighting outside Europe, questioning whether soldiers there are putting forth enough effort. Later in the article he praises the officers being produced by the School of Military Aeronautics in Egypt, writing that "we shall not fear when they, in their several capacities, have to dispute in the air the vital question of mastery with the Boche."[97] This suggests that the fighting the Royal Flying Corps in Egypt did against the Turks was not very significant and perhaps only a preparation for more serious conflict.[98]

The Gnome's contents demonstrated that aviators in Egypt were facing enemies on a regular basis in the air. One aviator participated in both an aerial fight at six thousand feet and a raid, within a seventy-two-hour period. Yet confidentially, he asked, "Can you tell me how to get back to France? This is a . . . country. There's no fun here nor any fighting."[99] The editor of *The Gnome* was surprised by the pilot's perspective on fighting in Middle East. However, the belief that the fighting outside Europe was less meaningful was fairly widespread. In the same issue of *The Gnome* was this statement:

A Correspondent reminds me that:—

"The Aeroplanes of this Brigade, this Brigade alone, are flying over the mountains of Macedonia, the plains of Mesopotamia, the forest clad highlands of East Africa, and the deserts of Sinai and Makar."

"Repeat this in a deep bass voice slowly! Try it!" he says.

He might also have included the Kingdom of Babylon and the Land of the Children of Ham.[100]

The encouragement to repeat "in a deep bass voice slowly" suggests soldiers did not take these roles as seriously as perhaps their instructors and leaders would have liked. Based in Palestine, *Chronicles of the White Horse* mocked the war efforts at where they were based with a cartoon.[101] Titled "What He Did in the Great War," it had two panels: the first "What Mother Thinks He's Doing" and the second "What He IS Doing." The first panel depicted a pitched battle, with guns and great crowds of soldiers, engaging in hand-to-hand combat. The second panel showed one British soldier supervising a local leading two packed camels and another soldier moving rocks from a pile, while behind them stretched an empty desert landscape. Though soldiers in Europe, too, were not in the frontline trenches every minute of every day, soldiers in the Middle East seemed to find any lack of fighting frustrating. Henry Hampton Rich was an officer at Kut-el-Amara with the 120th Rajputana. In an Imperial War Museum (IWM) interview he suggested, "It was a complete small sideshow. The campaign and Kut—it didn't matter, the objective was to beat Germany."[102] In his mind, the fighting was more reflective of the Indian than the British government. In another IWM interview, Leslie George Pollard, who went to Sandhurst and served in Mesopotamia, related that soldiers preferred to be in France. According to Pollard, the weather in Mesopotamia was hot, and there was nothing around.[103] For most Entente soldiers, the Ottoman campaigns were a second-class war.

Not only were the Ottomans looked at differently in conflict, but their future was also pondered on different terms. Writing about the bombing of a Turkish aerodrome, *The Gnome* informed its readers that bombs "were labeled with some endearing comments on 'What happens to Turkey when peace is signed.'"[104] Here, *The Gnome* hinted at the nature of the British and French ambitions in the Ottoman campaigns, which were largely imperial. The Ottomans were not another enemy to be challenged, defeated, and ultimately kept within its own boundaries. For the Entente powers, the Ottoman Empire was a pie awaiting division.

Conclusion

In a letter to his father on October 4, 1918, Lt. F. B. Turner wrote that "the war seems to be going fairly well on all the fronts."[105] Lieutenant Turner was fighting in Western Europe, where most of the public's attention was focused. Yet Turner had some curiosity about, and awareness of, fighting outside Europe. British and French trench newspapers demonstrate that the same traits were present within soldiers' public discourse. Although Western Front trench newspapers were centered on the experiences and views of their readers and contributors in Europe, they did not neglect all parts of the wider war. Soldiers valued fighting elsewhere based on proximity, perceived significance, and involvement of troops most like themselves. The war in Africa was virtually absent from the pages of trench newspapers, but the Ottoman campaigns received attention.

Writing about the diversity of Entente forces in the "Orient," the *Brise d'entonnoirs* punned that it was a veritable "macédoine," a fruit salad.[106] There may have been a diverse Entente fighting force in the East, with Australians, British, French, and Serbians, but the descriptions of the Ottoman lands and its people were anything but. Orientalist tropes from literature and academia were common in trench newspaper depictions of the Ottomans. In the poems of trench papers, the Ottoman Empire was an enchanted land with backward people, a mosque every ten feet, and harems in every courtyard. The genre was so well defined it could be easily transported for any context. An issue of the *Lead-Swinger* included "The Belgian Nights," a spoof of The Thousand and One Nights, with references to the "mighty Emperor of Ind, who strove against his potent foe, the Khizar-Wilhelm."[107] There was little change from the existing orientalist stereotypes in most European trench papers.

British and French trench newspapers produced outside Western Europe also continued to utilize orientalist tropes, even while they acknowledged their disenchantment with the "real Orient." Papers based in Egypt, Palestine, and Salonika show that Entente soldiers did not consider the Ottomans an enemy on par with the Germans, despite some meaningful losses at their hands. Within soldiers' trench discourses, the Turks were little more than the lackeys of the Germans.

British and French papers based outside Europe also demonstrate the extent to which soldiers understood the value of their fighting and themselves almost exclusively within the context of Europe. British and French trench authors outside Western Europe downplayed the significance of their campaigns and personal service. From southeastern Europe, a regular author in *La bourguignotte* began referring to himself as a *déraciné*.[108] One wonders if the *La bourguignotte* author, referring to himself as "uprooted" like the characters in Maurice Barrès's 1897 novel, *Les déracinés*, felt, like Barrès, that he was losing his connection with the nation due to remoteness of homeland and the fighting there.[109]

The limited number of trench papers from outside Western Europe considered here renders it difficult to draw definite conclusions about the experience of European troops in Mesopotamia and Africa. However, there does seem to be a contrast with papers from Europe, where interaction with colonial troops had the ability to destabilize prewar racial stereotypes. Whether because so many of the "others" in Africa and Mesopotamia were enemies or because of the racial hierarchies of the Indian Army or for altogether different reasons, orientalism may have been somewhat disproved by experience for Europeans in other parts of the world, but discourses about non-Europeans did not necessarily improve. In this case, the paucity of trench newspapers in places like Mesopotamia complicates any analysis of the contrasts with European papers, but a comparative study of soldiers' memoirs might prove very interesting.

For metropolitan soldiers fighting in Europe, the Ottoman campaigns were part of their consciousness of the wider war, but the historical significance of the region was based largely on European events and involvement. Based in Egypt, *The Gnome* tried to make sense of the relationship between East and West. In an article on "Gaza and the Crusades," an author wrote that "centuries pass and in the eternal ebb and flow of Occident and Orient, again Gaza becomes prominent."[110] A brief history of the Crusades followed, with the conclusion that "the Crusaders left Palestine and all the land and its Arab civilization succumbed to Turkish barbarism. In those dark ages, which have endured up to the present day, Gaza is unheard of."[111] Without the Europeans, Gaza disappeared from the narrative of world history. Trench newspapers in Europe and in Mesopotamia frequently suggested that the significance of Mesopotamia was determined by the involvement of Europeans. Soldiers rarely broke from this mold of thought, though this citation from the *Egyptian Gazette* that appeared in *The Gnome* demonstrates that some were aware of the power of broader thinking: "The gift of historical imagination is one of the rarest and most delicate ever vouchsafed to mortals, for it gives one the power to enter into the thoughts and feelings of men of other ages and of other countries, and doubtless it may be that there is some purpose in all this turmoil of history that breaks in ceaseless waves against the battered walls of Gaza."[112] Whereas those who served in the Near East had their stereotypes of the region challenged by reality, for very few Entente soldiers, in Europe or elsewhere, did their historical imagination broaden enough to see the region as more than a tide pool of Europe.

During the Great War, the fighting outside the West was the most obviously imperial. The composition of the fighting forces, the territory gained and lost, and the geography all made some recognition of imperialism unavoidable. Yet Entente soldiers in and from Europe were least interested in these most obviously imperial parts of the war. The wartime imperialism of the British and French seems to resonate with Bernard Porter's sense of absentminded imperialism. Though both the African and the Ottoman campaigns promised the gain of new territory to the British and the French, most European soldiers expressed little to no enthusiasm for new possessions. In a 1915 letter from France that discussed the other fronts, Edward D. Ridley wrote, "I see there has been a rumour about that the Huns were prepared to evacuate France and Belgium in exchange for all French Africa and the Congo. I expect they would be glad of the chance."[113] While Ridley meant that the Entente forces had the Germans on the run, his comment also suggests French Africa and the Congo were worth less to the Entente than France and Belgium. The colonies had less value. Admittedly, Ridley was British and less vested in those territories, but his perspective reflects the widely shared belief in the centrality of Europe among European soldiers. In a 1917 letter, Ridley wrote, "That we shall give back some of them, I do not doubt, but I think Togo Land should be given over to Belgium as part compensation, and I think we shall refuse to part with West Africa. East Africa we should, I think, give back after correcting the Portuguese frontier to its correct position before the Germans grabbed that bit. They ought to be allowed some colonies, because it would be fairer and more towards a peaceful settlement. We must avoid a mere armistice."[114] The notion of returning land to Germany would seem inconceivable in any other part of the world. Ridley did not consider the future of Alsace and Lorraine in terms of what would be "fairer" and help avoid "mere armistice." Other parts of the world may have been at stake in the war, but, for most trench authors, territory lost and gained outside Europe was collateral damage but for a few exceptions. As discussed in Chapter One, "The Great War in Imperial Context," Ottoman and African lands were spoils of war but not territory that could not be lost whatever the cost. Though many German and Ottoman lands would change hands after the war, territorial ambitions did not loom large in soldiers' discourses about justifications for the war. The fighting everywhere was about defeating the Germans, not acquiring colonies, in trench papers. If the war in Europe was largely fought against Germany and for democracy and the war outside Western Europe largely imperial, as historian Morton-Jack has suggested, trench newspaper commentary on other fronts suggests that, during the war, most Entente soldiers were not especially interested in perpetuating imperialism.[115] British and French soldiers may have belonged to empires, but in trench newspapers the expansion of those empires does not appear to have been a significant war aim.

FIVE

Why War?

Between 1931 and 1932, Sigmund Freud and Albert Einstein carried on a correspondence later published as the booklet *Why War?* The luminaries remembered the First World War and were anxious about the storm clouds gathering in Europe, during what we now call the "interwar period." Both Freud and Einstein were concerned with instinct, violence, and humanity's tendency toward aggression. Einstein wondered if sufficient supranational organizations could be created to control men's natures. *Why War?* suggested that many of the reasons for war were difficult to comprehend, emerging from the primal interior within. Both Einstein and Freud were writing at a remove from the Great War and both were from the Central Powers, but for the men of the Entente during the war itself, the reasons for war were not ambiguous or instinctual. In their trench writings, British and French soldiers gave clear and specific, if sometimes idealistic, reasons for fighting. Freud and Einstein believed that the true reasons for war lay far beneath the public causes, within what went unsaid. This chapter explores the given reasons for war within the public discourse of trench newspapers and how that related to broader civilian rhetoric about the war.

The primary cause of the war in trench newspapers was German aggression, against which British and French soldiers together claimed to be defending civilization and their homelands—very often "king and country" for the British and the *patrie* for the French. These themes reflected broader discourses about the war in society. The cause of civilization was portrayed by trench journalists and paid journalists alike and contrasted with kultur in their respective publications. The defense of home was likewise present in both the trench and civilian press, but in the trench press that defense not only was tied to country, such as England or France, but could reference smaller communities as well. That was especially true within French trench newspapers. For all of the nationalist rhetoric in wartime, a deep appreciation for smaller communities was in the trench press, as was a love of home that was connected to the nation but not always best defined by it.

The reasons given for war in trench newspapers also demonstrate an important boundary for understanding the role of empire within the Great War. Although their armies were imperially constituted and the soldiers were aware of other fronts, their own empires were not typically among the reasons British and French soldiers gave for why they were fighting. Soldiers borrowed slang from around their empires and served under former colonial generals, but, as argued by Bernard Porter in *Absent-Minded Imperialists* about the British Empire generally, in the Great War "the empire qua empire really did not seem to matter much" to many metropolitan troops as an explanation for their involvement in the war.[1] Empire was a fact of life but not typically a reason for fighting in the First World War. That is an important distinction but does not mean that empire did not play a significant role in shaping how metropolitan soldiers interpreted their struggle.

Keeping the Home Fires Burning

In his famous poem "The Charge of the Light Brigade," Tennyson wrote of the doomed brigade: "Theirs not to reason why, / Theirs but to do and die." But in British and French trench newspapers, trench authors gave many reasons why they were in the war. At times, the reasons given in trench papers were humorous. But when soldiers were serious, the reasons were very consistently tied to the defense of home. British soldiers wrote often of king and country. French soldiers gave their lives for France or the patrie. Those visions of home and country could sometimes be very local.

In 1915 the *Lead-Swinger* published a story titled "The Autobiography of a Biscuit Tin." The biscuit tin in question was an obvious stand-in for a soldier, and the narrative followed his journey as he went from an empty volunteer to being stuffed with food and sent to the front. Upon reflection, the tin concluded that "life in the real sense—strangely enough, a destructive sense—does not commence until after mobilization," but, even after rebirth into the harsh conditions of war, he was "still fired with a desire to serve my King and Country."[2] The biscuit tin was not alone. Service to king and country was a recurring theme in British trench newspapers throughout the war when motivations for fighting were discussed. In 1914 the *79th News* suggested that the war was for "King and country" and in 1915 echoed a presumed common sentiment with the phrase "God Save the King and Constitution Amen."[3] A war song appearing in the *"P.P."* in 1916 began, "Now, Colin joined the A.S.C. to serve our gracious King."[4] In 1917 the *New Year Souvenir of the Welsh Division* listed in the Welsh Division Alphabet "E—why England, for whom we are fighting. / Tho' its [sic] awfully boresome and rarely exciting."[5] From the early days until the end, the official reasons for fighting the war, within public discourse among soldiers, remained consistent: king and country.

The country that British soldiers fought to defend was typically described as England, even the English countryside, and it was often portrayed in a pastoral way. In *The Great War and Modern Memory*, Paul Fussell writes about

the elevation of the pastoral and the celebration of the country over the city among World War I soldiers as a continuation of the idea of imperialist exile from home, around
since the 1880s.[6] In their letters and imaginings, soldiers
fought to defend hillsides and family farms, not factories.
Wartime enlistment posters also utilized the themes of king
and country, often with rural overtones. One British poster
suggested, "Surely you will fight for your" with a picture of
the king and a map of Britain, with the word *and* between
them.[7] The same pastoral ideal was well recognized, and
sometimes satirized, in trench papers. The Christmas 1917
Wipers Times advertised an edition of itself as a tonic equal
to whisky: "Its pages carefully avoid all reference to war, and
recall the shaded peace of an English country lane, with the
birds singing, and the cows plodding their serene way to the
meadow where buttercups and daisies grow in rich profu-
sion. Where ever and anon the old village church bell rings
out its dulcet notes, and the little flying pigs—Oh Heavens! I
knew it was going to creep in somewhere."[8] A satirical advertisement in another issue of the *Wipers Times* attempted to
make the salient feel more like the familiar countryside as
it described "The Salient Estate," in terms that applied to
the country estates in England; it was complete with good
fishing and shooting.[9] Outdoor pursuits that took place in
nature were also popular when soldiers were at war; many
participated in cross-country runs. During one such out-
ing, Lieutenant F. B. Turner joined as many as four hundred to five hundred runners for a five mile run.[10] A 1915
Lead-Swinger Christmas story supplement, "Mystery of the
Manor House," began with a narrator walking "the hills and
peaks of Derbyshire, a joy to the eye" and describing the
scenic countryside.[11] The pastoral imagining of home that
Fussell identified in wartime poetry and literature was also
actively present in British trench newspapers.

The home that British soldiers fought to defend was typically national but could be built on regional and local connections. Kitchener's Army of volunteers contained the famous Pals Battalions, which allowed men who shared an occupation or interests and lived close to each other to enlist together and to serve alongside one another. This contributed to the regional and community-based feel of the army. English troops were the majority in the British Army, but British soldiers also hailed from Scotland, Wales, and Northern Ireland, all of which grew more distinct in the course of the twentieth century.[12] Invention or not, the Scottish Highland tradition and the distinctions of Welsh culture had both received considerable attention and research in the eighteenth and nineteenth centuries.[13] At times, trench newspapers acknowledged regional identities and distinctions among British soldiers. The *New Year Souvenir of the Welsh Division* included pieces in the Welsh language. In the November 1, 1917, *Wipers Times*, an item of correspondence from "Call Haine" of Bilge Villa, Bunkum, read,

> Sir,
>
> I wish to draw your attention to the shameful way in which no mention is made of the glorious Manxman in this war. We hear about the glorious Anzacs and Canadians—English county troops, Scotch, Irish, Welsh, and so on, but I have yet to see the gallant lads from the Isle of Man mentioned. Sir, they have done their bit with the best, and it is a very galling business for them to feel that their pluck is unnoticed. Trusting that the publicity given to the matter by means of your widely read paper will remove the injustice.[14]

For some soldiers, loyalty to "country" may have been understood in regional or local terms, though that was not the dominant tone in British trench newspapers, which largely reflected the kind of national identity present in the civilian press and in army recruiting posters.

As with the British, the French understood the war as a defensive effort, even more so because France had been invaded. As Stéphane Audoin-Rouzeau and Annette Becker argued in *14–18: Understanding the Great War*, men fought to defend the nation and civilization.[15] Trench newspapers confirm this view. In 1915 *La première ligne* described the fallen as having died for France and its Republic.[16] In 1917 *Le poilu du 6–9* included a poem dedicated to "young soldiers who died for the patrie."[17] These entries were typical. When men died in the war, trench newspapers asserted that they died for France or the patrie, as would postwar monuments. Though the rural ideal was less emphasized in French war literature, the patrie could also take on a rural guise. Some French papers, like *Le mouchoir*, included illustrations of the countryside, with damaged towns and churches. And, as with the British, trench papers largely upheld the same reasons for wartime sacrifice given in the civilian press or government posters.[18]

Among the significant distinctions between the British and the French was the French concept of patrie, which appeared often in trench newspapers. Men fought not just for France but also for their particular piece of France. British soldiers may have fought for similar reasons, but there was no conceptual equivalent in English. According to Eugen Weber, "The concept of the patrie, land of one's father, can mediate between private society (the family) and official society (the nation)."[19] Robert Gildea suggests that there were two patries, one petite and one *grande*.[20] Whether the patrie referenced within trench newspapers referred to the nation of France or to a more regional identity varied. In *Nos filleuls*, an article referred to the "true fraternity" of the provinces and insisted that in the war, it was not a matter of the southeast or the north or some other part of France fighting the Germans, but of the nation standing together.[21] *Nos filleuls* suggested a regional *union sacrée* on behalf of a larger patrie, but the existence of the argument itself suggests existing regional identifications. And in 1914 many French citizens certainly had very strong regional affiliations.[22] Caroline Ford's *Creating the Nation in Provincial France* has shown that not only did the residents of Brittany believe diversity and regional difference were part of nationalism but also many of their three hundred thousand conscripts in the Great War did not speak French.[23] Brittany may have been an exceptional case, but there were occasional columns in a number of French trench papers in regional tongues and other indications of strong regional identity. An issue of *La vie poilusienne* had an article in langue d'oc.[24] *L'echo des gourbis* had at least one article in a regional language, and *Le filon* had such articles in more than one issue.[25] The paper *Le pastis* even described itself as "essentially Marseillais." The editor claimed the journal was formed to counter jokes against the Marseillais, to strengthen the bonds among comrades from the mother-city, and "to propagate the culture and the Marseillais spirit among others, such as the Gascons, Vendéens, Bretons, etc etc" and "to teach them our customs and cuisine and by stories or figures of pronunciation, to inculcate in them, if possible, our accent."[26] Other sources confirm the existence of these strong regional identities in the trenches. In his war notebooks, Louis Barthas described serving alongside Bretons who regarded him with suspicion because of his accent and because he was not of their race, as he wrote, "Je n'étais pas de leur race."[27] In another entry recording joyous exclamations by his fellow soldiers, he included a phrase in Occitan about the *kronprinz*.[28] In his examination of wartime letters, Martyn Lyons did not find many French letters in regional languages, but he did find considerable evidence of regional identity and animus.[29]

Trench newspaper rhetoric about the defense of home was consistent with official government justifications for war and perspectives in the civilian press. A 1916 French exhibition poster showed a poilu looking on at a scene with a man plowing, led by a woman, possibly Victory or Marianne (a personification of the French Republic), carrying an olive branch.[30] Trench papers, British and French, evoked similar pastoral scenes of the nation. A poem in *Le poilu du 6–9* described a rural spring in France. The poem opened

> Printemps, joli Printemps de France,
> Cher messager des jour vainquers,
> Tu viens aujourd'hui dans nos coeurs
> Ouvrir la porte à l'Espérance.[31]

Not only did it describe the beauty of the French spring, but also in a later stanza the poem linked the white flowers of almond trees, blueberries, and red poppies with the victory to come and "Les trois couleurs de la Patrie!"[32] In Entente trench newspapers, the purpose of the war was primarily the defense of home. Though trench authors could make jokes about the reasons for war, like the British soldiers' song "We're Here Because We're Here," that was not the dominant sentiment, especially among the French, whose country had been invaded.

Soldiers wrote about defense of domestic communities, but those communities were rarely identified as extending beyond the nation. Aspects of empire were seemingly everywhere during the war, but empire was not viewed as an animating justification of the war for British and French soldiers from the metropole, who largely framed their participation in terms of country. When empire was a reason for Entente forces serving, it came from people of the colonies and Dominions. There were occasional references to empire in connection with metropolitan troops, such as the May 29, 1916, *Wipers Times* "Empire Day" issue.[33] A poem in a later edition of the *Wipers Times*, "To the P.B.I." (poor bloody infantry), concluded with "So here's to the lads who can live and can die, / Backbone of the Empire, the old P.B.I."[34] But even when soldiers understood that they were participants in empire, they most often framed their part in the war as helping their country. An article in "*P.P.*" titled "1917—The Year of Decision?" also spoke directly to the involvement of empires:

We are at last upon the threshold of a year which promises to be the most amazing and terrible in the history of the world. If we may judge from an almost universal opinion 1917 will witness the conclusion of a war so vast that all previous wars fade into comparative insignificance beside it. The future of the Great Empires and the fate of nations will be decided in the coming New Year, and probably there is not a man of the M.T. who does not already feel certain and assured in his own mind as to which of these Empires will emerge victorious from the gigantic struggle, and which will go under. When that day arrives—the day of the Triumph of the Allies—and nothing is more certain than the fact that it is well on the way, it will bring with it something which in the years to come, will last every man in khaki all his life and which, unlike most other things, will grow more wonderful with each succeeding year—and that will be the thrilling consciousness of having been one of those who helped contribute to the Triumph. There may not be any discernible glory in a man's allotted job, nor any apparent opportunity of gaining it—he may, indeed, be engaged in the humblest and most indistinguished work, but nevertheless, if he is obeying orders to the best of his ability, and making himself as good a soldier as he can, he "is doing his bit" as well as more brilliant men are doing their more brilliant bit. And a day will come when he will be able to say "*I* was one of those that helped the Old Country through!" It will mean more than, perhaps, most of us realize now. May this New Year bring that day.[35]

Though the author suggests that the war will determine the future of empires, he still concludes proudly that he is helping the "Old Country" through. Empire was an appendage to country, the primary cause for which soldiers fought. In French papers, metropolitan soldiers were even less often portrayed as participants in empire. The French emphasis on patrie was in many ways the inverse of empire.

Within trench papers, colonial troops and Dominion soldiers were more often seen as responding to the call of empire. And very often it was explicitly a "call" from empire in trench papers. A poem in *Kit-Bag* titled "Voices of Empire" had stanzas for Canada, Australia, and India, and included the following refrain:

> *We're coming to you, mother*
> *Coming to your call;*
> *We're sailing in the morning,*
> *But, as eve-tide shadows fall,*
> *We send you fondest greeting,*
> *We're longing for the fight,*
> *We're sailing in the morning;*
> *Good night, Homeland, good night.*[36]

The lines devoted to India included "We're coming in our thousands, / To uphold the Empire's might."[37] But even when papers acknowledged the origins of colonial troops, they were not always portrayed as fighting for empire. An issue of *Le poilu* celebrated the spahis for fighting for the benefit of the French patrie, while it emphasized that the North Africans had never before seen France.[38] As mentioned in an earlier chapter, even a parade of colonial troops could be portrayed as heroes for the Republic.[39] And in the special English edition of *Le poilu* for Americans, the poem "The Road to France" suggested that the Gurkhas had come to France on behalf of England, not empire: "To France— the trail the Gurkhas found / To France—old England's rallying-ground!"[40] An issue of the *Pulham Patrol* described a lecture on "Imperial India" held at the YMCA. "The lecturer pointed out how the peoples of Imperial India were throwing themselves heart and soul into the prosecution of the war on the side of the Allies, and gave convincing proof of their devotion to Great Britain."[41] To metropolitan trench authors, the British and the French empires were a source of primary allegiance for colonized peoples, but not themselves, and even that imperial allegiance was closely tied to the value of the metropole.

Both the British and the French empires were vast and significant by the time of the Great War. Both had dramatically expanded into Africa in the previous forty years. During the Third Republic, the French Empire had increased from 1 to 9.5 million square miles just in the time between 1880 and 1895.[42] Despite the obvious significance of empire, scholars find the support for empires more ambiguous. Neither the British nor the French public held a unified pro-empire position.[43] Mira Matikkala's *Empire and Imperial Ambition* and Gregory Claeys's *Imperial Skeptics* demonstrate the existence of anti-imperial sentiment in Britain before the war.[44] Many Britons were concerned about the costs of empire, some believed that the benefits of empire were class-specific, and the "little England" idea persisted.[45] The recent Boer War had certainly tarnished the idea of empire for some. Though the French public learned about the empire through media, French imperial expansion was largely driven by a "colonial lobby" of business and political interests.[46] Empire was promoted as a humanitarian endeavor that increased national prestige, though not everyone in the public believed it benefited the whole of France.[47] Support for empire was not universal, but as Timothy Baycroft has shown, "criticism of France's colonial expansion was never particularly vehement, and neither was it ever the primary platform of those who opposed it."[48] Lack of interest in fighting "on behalf" of empire in trench newspapers does not suggest a pro- or anti-empire view in the trenches but does demonstrate an absence of overwhelming enthusiasm for empire among soldiers during the war. The war was not typically posited as an opportunity for the British or the French empires by trench authors.

A related, and significant, question is the role of empire in British and French identity. In *Britons: Forging the Nation, 1707–1837*, Linda Colley argued that "Britishness" grew more defined "not because of any political or cultural consensus at home, but rather in reaction to the Other beyond their shores."[49] In addition to Protestantism and rivalry with the French, Colley suggests that the "acquisition of empire" shaped Britishness, which cannot be understood without reference to the rest of the world.[50] Others have had even stronger interpretations. In *Culture and Imperialism*, Edward Said argued that many things tied to Englishness and Frenchness were best understood as also being tied to empire. Said criticized Raymond Williams's work, writing, "I sense a limitation in his feeling that English literature is mainly about England, an idea that is central to his work as it is to most scholars and critics."[51] Rather, Said argued that English literature "makes constant references to itself as somehow participating in Europe's overseas expansion, and therefore creates what Williams calls 'structures of feeling' that support, elaborate, and consolidate the practices of empire."[52] If Said thought English literature, and identity, was about empire, the generation of scholars after him has striven to support that view. For example, Antoinette Burton's *At the Heart of the Empire* argues that "empire was not just 'out there' but a fundamental and constitutive part of English culture and national identity at home."[53] Other scholars have said the same for the French relationship with their empire, suggesting that it shaped identity and played a significant role in popular culture.[54] This is the position of the "new imperial history."

However, the presence of significant and defining links

between empire and metropolitan existence did not always lead to an identification with the broader empire by metropolitan residents. For example, despite the presence and significance of people from all over the empire, Britons did not consistently see their home countries as diverse, imperial centers. Confrontation with that reality could be jarring. An excerpt from the *Stretcher Bearer*, a soldiers' paper in the UK, demonstrates the gap. A contributor contrasted the area of Poplar with the area of Harrow. At Poplar, "one meets representatives of nearly all climes and nations: whites, yellowmen, half-castes and blacks—people who perform the rough and dirty work of the commerce of the world. Here, also, you hear a variety of lauguages [*sic*] and the majority of shop fronts, signs and placards, bear superscriptions in foreign tongues. Indeed, one can hardly imagine that one is on good English soil."[55] Twentieth-century Britain could not run without its empire, but that does not mean that Britons stopped seeing themselves as a people apart, even during the war with its reliance on the colonies. The same was true in France. As Timothy Baycroft writes, "What is striking is that while an absence of colonial images in any area of national representation is rare, it is equally rare for them to occupy a central or even prominent place in any dimension of the national or Republican discourse."[56] He considers the "place of the French colonial empire in the images and identity of the French nation" to be a "paradox of . . . omnipresence and marginality."[57] Trench newspapers do not clarify the investigation into public support for the British or the French empires. However, trench newspapers do make clear that however much their context was shaped by empire, most metropolitan soldiers viewed themselves as attached to a much smaller territorial unit, such as England, or the patrie.

In their trench papers, British and French soldiers framed the war as a defensive struggle to protect their homes and countries. Those countries were, at times, tied to an empire, but metropolitan soldiers did not envision themselves as fighting and dying for empire. Soldiers may have been loyal to their empires, but it was not their primary loyalty. Trench newspapers are consistent with Martyn Lyons's findings from soldiers' letters. Lyons found that for French soldiers, "their sense of national identity was narrowly territorial, and it did not envisage fighting to annex more territory," rather "the sense of French identity revealed by the poilus' letters was thus defensive and minimalist."[58] The homes that British and French soldiers had in mind to defend rarely extended beyond national borders.

European Civil War and the Defense of Civilization

According to their own words, British and French soldiers fought in the Great War to defend their homes and the cause of civilization. Like civilian counterparts, British and French trench authors also sometimes framed the conflict as a battle between Anglo-French "civilization" and German kultur. Civilization could extend to the whole of the Entente, but it did not include Germany during the war. In April 1917 *On les aura* listed countries that could claim the titles of civilization and humanity, which included all the Entente Powers and excluded enemies. Among the civilized were England, Australia, Belgium, Canada, China, Egypt, the United States, France, India, Italy, Japan, Montenegro, Portugal, Romania, Russia, and Serbia.[59] Echoing the ideals of civilization, *The Gasper* informed readers that the war was for the "rule of Law and ideals."[60] British and French soldiers saw themselves fighting to restore order, with decency. Those values were seen in stark contrast with the kultur that Germans proclaimed and the kultur that Entente soldiers portrayed in trench papers as a façade for barbarism and savagery.[61]

Much of what British and French trench authors said about the Germans would have been dismissed by Germans themselves. After all, they accused the British and the French of undermining civilization with their use of colonial troops in Europe. But kultur was something that Germans, too, recognized. Kultur had a long German history, as a distinctive sense of culture and civilization, one that had produced Beethoven and Kant and Schiller. It was defended in the much-maligned "Manifesto of the 93" by German intellectuals who sought to portray their country as humane and civilized. Kultur was not an opposite of civilization, but an alternative term and vision for it. In his pioneering work, *Rites of Spring: The Great War and the Birth of the Modern Age*, Modris Eksteins defined kultur as a matter of inner freedom and spiritual cultivation, which was contrasted with a concern with external form.[62] In the arts, kultur was intended for liberation of the self, for the victory of the spiritual over the material, of essence over externalities. Kultur was also a response to the Anglo-French domination of the world. Germany was attempting to gain more equal footing with its rivals in Europe, which had hampered German imperial expansion in places like Morocco and which had encircled Germany with alliances. England preached fair play, and France proclaimed universal values, but Germany's ambitions continued to be frustrated by diplomatic efforts and what seemed clear injustices. To many Germans, Anglo-French manners and international rule of law seemed driven by appearances and convention rather than principles and rights.[63] This was one reason that Germans viewed the Great War as a European civil war.[64] Kultur represented a competing value system for civilization, as defined by the British and French, which espoused principles of equality but refused to balance power with others.

In Entente trench papers, kultur had no aesthetic value or legal foundation. According to trench papers like *Le dernier bateau*, the edifice of kultur rested on the Boche's belief in his own superiority as the most perfect of men, and the remaining structure was built by pride, brutality, and hypocrisy.[65] In particular, kultur was linked to violence and militarism. *La bourguignotte* wrote satirically about a "kolossal kanon de 606," developed by "Kultur," which the most illustrious scholars of the German Empire were writing books about.[66] In the *Fifth Glo'ster Gazette*, a poet recounted being kept awake nights by "Huns sending over their message of hate / In support of Kultur's rights."[67] *Hate* was a slang term for shelling in the trenches. In the *Wipers Times*, a "BEF Alphabet" suggested the following:

> K's for the KULTUR beneficent Huns
> Endeavor to force down our throats with big guns:
> They send shells in packets, they send them in ones:
> But Kultur's NAR-POO in the trenches.[68]

Kultur was the fuel of the German war machine in trench papers and a direct threat to the sanctity of life for British and French soldiers and their communities. The seemingly senseless violence of German culture was frequently mentioned in trench papers. One issue of *Bleutinet* described a bombed hospital in Reims, which could have no strategic value; instead, the Germans pursued "destruction for the sake of destruction, killing for the sake of killing."[69]

One of the marks of advanced civilization in Europe at the time was the valuation of human life. Liberal reforms in Britain and France had sought to improve the position of the middle class and assuage the conditions of the working class and had gradually expanded the franchise through the nineteenth century. During the war, the British and French armies paid unprecedented attention to the bodies of individual dead soldiers, marking each grave and keeping a record of the dead. The value of the individual soldier had never before been so high, in part because they were understood as citizen-soldiers. This was especially true in France, where metropolitan soldiers were not subjects and, as Leonard Smith has shown, "by definition, the citizen-soldier will not entirely relinquish the rights of the citizen."[70] This appreciation for individual life and the dignity of the individual soldier was seen to be lacking in the German Army, according to many trench authors. In an issue of the *Wipers Times*, a poem "Profit and Loss" paralleled William Hohenzollern and his six sons with a Karl Baumberg and his family of seven sons and three daughters. At the outbreak of war,

> For reasons which they never knew Karl Baumberg's seven sons
> Were quickly clad in suits of grey and labelled 'food for guns,'
> Two rot in mud near Wipers, and another at Verdun,
> The Somme accounted for a brace and Passchendaele for one.
>
> The one remaining to old Karl is minus both his arms,
> His fighting days are finished, and he's sick of war's alarms;
> He grinds his teeth with fury, while old Karl hunts round for food,
> And his mother freely curses both the Kaiser and his brood.
>
> His one remaining sister (death has claimed the other two)
> Out of water and a horse bone tries to make a dish of stew,
> Comes a mandate "Our great Kaiser has another victory won
> Fly your flags and cheer, by order, for the victory of Verdun."
>
> Then old Karl, whose waking senses grab a fact both strange
>   and new,
> That the victories are worthless if they bring no end in view,
> And he curses Kaiser William who's the King of all the Huns,
> But his frau is quietly sobbing for—the Kaiser has six sons.[71]

Such portrayals depict the Germans as victims of their own senseless leaders, who care naught for their subjects and do not properly value human life. Even the frequent use of *Hun* as a negative descriptor for the Germans in British papers positions the Germans as lacking civilizational advancement.

British and French trench newspaper depictions of the

Germans reflected beliefs from outside the trenches, which circulated in wider society. Martha Hanna's excellent book *The Mobilization of Intellect* chronicled the work of French intellectuals to challenge German kultur. They publicly argued that "*Kultur* with its pervasive amoral mechanism had perverted their [Germans'] judgment and had directed Germany along a path of aggression and atrocities."[72] Public figures suggested that the German soldiers were "led by 'barbarians' whose indifference to culture was indisputable" and "German troops could have easily have murdered civilians, burned villages, raped women, and brutalized children, as atrocity tales circulating in France alleged."[73] Similar views existed in England. Lord Northcliffe, owner of the *Daily Mail*, described the German lack of virtue and civilization in his book *At the War*: "I was long loth to believe that the Germans selected churches as artillery objectives, but personal examination of more than 100 shelled towns proves it. And with the churches usually goes the churchyard; open coffins, shrouded corpses, and grinning skulls show that the modern Prussian takes as much pleasure in revealing the secrets of the grave as he does in the destruction of the enemy's wife and child."[74] Kultur was derided and portrayed as inferior by British and French civilian and trench authors.

Other parts of the world echoed the sentiments. Across the pond in the United States, intellectuals also attacked kultur. Historian William Roscoe Thayer, in his book *Germany vs. Civilization*, asserted that "these Teutonic masses, which resemble in so many points the Chinese rather than any European race, were slowly organized into a machine as vast as Germany itself."[75] Other public figures described Germany as an enemy of humanity.[76] In and out of the trenches, German attempts to justify the country's culture and its position in the war were met with harsh criticism in many countries. In many parts of the West, Germany seemed excluded from the circle of civilization.

Plenty of people were considered uncivilized in European history, like the Huns, which the Germans were so often called during the Great War. But the rhetoric of British and French dismissal of kultur in inter-European conflict alongside British and French assertion of their own civilization and its superiority during the Great War suggests the importance of empire in framing the war's context. At the time of the Great War, the rhetoric of civilization was closely linked to imperial causes. For the previous forty years, nearly all British and French imperial conflicts had been publicly justified, at least in part, by the claim of having superior civilization. Indeed, the project of imperialism was sometimes claimed to be *about* the expansion of civilization. In Britain, the Liberal Party justified colonialism as a humanitarian endeavor. France even officially considered its colonial endeavors to be part of a *mission civilisatrice.*[77] Together, in their imperial efforts, "Britain and France both claimed to be the spearhead of civilizing influences."[78] In their work, *Arguing about Empire*, Martin Thomas and Richard Toye explore imperial rhetoric in Britain and France. There are clearly parallels between British and French rhetoric about themselves during the war and the arguments made during imperial crises. For example, both Britain and France made claims of "legal rights, ethical superiority, and gentility" in the Fashoda Crisis.[79] The same types of claims are at play in Entente trench newspapers. Civilizational claims during the war demonstrate the persistence of imperial culture, even if most soldiers did not see themselves as agents of empire.

Just as the British and the French publics had been encouraged by colonial lobbies and business interests to see their respective country as an agent of improvement and inevitability in the rest of the world, so did trench authors sometimes see their struggle against the Germans during the war. The editorial in the 1917 Christmas issue of the *Wipers Times* explained that if the issue was short a few pages, that was because the editors had been obliged "to drop the pen for the sword, and go and liberate some more French villages, and thus fight the demon of oppression and barbarism, the last remaining relics of bestiality, brutality and Kultur."[80] They were up against "German despotism." As British and French soldiers sought to oppose brutality and restore order, they were drawing on a generation's worth of imperial rhetoric that helped shape the sense of civilization soldiers defended.

British and French metropolitan soldiers during the war saw themselves as defenders of the home front, which they saw as disconnected from empire, but soldiers' sense of civilization cannot be divorced from the existing rhetoric of empire. In *Culture and Imperialism*, Said set out to examine "how the processes of imperialism occurred beyond the level of economic laws and political decisions" and how they were "manifested at another very significant level, that of the national culture."[81] What would British and French identity have been without the contrasts between the metropoles and the colonies? What would their sense of civilization had been without imperialism?

Conclusion: At Home in Empire?

Within trench newspapers, British and French soldiers largely viewed their participation in the war as a result of German territorial aggression in Europe. The war was perceived as a threat to personal homes and a civilized way of life. The British and French empires became involved, but men from the metropole mostly fought for smaller territorial units and concepts like civilization. These views largely agreed with the public discourses of the civilian press and even official state propaganda.

The primary sentiment in trench papers was national, not imperial. British and French trench authors identified national motives in themselves and each other. A poem in *Wipers Times* titled "Mort pour la France" celebrated the sacrifice of a French soldier in this way:

Many the graves that lie behind the line,
Scattered like shells upon a blood-stained strand,
Crosses and mounds, that eloquently stand
To make a spot, that forms some hero's shrine.
And one, that nestles near a shattered pine,
Beside a war-wrecked wall, in barren land,
Is tended, daily, by a woman's hand,
Moistened by tears, that in her bright eyes shine.

But proud she was, and proud she still can be,
Love and patriot, both, she proudly reads
His epitaph. It dries her tears to know,
That he has purchased immortality:—
"Mort pour la France." He filled his Country's needs,
And though he rests, for France he'd have it so.[82]

Men were out to serve their country's needs, especially French men. As Jean-Jacques Becker put it, "They accepted the war because they were part of one nation and they tolerated it for the same reason."[83]

Metropolitan soldiers did not identify a strong connection between the causes for themselves being at war and their own empires. In this sense, trench newspapers bear out some of Bernard Porter's arguments. Porter argued that British imperialism "was of a kind that did not need to involve her greatly domestically," and so many British subjects did not think of it nearly as much as some historians suggest.[84] In this case, it seems that British and French soldiers often understood the war primarily domestically, especially the French. The empire was not under attack; France was. And, in some cases, what was defended was a political unit even smaller than the nation or home country—a local community. It is clearly not the case that everything seemed to be about empire for British and French soldiers during the war.

Yet despite the lack of enthusiastic identification with empire, there is a link between metropolitan soldiers and empire, if only because we cannot consider ideas of civilization in that era apart from ideas about empire. That connection may have been more implicit than explicit but demonstrates a way in which empire had shaped the context of most soldiers. Metropolitan soldiers fought on behalf of civilization to restore order and improve the world, maybe even to end war in Europe for all times. This sense of civilization and the trajectory of improvement reflects not only the values of liberalism and belief in European progress but also the logic of European imperial endeavors. The relationship between the wartime vision of civilization and colonial rhetoric reinforces the existence of imperial culture *and* the need for "semantic precision" in seeking to understand imperial culture.[85]

Many people have written about the shocks that accompanied the Great War. One was the descent into what was called the "troglodyte" world, so well portrayed at the time in works like *Le feu* and analyzed later in works like *The Great War and Modern Memory*. The sight of soldiers covered in mud and lice, occupied with the business of basic survival and killing was a stark contrast for people who saw themselves as civilized. The severity of the war and its duration was also a shock, not just to soldiers but also to the public. This was, in part, because many Europeans considered themselves at a civilizational stage that was nearly done with war. The brutality and hatred and extreme loss of life in the Great War threw some people into a state of disillusionment about their societies and values. But not everyone found the barbarism of wartime a reflection of their own flawed selves and societies, as Freud would have it. During the war, some Entente soldiers and civilians saw the barbarism of the Great War as something they had been dragged down to by an inferior enemy. The relationship between portrayals of German inferiority and the language of empire will be explored in the next chapter.

SIX

The Imperial Enemy?

The most traditional way to understand the Great War has been primarily as a European conflict, one that shattered the innocence of the twentieth century. In *The Lost Generation*, Reginald Pound described the soldiers of the Great War as the "last to play with tin soldiers" rather than mechanical toys and the "last to be brought up in sailor suits."[1] The Great War has even been referred to as a "European civil war" by those who look at the war primarily as a European conflict. After all, the czar of Russia, king of England, and kaiser of Germany were all cousins, and Germany's rising status and kultur was a challenge to the balance of power in Europe and Anglo-French cultural dominance. However, more recent scholarship has redirected attention to the broader context and reach of the Great War. The war was perhaps the apotheosis of the British and the French empires, and it was the final act of the Austro-Hungarian, German, Ottoman, and Russian empires. Men and material came to Europe from all over the globe, and the wins and losses were felt far away too. Germany's territorial losses exceeded a million square miles, almost all outside Europe. British and French soldiers may have fought for their home countries, but their empires were enlarged by the Entente victory, and their surviving empires overshadowed others.[2] The war was much more than a conflict within Europe, and its consequences reverberated around the globe.

Despite the imperial advantages of their victory and the

imperial nature of campaigns outside Europe, British and French trench authors did not indicate their own imperial ambition or advantage as an aspect of the war. Instead, imperial ambition was assigned to the Germans, as an inferior incentive for war. After all, wartime Germany was the Second Reich, and Wilhelm was the emperor of Germany. Trench papers did not tire of referring to the "imperial" kaiser or his "Hun Empire." German kultur could also be tied to imperial ambition. In framing their own defense of homeland, British and French trench authors could go so far as to adopt anticolonial rhetoric, which seemed to undercut the legitimacy of imperialism. Yet, paradoxically, British and French soldiers' depictions of the German enemy also relied on colonialist rhetoric, which portrayed the Germans as an inferior race, responsible for causing disorder that needed to be resolved by their Anglo-French superiors. In trench papers, Germany was both a dangerous imperialist force within Europe *and* home to a rebellious inferior race. In this light, the "European civil war" was one in which the problems were familiarly colonial, as were the solutions.

This chapter emphasizes the way in which Entente understanding of the war was shaped by colonial rhetoric and violence and also underscores that although British and French metropolitan soldiers borrowed liberally from the rhetoric of empire to describe their plight in the trenches, they did not see much, if any, connection between their own actions and imperialism. The previous chapter outlined how Entente soldiers saw themselves as defenders of their homes rather than their empires, with some justification. Soldiers also seemed unaware of the implications of their home countries' imperialism outside the war. Criticism of German imperialism did not automatically lead to critique of Britain or France's approach to empire. This seeming dissonance reveals an interesting relationship between the British and French and the relevant terminology—in particular, the word *imperialism*. Further, while British and French trench authors were far from dismissive of empire on the whole, their accusations against the Germans suggest an awareness of its dangers and the use of brutality in its methods.

Germans: The Dirty Race?

A column in a 1916 issue of *Bleutinet* exclaimed passionately that in German atrocities "we always recognize there the dirty race (*la sale race*)" that pursues evil for evil's sake and is led by "monstrous ambitions."[3] Though in the early twentieth century, *race* was sometimes used with regard to nations, the denigration is still striking. After the war, the Germans would be dismayed by Article 231 in the Treaty of Versailles, the war guilt clause, but it must have been no surprise to Entente soldiers from the Western Front, who consistently understood the war to be a result of German aggression. There were other Central Powers, but they were not significant in the public discourses of the trenches unless faced directly, and, even then, those allies could be discounted. The Germans were called various things by trench authors: "Fritz," sometimes in a more casual or endearing way by the British; "Huns," more critically by the same; and "Teutons," occasionally. To the French they were most often "Boches" and referred to jovially much less frequently. In many places they were described much like they were in *Bleutinet*, as a separate race and one inferior to the British and the French. These descriptions reflected the existing rhetoric of empire, demonstrating how the war's violence was understood in relation to prewar colonial violence.

There was, at times, a close kinship between the language used to describe the Germans and the language that had been used by Europeans for a generation to describe people subject to their colonization efforts. In French papers, the Germans could be "savage hordes" or "barbarians."[4] Their humanity could even be questioned by trench authors. Before the war, colonial peoples had been displayed in Europe for some time, a practice which denigrated their humanity. An issue of the British paper *The Dump* included a drawing of a young girl with her mother looking at a monkey in a cage affixed with a sign, reading, "Fritz, Almost Human." In the caption, the young girl said to her mother, "Mummy Mummy you never told me they'd got a prisoner."[5] In their trench papers, the French questioned German humanity more frequently than the British. *Le poilu* defined *Boches* as a type of animal.[6] *La première ligne* described the Germans as types of pigs—Bavarian, Saxon, Prussian, and so forth—in response to an alleged decree about exterminating pigs in Germany.[7] These types of definitions were not always present, but they were not at all exceptional. An issue of *Le poilu sans poil* showed a happy poilu kissing a girl in front of a Christmas tree, decorated with decapitated German heads—an angry kaiser serving as the tree's star.[8] Kultur itself was a "jewel" of Boche brutes.[9] The alleged inferiority of the Germans, and their questionable humanity, was made explicit in British and French trench papers.

Depicting the Germans as culturally and excessively prone to atavistic violence linked Germans and colonized peoples more implicitly. The Germans were prototypical heathens in a 1917 issue of *Bombes et pétards*, which included correspondence between Wilhelm and Satan.[10] Atrocity tales reinforced their inhumanity. A poem in *Le poilu marmité* titled "An Eye for an Eye" accused the Germans of killing women and infants with gas attacks in their attempt to build an empire.[11] The drawings of ruins in French trench papers were not just reflections but also projections of fears of what might sweep through the rest of France. In the oft-quoted *Good-Bye to All That*, Robert Graves insisted that although he discounted 20 percent of the atrocity accounts, his disgust at the German violation of Belgian neutrality was what prompted his enlistment.[12] That sentiment was also present in trench papers. Depictions of the Germans resembled descriptions of non-European people as dangerous and aggressive. In an illustration from *The Dump*, a winged Victory, with a shield and an English bulldog by her side, defeats the gruesome skeleton of militarism armed with a scythe, accompanied by a pint-sized devil kaiser with horns and pitchfork.[13] It is reminiscent of the images in works like Kipling's "The White Man's Burden," which described colonized people as "half devil and half child."

In the face of such disorder and despicable behavior, trench authors emphasized their own role in bringing civilization and enforcing order. In the *Wipers Times*, a poem suggested the following:

> Now we have arrived in pastures new,
> Where the Hun's taking lessons that once he gave.
> Here's the best of good luck to all of you
> In the teaching of blackguards how to behave.[14]

The idea of "teaching blackguards how to behave" closely paralleled the "civilizing mission" of European colonialism. Entente soldiers were portrayed as knowing how to put the Germans in their place. An issue of *Le poilu du 37* had a drawing of a French soldier riding a *Pickelhaube*-wearing German prisoner, like a "camel."[15] In trench papers, Germans were rebellious and dangerous inferiors who needed to be taught a lesson by more civilized peoples. British and French soldiers considered themselves up to the task.

The previous chapter linked the defense of civilization to the colonial context of Entente countries, but depictions of German savagery and inferiority make an even stronger case for a connection between wartime defensive rhetoric and prewar justifications for British and French imperial expansion. The British had long used "imputed barbarism to justify, and even ennoble, imperial ambition."[16] The French, too, had cloaked their colonialism in "humanitarianism."[17] In *Rites of Spring*, Modris Eksteins notes that the British concept of civilization was closely linked to Britain's imperial mission "of teaching . . . the rules of civilized social conduct, the rules for 'playing the game.'" The British mission was to introduce "lesser breeds," to use Kipling's words, to "the law."[18] This was very much the rhetoric within trench newspapers, now applied to the Boches, which justified British and French violence within Europe. Papers like *Bochofage* were explicitly for Boche eaters.

The language surrounding justifications for the war in trench newspapers indicates just how important colonial logic and rhetoric were for interpreting the war in Europe. Edward Berenson's book *Heroes of Empire* chronicles five charismatic British and French colonial figures who gained hold in the public eye. According to Berenson, "to qualify as genuine national heroes in the second half of the nineteenth century, they had to be peaceful conquerors—or appear as such—capturing territory in a 'civilized,' humane way or defending civilization against barbarism with their heroic acts."[19] British and French soldiers were explicitly told to consider themselves defenders of civilization against barbarism during the Great War.

Trench paper accounts of Germans as racially inferior reflected broader public discourses. Martha Hanna's *Mobilization of the Intellect* explores many of the ways that French public intellectuals confronted German culture. One French pamphlet even warned that Germans could be detected by odor and urinated through their feet.[20] Though those claims seem ridiculous, wartime Britain and France were awash in materials that minimized German humanity. In *At the War*, Lord Northcliffe wrote that "the faces of our soldiers, unlike those of the Germans, are full of individuality."[21] Northcliffe was the owner of the *Daily Mail* and *Daily Mirror*. In 1918 G. Hamilton MacLeod published *The Blight of*

Kultur, in which he wrote that the term "*Hun* conveys just the proper amount of loathing with which we must regard for many a long day to come the apostles of arrogance, brutality and kultur."[22] From the pulpit in London, Bishop Arthur Winnington-Ingram was notorious for his xenophobic sermons in defense of the war effort. Many public figures and much of the popular press in Britain and France portrayed the Germans as unequal partners in civilization and the war. The same was sometimes true in the Dominions. In her research on Australian depictions of the Germans, Emily Robertson found similar patterns. Looking specifically at the art of Norman Lindsay, Robertson has argued that "Lindsay's 'Hun' was closely modeled on anti-Asian and anti-African British imperial atrocity propaganda that long preceded the Great War."[23]

Entente heroism was encouraged by depicting Entente soldiers in ways that emphasized their humanity and ennobled their sacrifice. A poem in *Le poilu du 6–9* in honor of the young dead began as follows:

A vingt ans que la vie est douce et semble belle!
Que de rêves d'amour, de joie et de bonheur;
Et cependant la voix du devoir les appelle,
Il faut, pour la Pays, mourir au champ d'honneur

Le sacrifice est grand! Mais Dieu, puissant et safe,
Récompense toujours ceux qui l'ont mérité.
S'Il demand beaucoup, Il done advantage:
Votre fils et heureux et pour L'Eternité.[24]

Trench newspaper depictions of characteristic national values and manliness sometimes also seem shaped by a sense of self that came, in part, from racial distinctions learned through imperialism. The *Stretcher Bearer* described a Lieutenant Langdon leaving for active service in this way: "In the world of sport, Mr. Langdon proved himself a strong swimmer, a sound cricketer, and a splendid tennis player, but the fine sporting spirit with which he was imbued characterised all phases of his activities. It was the fine spirit of the white man—the good old Guy's spirit of which stuff Englishmen are made."[25] Despite the dehumanizing existence of life at the front, Entente soldiers did not dehumanize each other in print as they did the Germans. According to Libby Murphy, even downtrodden and discouraged poilus could qualify for a picaresque depiction, as "an unheroic and morally pliant everyman who is forced to fend for himself to survive in a chaotic and hostile world governed by chance."[26] On the British side, Murphy highlights Old Bill, the Bruce Bairnsfather character whose experience of the war is unglamorous but full of perseverance. Even if Entente soldiers did not always write about the Germans as depraved monsters, they essentially never wrote about themselves that way. Even their less impressive representatives had a basic human dignity that was, at times, denied to German counterparts.

Although Entente trench authors in Europe did not see themselves as the vanguards of empire, their depictions of Germans clearly demonstrate the primacy of imperial experience in shaping the "us" and "them" of the war. War relies on othering in order to justify killing. Some of the most recent and ready-to-hand practices of othering for most Europeans came from imperialism. After all, the majority of conflicts that European countries had been involved in during the previous fifty years had been colonial. As Edward Said writes in *Culture and Imperialism*, although identity is not static, "throughout the exchange between Europeans and their 'others' that began systematically half a millennium ago," one consistent idea "is that there is an 'us' and a 'them.'"[27] The rhetoric of colonial others was available to the men in the trenches and they made use of it. Though Europeans also obviously experienced distinctions of class and gender and nation, the language used to describe colonial others seems to have been widely adopted in the trench papers for the purpose of distinguishing the Germans.

Understanding audience is key to understanding these discourses. Public discourses about the enemy served a purpose. As Karl Marlantes, Vietnam veteran and Rhodes Scholar, points out in his book *What It Is Like to Go to War*, "pseudospeciation" makes it easier to kill the enemy, and those who dedicate their wartime actions to a cause are less affected by guilt.[28] Emphasizing to each other that the Germans were Boches and brutes and that fellow trench authors were fighting on behalf of civilization likely helped the men in the trenches to encourage each other and to avoid guilt for participating in killing. Entente soldiers needed to find meaning in their labor and persist in the cause, just as the people at home needed to believe in the cause that asked for their sons and husbands. That colonial rhetoric seemed so compelling in the Great War suggests that it may have been quite convincing for the purposes of the British and French empires in the years before the war.

Despite the significance of Entente soldiers seeing Germans this way, we should not assume that they only saw them through the lens of colonial rhetoric. Trench authors referred to Germans in a variety of ways and teased them with all means available. In a Christmas issue, *Le cafard enchaîné* had a cartoon of a German soldier treed by a poilu with a bayonet, crying out "O! Tannenbaum!"[29] And although the French, especially, frequently wrote about the Germans, both the British and the French wrote about home more often than they wrote about the enemy. Entente soldiers seemed convinced that Germany was responsible for the war, but the Germans did not entirely define the war experience for Entente soldiers. War was also about enduring mud and bad weather, suffering through separation from family, finding comradeship and tension in the trenches,

and much more. The Germans were not even the only enemies. The war was also against rats, as shown in a cartoon
in *Bleutinet* about a "nocturnal offensive." In the drawing,
a pipe-smoking soldier with a stick chases one rat, while
another is already under his boot.[30]

It should also be remembered that there were still distinctions between portrayals of the Germans in public discourses and more private discourses, like diaries and personal
letters. Private writings could be more or less tolerant of
the Germans than public narratives. In a letter received by
the Cambridge librarian Francis Jenkinson, T. Knox-Shaw
described the deportation of girls from Lille for their safety
as the Germans advanced and concluded with "God, How
I hate the Boche."[31] Such frank hatred of the enemy was
often absent in British trench newspapers. Though French
trench newspapers preferred the derogatory term *Boche*,
many private diaries and letters of French soldiers spoke
of "Germans."[32] In Henri Barbusse's famous novel, *Le feu*,
a character claims he would rather skewer a German than
a pig.[33] However, in his letters to his wife, Barbusse wrote
that although Germany attacked France and began the war,
"the current crisis is the logical and fatal consequence of
national vanities, and each takes part of the responsibility."[34] The hatred of the Germans and the criticisms of kultur within trench newspapers reflected the general public
discourse among soldiers but, at times, magnified or damp-
ened personal taste.

Imperial Aggressors

Paradoxically, when the Germans were not accused of being
like Kipling's "sullen peoples" both "half-devil and half-
child," they were accused of being imperial aggressors and
seeking to build a colonial empire in Europe. Germany's
overweening ambition was a frequent topic in trench papers.

One example is the earlier-referenced "Austrian legend" told in a French paper—when ambassadors of the Great Powers went to heaven for mediation of peace, God could not even leave his throne for "a single moment," because Emperor Wilhelm would seize it.[35] A starker portrayal of unholy ambition for empire appeared in the *Fifth Glo'ster Gazette*. In the "Song of the Hun-Eagle," the German imperial eagle sings:

I am the bird of birds. Of Night
The symbol and the hope.
Supreme, I bask in Kultur's light
While men in darkness grope.

My home upon Vainglory's peak
O'erlooks the lordly Rhine:
Yet still unsatisfied I seek
The Earth—which should be mine.

Contempt I hiss at people who
Quote "Nations Law"—such stuff!
My piercing eye sees clearly through
Their sentimental bluff.

'Tis obvious that fair words conceal
Mere rank hypocrisy.
And so I answer each appeal
With just ferocity.

How righteously I strafe the foes!
—It should be told in rhyme—
And how my pent up hate o'erflows,
Imperial, sublime!

With what a grip my claws and beak
Can fasten, clutch and tear!
Yet 'gainst the British Lion meek,
French Cock, and Russian Bear.[36]

The "Hun-Eagle" finds his "imperial" hate to be "sublime" and sets his sights on the entire earth. Other trench papers suggested the same. *Le poilu du 37* directly accused the Boches of attempting to build an empire through the war.[37] Within French trench newspapers, the "imperial Kaiser" and "imperial Germany" were frequently used terms. The terms were less common in British papers, but the sentiment was often there. A three-act burlesque in *The Gasper* titled "A Scrap of Paper" included these lines by the kaiser: "Kaiser: Ach! But victory is now mine! Shades of Thor shine now on thy son! Spirit of Allah! Der means of our By-Kultur-made-certain victory are now in the hands of thy Greater-than-Mahomet prophet. We shall sweep them into der sea, we will walk over their contemptible little Army, Calais is mine! Petrograd is mine! Paris is—"[38] To some Entente soldiers, the war in Europe was a demonstration of German kultur in action, and the result was imperialism. Ironically, whereas Germans protested the Entente use of colonial troops within Europe, in trench newspapers British and French soldiers suggested it was the Germans who were inappropriately expanding empire and bringing it home. The German Army seemed to treat the borders and populations of Europe much like Europeans had treated overseas lands and peoples. The treatment of Belgium was taken to be an instructive example.

A helpful parallel to this understanding of Germany is found in *Imperial Sceptics: British Critics of Empire, 1850–1920*, by Gregory Claeys. Claeys writes that "through the great age of modern imperial expansion, from the late fifteenth to the mid-twentieth century, then, three main arguments underpinned European justifications for conquering the rest of the world: the superiority of Christianity; the supremacy of European civilization; and the greater economic efficiency of more 'advanced' peoples in developing the world's resources."[39] For many Entente soldiers and civilians, these were the kinds of claims made by Germany.

Trench papers had strong negative reactions to reports of Germans preaching, "Gott strafe England" or proclaiming, "Gott mit Uns," which suggested a privileged relationship between Germany and the Divine.[40] Germany was also accused of attacking the map of Europe to spread kultur and carry out economic exploitation. The *79th News* shared a "stirring address" given by Father Bernard Vaughan to the Cameron Highlanders entitled "For Honour, Truth, and Freedom." Father Vaughan warned that

> Germany was out to reset the map of Europe, and to reconstruct the nations of the earth. The war party was determined to justify to its people its vast armaments. It had sat on the safety valve long enough, and now it promised its teeming population nothing less than the French Colonies for its expansive interests and enterprise. The lust of power and the greed of gain had atrophied Germany's moral sense, so that in its intoxication it altogether forgot these principles upon which alone civilised nations can live and flourish.[41]

Father Vaughan's interpretation of German "lust of power and the greed of gain" could be compared to what outside of Europe might have been considered, in Claeys' description, "greater economic efficiency of more 'advanced' peoples in developing the world's resources." British and French powers were at the table for the Berlin Conference of 1885, but when they found European territorial boundaries challenged by Germans without local populations being consulted, they found it deeply unsettling and a threat to civilization.

According to the work of Heather Jones, the perception of wartime Germans as imperial aggressors was mirrored in the civilian press and reflected some German policies.[42] Not only was Germany consciously a Reich during the war, but also within Germany some people argued that "the best way to defend the Reich was to expand it—by creating a new colonial periphery under German control."[43] Though the public was divided on the idea of a colonial periphery in Europe, Germany did develop "territorial designs" during the war for parts of Eastern Europe.[44] Germany also used "some colonial forms of coercion against white populations in Europe" during the war, which was "new and radical," even if those forms of coercion were inspired by other European empires.[45]

Resistance to German aggression could even be portrayed as almost anti-imperial in trench papers. In the *Lead-Swinger*, the poem "To the 'Slackers' at Home" warned its readers:

> But now we know, what we knew not then,
> That this war is not a joke;
> And that what we want is men—more men
> To throw off the Teuton yoke.
>
> The lads who have gladly given their all,
> In England's cause and name;
> Surely you hear their spirits call,
> And the call is a cry of shame.[46]

For the author, the war carried with it the threat of the "Teuton yoke." Men were needed to sacrifice for "England's cause and name," lest she be swallowed up by German expansion. Rather than seeing the war as a struggle between empires, this trench author warned the men of England about the threat of Teutonic aggression. To fail to fight it would bring great shame on the men of England.

The link between accusations of imperialism against Germany and prewar empire was sometimes explicit, because trench papers occasionally even utilized imagery from prewar colonial scandals or referenced prewar crimes. In the civilian press, the German killing of civilians in the invasion of Belgium was compared with German atrocities against the Herero, and "allied propagandists damned such practices as 'colonial.'"[47] This approach was mirrored in trench papers.

Within trench newspapers, the Germans in Europe sometimes evoked historical imperialism or European imperialism in Africa. In *Poil . . . et plume* the "Huns" were described as Assyrians, intent on enslaving an entire people and hardly content with reducing the inhabitants of Lille to slavery.[48] A poem in *L'écho des guitones* described a poilu as like a lion, using his knife to stop the heart of the enemy, "to vanquish slavery," which he must do unless he would "lose his existence and his liberty."[49]

In particular, the scandal of "Leopold's Congo" seems to have provided a great deal of material for the atrocity tales of the "Rape of Belgium," in the regular press and in trench newspapers. In the nineteenth century, Belgium's King Leopold II had essentially transformed the whole of the Congo into a plantation, wherein slavery and violence were used to extract huge amounts of rubber and ivory, for tremendous profit. "Leopold's Congo" became one of the first international human rights scandals, and Western press coverage of the scandal included drawings and photos of men, women, and children whose hands had been cut off in the pursuit of profit.[50] Not long after, the related French scandal in the Congo, also publicized in England, "reproduced all the elements of a mainland crime story" with descriptions of mistreatment, murder, and disfigurement.[51] These images and stories from the media provided trench authors with a vocabulary for depicting German violence. Striking trench-paper images of Germans directly evoked the Congo abuses. A drawing in *Le mouchoir* depicted Wilhelm at the Cathédrale d'Angers, a murdered baby with missing hands and feet on the ground before him, and three handless children reaching for him along with a retinue of skeletons, while he recoils in horror.[52] The only things missing are the rubber trees. An illustration by Paul Iribe in the French *Télé-Mail* depicted a German with a dramatic mustache and Pickelhaube, decorated with an Iron Cross, looming over hundreds of skulls, which frame a medal of the Kaiser inscribed "Gott mit Uns."[53] These images bear strong resemblances to popular press images of Leopold's scandal in European newspapers.[54] Within trench newspapers, it seemed that the Germans had learned the lessons of colonialism in Africa and brought them back to haunt Europe.

The close link between the accusations of imperialism leveled at the Germans and the imagery and press of prewar colonial scandals emphasizes that the language and images of empire saturated the war. Germans were viewed in colonial terms as uncivilized people and yet were resisted in an anti-imperial way. The anti-imperial images used against Germany in trench newspapers were not born with the war; they were culled from earlier perspectives and media accounts on what it meant to conquer and subjugate other people. It seems that part of the reason the Great War was viewed as a struggle for "civilization" was because colonial violence provided the lens for viewing the violence of the Great War.

This can also be seen clearly in civilian publications from the war. In 1915 Charles Andler published *Pan-Germanism: Its Plan for German Expansion in the World*, which argued that Germany was pursuing continental domination.[55] There were other similar works. In 1918 G. Hamilton MacLeod published *The Blight of Kultur*, which took on the relationship between the Germans and empire directly and argued against "the pernicious influence of the Germans" on "our imperial policy."[56] MacLeod outlined what he perceived to be the German imperial designs on Australia and interference in India.[57] The German Empire had to be halted because "the outstanding truth is that Germany's methods of colonizing are a disgrace to civilization and a menace to the peace of the world. It knows nothing within its own confines of freedom, and what it transports beyond its borders is the tyranny of militarism. Where the teeth of kultur have been allowed to get a grip, we find nothing but cruelty, oppres-

The Imperial Enemy?

sion and moral death."[58] For MacLeod, the treatment of the Herero was typical for the Germans. Kultur was an imperial threat within Europe.

Although trench paper accusations of German imperial aggression demonstrate the presence of a culture shaped by imperialism, they also bear out the skepticism of Bernard Porter about European identification with empire. For most Entente trench authors, imperialism was something other people did. In *The Absent-Minded Imperialists*, Porter highlights that in the early nineteenth century, "when Britons used 'imperialism' then it was usually to describe hated French Bonapartism, which is one reason why they denied its application to themselves."[59] That pattern appears to have persisted into the Great War. As Porter further explains, the British middle class "attitudes to the empire" were not all "imperial ideas" but often came from "home-grown ideologies, rooted in the middle classes' domestic rather than their imperial functions."[60] Other scholars have made similar points. Mira Matikkala's *Empire and Imperial Ambition* also offers a helpful perspective. Matikkala argues that while many British people understood empire in purely geographic terms and even anti-imperialists supported the settler colonies, imperialism was understood by those opposed to it as "illiberal authoritarianism" that threatened liberalism and civic virtue at home.[61] Many people in Britain made a distinction between empire and imperialism, and that distinction appears to have followed the men into the trenches.

The French also had a challenging relationship with the idea of imperialism. The France of the Great War was the Third Republic. French republicanism, with its legacy going back to the French Revolution and its alleged universal values, made empire a bit of a conundrum. In *A Mission to Civilize*, Alice Conklin writes that "republican imperialism should have been a contradiction in terms—a nation of *citoyens* cannot by definition possess *sujets*."[62] The French resolved the conflict by envisioning their empire as a "civ-ilizing mission," to spread republican values.[63] Even with direct interventions and territorial acquisitions, as in Tunisia, the French "claimed their actions were taken to uphold better standards of governance and to restore regional order. At the rhetorical level, if not at the practical one, imperialism was eschewed."[64] During the war, Senator Bérenger even used successful recruiting campaigns in Africa to claim that *La France coloniale* was no longer separate from *la France d'Europe*.[65] The French, too, seemed too convinced of their humanitarian efforts to see themselves as imperialists. Imperialism was a problem of other empires.

When Entente trench papers did address the British and French empires directly, those empires were seen as harmonious and separate from imperialism. In a 1916 issue of *Kit-Bag*, Sapper S. Lewis wrote confidently that "after the war," our "Empire will emerge stronger than ever. Our flag will in the name of freedom fly over lands where once flew the flag of tyranny and oppression. The colonies once owned by Germany will awake to a far finer destiny, smaller nations will at last be able to live in peace without fear of oppression."[66] There was considerable optimism about the condition of belonging in the British Empire. The *Stretcher Bearer* reflected on the mixing of people in hospitals during the war and concluded, "The meeting of Scotsman and Southerner, Londoner and Provincial, Irishman and Englishman is bringing about an interchange of thought that will materially alter British politics as soon as the boys return home. There are the Canadians, too, with their independent thinking and initiative. Now that the Australians and New Zealanders have come there will be a veritable formation, in France, of an almost indissoluble bond of Empire, which I do not doubt, will have vast influence on the future of the world's history."[67] In that example, the fate of nonwhite members of empire is notably not even considered. French papers, too, suggested that their empire was benevolent and only improving through the war. In 1916 *La vie poilusienne* suggested that after the war French colonies would become successful again and a new happiness would spring up in the old French soil, while the Central Powers, annihilated by a costly and difficult war, would see their hope to compete with the Britannic Lion crumble.[68] British and French trench authors' views of their own empires seem largely aligned with pro-empire rhetoric, which emphasized humanitarianism and liberalism.

Although *imperialism* was not a positive term, *empire* was not inherently a negative one. Not only were the British and French empires not directly criticized, but also the term *empire* could even be adopted for other contexts. On occasion, trench authors referred to themselves as participants in empires of the trenches, still very distinct from German imperialism. *L'écho du boqueteau* wrote that the "Central Empires" were endangered by the coming "moment of advance by all the *poilus* of all the fronts of Europe and of the Orient, the liberating and glorious moment of definitive emancipation, in the same blow, of the people oppressed by Pangermanism and the troglodytes of the empire of the trenches . . . liberty!"[69] The so-called French empire of the trenches stood only to exterminate Pan-Germanism. The British sometimes referred to the "hut empire" on their lines that stood against the German tide. The British and French accepted their "empire of the trenches," which was opposed to "imperialism."

Trench newspaper references to empire are not conclusive about enthusiasm for it, but they do indicate that there was not widespread enthusiasm for imperialism and what it was taken to mean. Whether or not the "little England" ideal was popular or the French colonial lobby was not entirely successful, anti-imperialist rhetoric had found some place in popular consciousness. Colonial violence had become a strong metaphor for excessive and inappropriate violence. Although soldiers did not suggest that their own empires should be dismantled, awareness of colonial scandals suggests that imperialism was understood to be a Hobbesian approach to government at best. The distinction documented by Matikkala is crucial. *Empire* itself was not a dirty word, but to be the object of someone else's imperial ambition was horrible indeed.

Here, too, the use of imperial rhetoric should not be exaggerated. Germans were not exclusively described as imperial aggressors. And the German Army could be linked to death without evoking colonial atrocities. In a drawing from *La bourguignotte*, a group of Germans, one with a bloody hand, stood aghast as a large figure of Death loomed near them, with the caption reading, "They dread death."[70] No doubt the judgment that accompanied death was most terrifying. In that same issue, the futility and senselessness of the German effort was highlighted in other ways. According to one humor column, suicide had become a dangerous epidemic in the German Army—and was now punishable by death.[71] And the struggle against the Germans could also be framed using older imagery, such as that of the Crusade, which has been explored so well by other scholars. An example of an older conflict being used to interpret the Great War can be found in a rhyming letter from a father to a son in *Le poilu du 37*. The letter encouraged the reader that Wilhelm would be vanquished, by the "God of the Francs, the God of Joan of Arc!"[72] Nineteenth and twentieth century imperialism was not the only angle from which to interpret the Great War.

The significance of imperial rhetoric in framing German aggression is not that it was the exclusive approach to understanding the war. It is significant because its presence demonstrates the extent to which the language of colonialism and awareness of adventures and atrocities outside Europe had permeated the public consciousness. The language of

The Imperial Enemy?

empire was not the only vocabulary available to help make sense of the war, but it was certainly part of that vocabulary, implicitly and explicitly. In this way, trench papers reveal that prewar colonial violence sometimes shaped how Entente soldiers interpreted the violence of the Great War.

Conclusion

Within trench newspapers, British and French soldiers largely viewed their participation in the war as a result of German territorial aggression in Europe. The war was perceived as a threat to personal homes and a civilized way of life. The British and French empires became involved, but men from the metropole mostly fought for smaller territorial units and concepts like civilization. These views in trench papers largely corresponded with the public discourses of the civilian press and even official state propaganda.

If British and French soldiers at times seemed ambivalent about the idea of empire as a cause in trench papers, their use of imperial rhetoric demonstrates clearly the ways in which empire had permeated their consciousness. Trench newspapers demonstrate that consciousness of empire was an interpretive filter for many soldiers' understandings of the Great War. Descriptions of the Germans in trench papers included racial distinctions, denigration of their traditions and culture, and the devaluation of kultur, which the Germans publicly championed. Berenson writes that in "the need to rescue innocents from subject peoples that no longer knew their place" was a key justification for colonial ventures.[73] It was practically the same argument that made the invasion of Belgium a cause for war. British and French trench authors commonly viewed Germans from a colonialist perspective. The link to colonial rhetoric could even be one reason why the war was viewed as a struggle for civilization.

British and French trench authors also portrayed themselves as anti-imperial fighters. The Germans stood accused of bringing overseas-style empire home and seeking to impose themselves as imperial overlords in Europe. Trench newspapers, as well as books and pamphlets from public figures and academics, reinforced the notion that Germans believed they had superior technology and beliefs that should be spread. Rather than importing colonial troops, as did their opponents, the Germans had imported oppressive and brutal tactics from the colonies. They were also accused of seeking to dominate Europe solely for the purpose of exploitation, suggesting that many believed that colonies had a similar function, despite the humanitarian rhetoric.

Though British and French trench and civilian authors distinguished between their empires and that of Germany, the use of imperialism as indictment suggests a crack in the façade of imperial culture. People were obviously aware that the methods of empire could be brutal and oppressive. The critiques of alleged German wartime imperialism also repurposed images and concepts from earlier colonial scandals and debates, suggesting a deeper hold in the public consciousness of colonial violence. Even if British and French trench authors believed their own empires to be benevolent associations, within trench newspapers imperialism seems to be a description for a tyrannical form of government, a very serious comment on the understanding of European expansion. Empire was one thing, but when subjected themselves at home to the same type of behavior practiced overseas, many Entente soldiers found imperial practices objectionable and claims from one country about higher civilization or religious destiny to be offensive. While the war may not have turned a majority of soldiers against empire, it certainly created space for a new perspective on the experience of it.

What do these findings in Entente trench newspapers suggest about imperial culture? In *Absent-Minded Imperialists*, Bernard Porter argues that when it came to nineteenth-

and twentieth-century Britain, "there can be no assumption that she was 'steeped' in imperialism, by any useful definition. Efforts to discover this in the fabric of her society are fundamentally misconceived."[74] Porter's work was in opposition to the new imperial history, demonstrated in the works of scholars like Edward Said, John MacKenzie, and Antoinette Burton. Porter did not deny the significance of empire in nineteenth- and twentieth-century Britain but did deny its hold on the public consciousness. Imperialism fueled the British economy, but, according to Porter, it did not generate much interest or enthusiasm for much of the nineteenth century.

It would be an overstatement to suggest that trench newspapers were full of imperial discourses and that the only way that Germany was interpreted was through an imperial lens. Trench newspapers existed primarily for the purpose of entertainment and were more concerned with the experiences of their readers than anything else. Even references to German "misinformation" was fodder for sillier humor. For example, a joke in *Trot-Talk* relayed, "A German Paper states that 'England has leased Calais from France for 99 years.' How silly these German Papers! As if we shall not have need of Calais for the *whole* War!!"[75] Not everything was atrocity tales and murdered Belgian babies.

However, trench papers clearly demonstrate that imperial rhetoric was used, at times, to interpret German actions and the threat that Germany was perceived to pose to Britain and France. Whether because of the press coverage of Leopold's Congo or the Boer War, images and ideas from the world of empire was part of metropolitan Entente soldiers' consciousness. Descriptions of the Germans as barbarians and heathens seem to suggest an acceptance of the justifications of existing empires typically provided in the British and French popular press. Yet, for Entente soldiers, the war was not about British and French empires. In con-

trast, the use of *imperial* in trench papers was very negative, indicating an awareness of the abuses of the system
and its dehumanizing approach to others. Trench newspapers suggest that empire did have a place in Entente consciousness, even though existing understandings of empire
and imperialism were complicated.

Conclusion

This book has emphasized that the Great War took place, and was understood, in an imperial context. Even for metropolitan soldiers serving in Europe, features of the war were inseparable from empire, from trench slang to serving alongside colonial troops to fighting in Mesopotamia. The chapters of this book have shown different ways in which empire was a factor in British and French soldiers' experience and perceptions of the war. Just as Timothy Baycroft discusses images of French colonialism as being best described through "omnipresence and marginality," this book has explored the omnipresence of empire in soldiers' discourse of the Great War despite its seeming marginality.[1] Never the central preoccupation of British and French trench newspapers, empire was also never entirely absent.

Commenting on the Great War, and the histories that would be written about it, Sir Gen. James Willcocks, who served with the Indian Army, wrote, "What an opportunity for still closer welding together the divers races and peoples that combine to make the Empire of Great Britain."[2] Colonial troops prompted some of the most overt discourses on empire within trench newspapers. The chapter "Men on the Margins," which examined soldiers' discourse about colonial troops, illustrated both the continuation of old stereotypes and the challenges to those stereotypes created by the war. New opportunities for interactions created the possibility of new narratives about non-Europeans in the British and the French empires. Descriptions of men from India and Africa, and their reasons for fighting, revealed ways that British and French soldiers understood and imagined their own respective empires. The valuation of colonial troops, and the limits of that valuation, spoke about how the war stretched dynamics within the surviving combatant empires.

Although the war created new and sometimes quite positive views of colonial others on the Western Front, the same was not necessarily true for fighting outside Europe. The chapter "Other Fronts, Other Wars?" demonstrated the extent to which soldiers relied upon orientalist tropes to represent the Ottoman Empire in trench newspapers. That orientalism extended to seeing the Ottomans as weaker partners in the Central Powers, subject to German domination, with few or poorly identified goals of their own in the war. By engaging with British and French papers from the Ottoman campaigns, the chapter also demonstrates that the war forced many soldiers outside Europe to confront those stereotypes. British and French soldiers in Egypt and Mesopotamia found themselves far from the pages of The Thousand and One Nights. But that new experience did not automatically translate into new appreciation for local people, and many metropolitan soldiers who served elsewhere saw less value in the fighting outside Europe. The old geographic hierarchies persisted. The new interactions that accompanied the war did not always lead people to change their minds about the impressions of others that they brought into the war.

Perhaps most revealing about the prewar imperial context and understandings of empire were the depictions of Germany in trench newspapers. As shown in the chapter "The Imperial Enemy?" British and French soldiers used the rhetoric of empire to make sense of Germany and to justify their own involvement in the war. Denigrations of Germans as inferior and barbaric people echoed prewar European rhetoric surrounding colonized peoples. Accusations of German imperialism in the war included adopting the very imagery of prewar colonial scandals to describe German wartime activities. The alternating imagery is interesting in itself, but more importantly, it emphasizes the extent to which imperialism could serve to describe excessive and inappropriate violence. With respect to their own empires, British and French trench authors demonstrated confidence in their humanitarian mission. At the same time, empire was not a cause that British and French soldiers often described themselves willing to die for, potentially undermining or transcending the image of the imperial hero so prominent in prewar music halls.

The chapter "Why War?" highlights the limitations of empire in capturing the war experience of Entente soldiers. Despite use of prewar colonial imagery and the rhetoric of civilization, itself shaped by empire, British and French soldiers did not see their participation in the war as part of an imperial project. They did not even typically identify themselves as members of empire, preferring instead to demonstrate allegiance to their country or local community. Men fought and died for the patrie, not imperial glory. However much the context of the war was shaped by empire, empire was not at the forefront of Entente soldiers' consciousness about the war. This, too, is an important aspect of British and French imperial culture.

The issues raised in the introduction should now be addressed. To what extent did soldiers, among themselves, see the war as a matter of conflict between empires, and how did they process the cultural encounters within and between empires? In the identities and communities that they created and carried through the war, when and how did empire matter? It seems clear that in the public discourse of the trenches, Entente soldiers did not see the war primarily as a matter of conflict between empires. It might be understood as a war of imperial aggression by the Germans, but it was resisted by countries that happened to have empires to call upon. Despite the growth of the British and French empires through the war, Entente soldiers did not perceive the war as an opportunity for imperial advantage. This is a pretty stark contrast to the meaning of the war for many colonial troops, some of whom premised their involvement on an improved position within the empire for their homelands after the war and many of whom could not have conceived of their involvement in the war apart from participation in empire.

Entente soldiers processed cultural encounters within and between empires in a variety of ways but often made use of prewar hierarchies and ideas. Together the chapters of this book reveal the extent to which soldiers were familiar with the rhetoric and imagery of their empires. British and French soldiers entered the war equipped with stereotypes about the people who served as colonial troops that borrowed from advertising, the popular media, and recent military conflicts. Trench authors wrote about the war outside Europe using the kind of "allegorical signifiers" from literature and advertising that David Ciarlo has analyzed, which had little relation to actual people or places.[3] But trench newspapers also demonstrate that new contact and experiences with colonial people or the world outside Europe, through the war, had the ability to destabilize the ideas and imagery that held sway before the war.

In the identities and communities that Entente soldiers created and carried through the war, empire mattered as an available interpretive lens. This book demonstrates the significant role of colonial violence in shaping soldiers' vision of the war, and potentially, modernity. Scholars have explored the ways in which the Herero genocide affected German policy and opinion, shaping understandings of violence and the role of the imperial state.[4] By using the imagery of colonial scandal to describe German behavior in Belgium and elsewhere, trench newspapers demonstrate that understand-ings of empire provided analytic tools for interpreting the war. Some British and French soldiers saw themselves as resisting imperial aggression and as potential victims of colonial-style violence. It may even be the case that one reason the Great War was perceived as a struggle for "civ-ilization" by Entente powers is because the war was being interpreted through the rhetoric and reasoning of empire. If so, colonial violence significantly shaped understandings of modernity by first influencing the perception of one of the earliest thoroughly modern wars.

The history of imperial culture is still an evolving field. Empire has gone from being ignored to being omnipres-ent in European history. In his criticism of some works of imperial history, Bernard Porter identified two problems:

> One is a rather loose and inclusive use of the word "impe-rial," to cover any *foreign* feature in British society irre-spective of whether it was the result of Britain's overseas dominance or not. (The idea of "dominance" is surely essen-tial to any useful definition of "imperialism.") The second is a tendency, especially among literary and cultural "theo-rists," who do not usually know much history, to *assume* an imperial dimension to just about everything in British soci-ety, and so to impose an imperialist reading on it whether the empirical evidence for it is there or not.[5]

This book has tried to navigate between that Scylla and Cha-rybdis. *Empire Between the Lines* does not argue that the war was primarily understood as an imperial event by Entente soldiers from the metropole. It clearly was not. However, the war was also clearly an experience of empire for many of those soldiers. Whether through trench slang, the lead-ership of former colonial officers, interactions with colo-nial troops, or awareness of the broader context of the war, Entente soldiers were confronted with aspects of empire.

Some of those soldiers changed some of their perspectives of others as a result. The war itself also cannot be fully grasped by scholars apart from empires, because empires provided so many of the resources and some of the settings of the conflict. This book does not argue, though, that soldiers were incapable of comprehending the war, in a manner satisfactory to themselves, without a sense of their place in their respective empires. At the same time, this book should make clear that imperialism *did* provide an interpretive lens to understand the Great War, one that many soldiers made use of and that had some currency in the community of the trenches.

Apart from questions of imperial culture, the study of trench newspapers also demonstrates the significance of differences between types of war literature. War historians have long preferred single-author narratives, but trench newspapers bring to light the community of the trenches and the newspapers' various writing conventions. While this study takes a thematic look at trench newspapers, it nonetheless highlights the diversity of types of writing within them and the widespread use of satire and humor. Much more remains to be said about the variety of genres within trench newspapers, such as one-act plays, satirical advertisements, sporting columns, and correspondence sections. Often anonymous and always collective endeavors, trench newspapers also relate differently to the individual. Trench newspapers were not the product of modern, rational, Robinson Crusoes. The relationship between the individual and the collective, not just as members of the military or participants in the Great War but as participants in war literature, merits further investigation.

Trench newspapers, by their very nature, underline the importance of considering intended audience when approaching war literature. After being injured in the Great War, Ernest Hemingway wrote a letter on October 18, 1918, to his parents, intending to reassure them about his health and state of mind. He said, "And it does give you an awfully satisfactory feeling to be wounded, its getting beaten up in a good cause. there [*sic*] are no heroes in this war. We all offer our bodies and only a few are chosen, but it shouldnt reflect any special credit on those that are chosen. They are just the lucky ones. I am very proud and happy that mine was chosen, but it shouldnt give me any extra credit."[6] Almost a month later, on Armistice Day, he wrote to his sister Marcelline confidentially that "the Doc says that I'm all shot to pieces, figuratively as well as literally. You see my internal arrangements were all battered up and he says I wont be any good for a year. So I want to Kill as much time as I can over here. If I was at home I'd either have to work or live on the folks. And I cant work. I'm too shot up and my nerves are all jagged."[7] Like every author in the conflict, Hemingway adjusted his message for his audience, based on what he wished to communicate and what he thought it could or should know. Although in war literature soldiers often seemed alienated from the home front, in trench newspapers they longed for nothing more than leave.[8] So much attention to the war's literature and poetry has emphasized the horror of the conflict and the alienation of the men who fought. Certainly, some aspects of the war were "beyond words" as Jay Winter has said.[9] But soldiers also used trench newspapers to encourage and amuse each other during the war. Despite its presence, horror was not the only experience in the trenches.[10] When analyzing war writing, it is important to always discuss audience and authorial intent.

This study has attempted a transnational or broader "European" approach to history. This book has sought to consistently and equitably utilize both British and French primary sources, rather than relying on secondary sources for half of the content. Bringing together British and French soldiers' discourses acknowledges that British and French soldiers fought within the Entente Powers, not just for or with Britain or France. Trench authors suggested the war was in defense of a shared Anglo-French "civilization"; looking at British and French sources together allows examination of that shared culture. This book has also attempted to put Europe into broader context, by studying British and French metropolitan soldiers in the context of empire. As David Cannadine said, and as quoted earlier, "Britain was very much a part of the empire, just as the rest of the empire was very much part of Britain."[11] The same was true for France. We will miss much about the nature of twentieth-century empires if we refuse to consider the relationship of their parts to the whole.

This study also suggests areas of future research into the interwar period. In particular, postwar discourses of race could be compared to soldiers' constructions of race within trench newspapers. Between the competing wartime images of *l'ami noir* and colonial savagery, which of the two gained more traction among the public after the war, and why? Were there any appreciable differences between civilians and veterans on the subject? Though the war seemed to open new possibilities for citizenship in French West Africa, especially for veterans, access to citizenship actually declined. Only eighty-eight Africans were granted citizenship in the decade following the war.[12] How did the struggle for greater rights within empire—in India, the Dominions, and French colonial possessions—affect the constitution of the memory of the war in Europe? Although some scholars have researched the relationship between empire and war memory, it might be interesting to explore that in connection with postwar veterans' associations in Europe.[13]

The most obvious direction that this study suggests for additional research into trench newspapers themselves also involves the postwar period, above all into the trench newspaper associations that outlasted the war. The paper *Le poilu* had issues as late as 1920. The French trench-paper association, Amicale des Journaux du Front, continued its activities through the 1920s. What role did this association play in the lives of its members, and what were its chief activities? How did members make the decision to let the organization lapse? What was the status and position of the organization at the outbreak of World War II? How did trench newspapers serve as a *lieu de mémoire* for soldiers in Britain and in France?[14] In 1918 a Captain Laski wrote to Francis Jenkinson, the librarian of the War Reserve Collection at Cambridge:

> Dear Sir,
>
> While in hospital I am trying to get together a collection of regimental magazines. I note in a copy of your yearly report a list of such publications.
>
> I should be extremely grateful if time could be spared to give me the address to which to write & for which I venture to attach a list of titles.[15]

Who made most use of the War Reserve Collection at Cambridge University, and other collections like it, after the war? What happened to the private collections created by soldiers? This book has focused strictly on the lives of wartime trench newspapers, but their afterlives are also fruitful ground for historical inquiry.

The final direction of future research suggested by this study is into those areas presently omitted: Dominion and colonial trench newspapers and POW and hospital papers. J. G. Fuller's *Troop Morale and Popular Culture* does analyze Dominion papers but does not specifically interrogate the role of empire. Colonial trench newspapers existed, but their limited number may make them difficult to study conclusively. POW and hospital papers could be compared with trench journals from the front for a richer understanding of the war experience, including the broader spectrum of experience that included hospitalization and captivity. POW papers were also subject to different forms of censorship, which presents a useful case for comparison and may represent an interesting intersection of German and Entente trench papers.

The Great War provided striking evidence that the interdependencies and interconnections of modern societies were partially constituted through empire. Soldiers fought the war on behalf of nations that were inseparable from empires. This study has shown the "omnipresence and the marginality" of empire in the discourse of British and French soldiers. Within trench newspapers, soldiers connected empire to perceptions of their allies, their enemies, the wartime objectives, and the geography of the war. A relationship between the war and empire not just is present in the work of recent historians but also existed within soldiers' discourse during the war. Analyzing that relationship improves our understanding of empires and the war experience.

Keeping all of that in mind, one should remember that the primary purpose of trench papers was not to address serious topics but to avoid some of them. In the face of horror, trench papers offered attempts at hilarity. Even serious subjects were often approached in a silly manner. One issue of *Trot-Talk* told readers that "in spite of the importance of the Brest-Litovsk negotiations, it is not proposed to alter the title of this Magazine to '*Trotsky-Talksky*,' as has been suggested."[16] Trench newspapers wanted to make their readers smile, to better survive the war. Our investigation should not forget that, even as it attempts to better understand the British and French empires, which "whether in the process of expansion, or when faced with external challenges, internal violence, and ultimate contraction . . . rose and fell together," and were the empires that best survived the war.[17]

NOTES

Introduction

1. Titles include *Ten Days with the Indian Army Corps* by Eyre Chatterton, the Bishop of Nagpur; *India's Contribution to the Great War*, published by the Government of India in 1923; and Alphonse Séché's *Les Noirs*, 1919.

2. Some examples include Ellinwood and Pradhan, *India and World War I*; Chakravorty, *Indian Nationalism*; Nasson, *Springboks on the Somme*; Davis, *Ends and Means*; R. Ford, *Eden to Armageddon*; Nunn, *Tigris Gunboats*; Porte, *Du Caire À Damas*.

3. John Morrow's *Great War* (2004) makes a similar effort.

4. Myron Echenberg's *Colonial Conscripts* (1991) used a longer timeline but also contributed to knowledge of the *tirailleurs sénégalais* in the Great War.

5. Chakrabarty, *Provincializing Europe*.

6. That includes Stovall, "Color Line behind the Lines," 737–69, and Peabody and Stovall, *Color of Liberty*.

7. Beaver, *"Wipers Times,"* 45.

8. Eksteins, "All Quiet on the Western Front," 345–66; Fussell, *Great War and Modern Memory*.

9. Joseph Galatier, "Journaux du front," *Le Temps*, April 20, 1915.

10. Seal, *Soldiers' Press*, ix.

11. Osborn, "Trench Journals," 482.

12. Winter and Robert, *Capital Cities at War*, 9.

13. Grayzel, *Women's Identities at War*, 3.

14. Baycroft, "Empire and Nation," 149.

15. French, "Strategy of the Entente Powers," 56.

16. Stoler, *Carnal Knowledge and Imperial Power*, 141.

17. Cooper and Stoler, *Tensions of Empire*.

18. Gleisner, "Soldier-Poet or Écrivain-Combattant," 1.

19. Cooper and Burbank, *Empires in World History*, 8.

20. Cooper and Burbank, *Empires in World History*, 8.

21. Matikkala, *Empire and Imperial Ambition*, 12.

22. Cannadine, *Ornamentalism*, xvii.

23. Schneer, *London 1900*, 10. Another excellent example is Ciarlo, *Advertising Empire*.

24. Langbehn and Salama, *German Colonialism*; Evans, *Empire and Culture*; Thompson, *Empire Strikes Back?*

25. Smith, *Between Mutiny and Obedience*, xv.

26. Séché, *Les Noirs*, 235.

1. Great War in Imperial Context

1. Chakravorty, *Indian Nationalism*, 8.

2. Chakravorty, *Indian Nationalism*, 11.

3. Government of India, *India's Contribution*, 69.

4. Ellinwood and Pradhan, *India and World War I*, 51.

5. Streets, *Martial Races*.

6. Chakravorty, *Indian Nationalism*, 15.

7. See Omissi, *Indian Voices of the Great War*, which elaborates on this view.

8. Bhownaggree, *Verdict of India*, 39.

9. Government of India, *India's Contribution*, 175.

10. Chakravorty, *Indian Nationalism*, 239.

11. Chakravorty, *Indian Nationalism*, 109.

12. Bhownaggree, *Verdict of India*, 12.

13. Nasson, *Springboks on the Somme*, 5.

14. *Dead Horse Corner Gazette*, October 1915, 4, CUL.

15. Shurtleff, foreword, x–xi.

16. Cook, "Immortalizing the Canadian Soldier," 48.

17. Keshen, "Great War Soldier as Nation Builder," 4.

18. Lloyd, *Battlefield Tourism*, 214.

19. Fuller, *Troop Morale and Popular Culture*, 160–74.

20. Lloyd, *Battlefield Tourism*, 191.

21. Nasson, *Springboks on the Somme*, 35.

22. Nasson, *Springboks on the Somme*, 244.

23. Nasson, *Springboks on the Somme*, 157.

24. Nasson, *Springboks on the Somme*, 160.

25. Nasson, *Springboks on the Somme*, 129.

26. Maguire, *Contact Zones*, 82–83.

27. Costello, *Black Tommies*.

28. Frémeaux, *Les colonies dans grande guerre*, 11.

29. Fogarty, *Race & War in France*, 17. For more detailed information, see Klein, *Slavery and Colonial Rule*.

30. Echenberg, *Colonial Conscripts*.

31. Fogarty, *Race & War in France*, 24.

32. Fogarty, *Race & War in France*, 27.

33. Frémeaux, *Les colonies dans grande guerre*, 79, 83, 84.

34. Ecole Militaire de L'Artillerie et du Genie, *Role de l'officier*, 160.

35. Ecole Militaire de L'Artillerie et du Genie, *Role de l'officier*, 163.

36. Conklin, *Mission to Civilize*, 166.

37. Fogarty, *Race & War in France*, 1.

38. Frémeaux, *Les colonies dans grande guerre*, 15.

39. Lunn, *Memoirs of Maelstrom*, 59.

40. Lunn, *Memoirs of Maelstrom*, 145.

41. Lunn, *Memoirs of Maelstrom*, 145.

42. Klein, *Slavery and Colonial Rule*, 217–18.

43. Diallo and Senghor, *White War, Black Soldiers*, 71.

44. Digre, *Imperialism's New Clothes*, 22.

45. Nasson, *Springboks on the Somme*, 162.

46. Strachan, *To Arms*, 497.

47. Pradhan, *Indian Army in East Africa*.

48. Digre, *Imperialism's New Clothes*, 34.

49. Strachan, *To Arms*, 503.

50. Farwell, *Great War in Africa*, 57.

51. Pradhan, *Indian Army in East Africa*, 146.

52. Pradhan, *Indian Army in East Africa*, 32.

53. Strachan, *To Arms*, 584.

54. Digre, *Imperialism's New Clothes*, 88.

55. Pradhan, *Indian Army in East Africa*, 51.

56. Davis, *Ends and Means*, 18.

57. Bruce, *Last Crusade*, 3.

58. R. Ford, *Eden to Armageddon*, 299.

59. R. Ford, *Eden to Armageddon*, 399.

60. Singha, *Coolie's Great War*, 155.

61. Jarboe, *Indian Soldiers in World War I*, 212–15.

62. Singha, *Coolie's Great War*, 41.

63. Nunn, *Tigris Gunboats*, 6.

64. Davis, *Ends and Means*, 208.

65. Carver, *Turkish Front*, 101.

66. Carver, *Turkish Front*, 101.

67. Nunn, *Tigris Gunboats*, 279.

68. Fogarty, *Race & War in France*, 13.

69. Hanna, *Your Death Would Be Mine*, 3–7.

70. Greenhalgh, *Victory through Coalition*, 8.

71. Gildea, *Children of the Revolution*, 443.

72. *Glo'ster Gazette*, no. 19, June 1917, 25, CUL.

73. *Lead-Swinger*, vol. 1, no. 6, Christmas 1915, 5, CUL.

74. Nasson, *Springboks on the Somme*, 12.

75. *Stretcher Bearer*, vol. 1, no. 1, October 1915, 3, general holdings, British Library.

76. MacKenzie, introduction to *Popular Imperialism and the Military*, 7.

77. MacKenzie, introduction to *Popular Imperialism and the Military*, 3.

78. Berenson, *Heroes of Empire*, 10, 20, 54.

79. Berenson, *Heroes of Empire*, 79.

80. Berenson, *Heroes of Empire*, 169, 172.

81. Berenson, *Heroes of Empire*, 192–93.

82. Berenson, *Heroes of Empire*, 262.

83. Wilder, "Panafricanism and Republican Political Sphere," 251.

84. Pegler, *Soldiers' Songs*, 14.

85. Pegler, *Soldiers' Songs*, 62, 195, 131.

86. Brewer, *Tommy, Doughboy, Fritz*, 49, 28.

87. Downing, *Digger Dialects*, 8, 39.

88. Sainéan, *L'argot des tranchées*, 55–59.

89. Murphy, *Art of Survival*, 44.

90. Winter, *War beyond Words*, 2.

91. Sainéan, *L'argot des tranchées*, 137–38.

92. Murphy, *Art of Survival*, 52.

93. Sansom, *Letters from France*, 111–12.

2. Christopher of Whisky Fame

1. Beaver, *"Wipers Times,"* 5.

2. *Lead-Swinger*, September 18, 1915, 2, CUL.

3. Audoin-Rouzeau, *Men at War*, 21; Seal, *Soldiers' Press*, 194.

4. The sometimes-sporadic nature of printing and short lives of some titles can make it hard to do quantitative analysis or observe trends within some individual papers.

5. *Le Poilu*, no. 38, November 1917, HIST.

6. *Pennington Press*, vol.1, no.1, September 1, 1916, 2, CUL.

7. *Le Poilu du 6–9*, no. 8, March 1917, 1, print collection 12, S-100, UPENN.

8. Fussell, *Great War and Modern Memory*; Graves, *Good-Bye to All That*; Hynes, *War Imagined*; Todman, *Great War*; Winter, *Sites of Memory, Sites of Mourning*.

9. Audoin-Rouzeau, *Men at War*, 19.

10. Seal, *Soldiers' Press*, ix.

11. Audoin-Rouzeau, *Men at War*, 19.

12. In the Cambridge University Library War Reserve Collection, items vary in size from ten centimeters in height to twenty-seven.

13. Fussell, *Great War and Modern Memory*, 156.

14. Fussell, *Great War and Modern Memory*, 158.

15. Gleisner, "Soldier-Poet or Écrivain-Combattant," 9, 11.

16. Fuller, *Troop Morale and Popular Culture*, 11.

17. Audoin-Rouzeau, *Men at War*, 9.

18. Audoin-Rouzeau, *Men at War*, 9.

19. *Thumbs-Up*, vol. 1, no. 2, March 1916, 39, general holdings, British Library.

20. Seal, *Soldiers' Press*, 2–3.

21. Gleisner, "Soldier-Poet or Écrivain-Combattant," 7.

22. Crouthamel, *Intimate History*, 4.

23. Nelson, *German Soldier Newspapers*, 13, 27.

24. *Le poilu*, no. 38, November 1917, HIST.

25. *Les boyaux du 95ème*, no.1, n.d., 2, HIST.

26. *La marmita*, no.17, December 15, 1915, 1, print collection 12, S-159, UPENN.

27. *Le mouchoir*, March 1, 1917, 3, HIST.

28. *The Dump*, Christmas 1916, 1, CUL.

29. In her translation of Audoin-Rouzeau's work, Helen McPhail defined *cafard* as "a deep melancholy, an overwhelming sense of depression and misery which has no precise linguistic equivalent in the English vocabulary of the Great War." McPhail, translator's note, viii.

30. Gleisner, "Soldier-Poet or Écrivain-Combattant," 10.

31. Osborn, "Trench Journals," 481.

32. When it began, *Punch* called itself the London *Charivari*.

33. Beegan, *Mass Image*, 5, 39.

34. "P.P.," vol. 1, no.11, November 10, 1916, 3, CUL; "P.P.," vol. 1, no.12, November 17, 1916, 12, CUL.

35. *Lead-Swinger*, no. 5, November 27, 1915, 20, CUL.

36. *Fifth Glo'ster Gazette*, no.15, October 1916, 9, CUL.

37. *Trot-Talk*, vol.1, no. 2, April 1, 1918, 1, CUL.

38. *Brise d'entonnoirs*, no. 15, October 15, 1917, 4, BDIC.

39. *Le klaxon*, no. 9, September 1916, 4, BDIC; W. L. Murphy to Francis Jenkinson, August 5, 1917, 6444/M/11, Francis Jenkinson Papers, CUL.

40. Anthony M. Ludovici, *The Secret of Laughter* (London: Constable, 1932), quoted in Holland, *Laughing: A Psychology of Humor*, 45.

41. Holland, *Laughing: A Psychology of Humor*, 83.

42. Lipman, *Laughter in Hell*, 16.

43. Beaver, "Wipers Times," 215.

44. Frankl, *Man's Search for Meaning*, 63.

45. Frankl, *Man's Search for Meaning*, 61.

46. Fine, "Dying for a Laugh," 193.

47. Fine, "Dying for a Laugh," 187.

48. Smith, *Between Mutiny and Obedience*, 98.

49. Fuller, *Troop Morale and Popular Culture*, 19.

50. For example, the British still practiced "Field Punishment No. 1," which "consisted of being strapped or tied spread-eagled to some immobile object: a favorite was the large spoked wheel of a General Service Wagon." Fussell, *Great War and Modern Memory*, 118; Freud, *Jokes and Their Relation*, 160.

51. Erasmus, "Letter to Dorp," 145.

52. *Lead-Swinger*, no.4, November 6, 1915, 20, CUL.

53. Erasmus, "Letter to Dorp," 145.

54. *H.C.B. Gazette*, Spring Double Number, n.d., 7, general holdings, British Library.

55. *Thumbs-Up*, vol.1, no.1, February 1916, 3, general holdings, British Library.

56. *Thumbs-Up*, vol.1, no.1, February 1916, 175, general holdings, British Library.

57. *Fifth Glo'ster Gazette*, no. 23, July 1918, 4, CUL.

58. *Staff Herald*, May 29, 1916, 7, IWM.

59. *H.C.B. Gazette*, Spring Double Number, n.d., 3, general holdings, British Library.

60. *H.C.B. Gazette*, Spring Double Number, n.d., 3, general holdings, British Library.

61. *Le bochofage*, 1916, 1, HIST.

62. Herzog, *Dead Funny*, 1–2.

63. For more on this subject, see Becker, *Great War and French People*; Watson, *Enduring the Great War*.

64. Audoin-Rouzeau, *Men at War*, 95.

65. *Lead-Swinger*, no. 4, November 6, 1915, 17, CUL.

66. *Le Filon* (March 1, 1917), 1. BDIC. *"Ne bourrant pas le crâne."*

67. E. D. Ridley to his mother, August 5, 1914, 7065, E. D. Ridley Papers, CUL.

68. E. D. Ridley to his mother, January 21, 1915, 7066, E.D. Ridley Papers, CUL.

69. *Le rire aux eclats*, January 1917, 3, UPENN.

70. Harold Essex Lewis, interview by Nigel de Lee, 1986, audio, 28:31, 9388, IWM, https://www.iwm.org.uk/collections/item/object/80009177.

71. *Fifth Glo'ster Gazette*, no. 18, April 1917, 14, CUL.

72. *Face aux Boches*, no.2, September 1915, 1, BDIC, A1, N2; *L'écho des guitounes*, no. 25, July 31, 1916, 1, print collection 12, S-160, UPENN; *Le bochofage*, no.5, December 25, 1916, 1, print collection 12, S-154, UPENN.

73. Embusqués were shirkers who were not in the army and/or the men in "softer" positions in the military, away from the front and presumably safe from danger.

74. *Fifth Glo'ster Gazette*, no. 13, July 1916, 1, CUL.

75. Gleisner, "Soldier-Poet or Écrivain-Combattant," 6.

76. Scott, *Domination and Arts of Resistance*, 5.

77. Scott, *Domination and Arts of Resistance*, xii, 188.

78. Sansom, *Letters from France*, 195.

79. Patrick Beaver, interview by BBC, 1973, IWM (source removed).

80. Audoin-Rouzeau, *Men at War*, 34.

81. Fuller, *Troop Morale and Popular Culture*, 4.

82. Fuller, *Troop Morale and Popular Culture*, 9.

83. Smith, *Between Mutiny and Obedience*, 80, 87–88.

84. Allen, *In the Public Eye*, 43, 59.

85. Allen, *In the Public Eye*, 135, 185, 192.

86. Brown, *Victorian News and Newspapers*, 273; Altick, *English Common Reader*, 240–60.

87. Fussell, *Great War and Modern Memory*, 164.

88. Fritzsche, *Reading Berlin 1900*, 1.

89. Lyons, *Writing Culture of Ordinary People*, 12.

90. Gleisner, "Soldier-Poet or Écrivain-Combattant," 1.

91. *H.C.B. Gazette*, vol.1, no. 2, March 1916, 39, general holdings, British Library.

92. Lyons, *Writing Culture of Ordinary People*, 76.

93. Smith, *Between Mutiny and Obedience*, 84.

94. RME, "The Disc Identity," 107.

95. Sainéan, *L'argot des tranchées*, 6.

96. Beaver, "*Wipers Times*," 161.

97. Williamson, foreword, ix–x.

98. "Un journal de tranchées, et c'est notre cas, est un organe permettant à tous les poilus d'un meme regiment de communier dans la meme pensée, de se sentir les coudes, dirions nous dans notre langage, mais pour mener à bien la tâche est rude." L'Homme des Bois [pseud.], "Des Marraines!! Des Abonnements!!," *Brise d'entonnoirs*, no.1, July 1916, 2, BDIC. *Poilu*, "hairy one," was a nickname for a French soldier.

99. Das, *India, Empire*, 31.

3. Men on the Margins

1. Strachan, *To Arms*, 497; Chakravorty, *Indian Nationalism*, 11.

2. Chakravorty, *Indian Nationalism*, 11; Fogarty, *Race & War in France*, 24–27.

3. Among those works which stand out about soldiers' experiences are Lunn, *Memoirs of Maelstrom*; Omissi, *Indian Voices of the Great War*; Antier-Renaud and Le Corre, *Les soldats des colonies*. Notable works that explore the imperial nature of the war include Strachan *To Arms*; Frémeaux, *Les colonies*; Fogarty, *Race & War in France*; Liebau et al., *World in World Wars*; Das, *Race, Empire*; Fogarty and Jarboe, *Empires in World War I*.

4. Cooper and Burbank, *Empires in World History*, 16.

5. Das, *India, Empire*, 125.

6. *Le poilu*, April 18, 1915, 1, 12424, HIST.

7. "P.P.," vol.1, no.13, November 24, 1916, 7, WRB 496, CUL.

8. Though not discussed in this chapter, the Canadians, South Africans, and ANZAC troops also received attention in British and French trench newspapers.

9. Stovall, "Color Line behind the Lines," 741.

10. Stovall, "Color Line behind the Lines," 767.

11. Guoqi, *Strangers on the Western Front*.

12. *Pennington Press*, no. 3, September 13, 1916, 3, WRB 496, CUL.

13. *Le dernier bateau*, no. 2, October 1, 1915, 6, A1, N2, BDIC. *Le dernier bateau* means "the last boat."

14. *Trot-Talk*, vol. 1, no. 2, April 1, 1918, ix, WRB 520, CUL.

15. Ramamurthy, *Imperial Persuaders*, 93.

16. For an in-depth discussion, see Richards, *Imperialism and Juvenile Literature*.

17. Schneider, *Empire for the Masses*, 40.

18. See Stocking, *Victorian Anthropology*. Pro-empire and anti-empire voices were in Britain and France, but neither side was entirely free of racialized thinking.

19. Pieterse, *White on Black*, 77–78, 88.

20. Ramamurthy, *Imperial Persuaders*, 105–6.

21. Fogarty, *Race & War in France*, 100.

22. Merewether and Smith, *Indian Corps in France*, 481.

23. Nelson, *German Soldier Newspapers*, 133. For general information, see also Le Naour, *La honte noire*.

24. Ray Costello's *Black Tommies* (2015) tells the tale of British West Indian soldiers and the challenges they faced trying to serve alongside other British soldiers in Europe. Lucas, *Empire at War*, 394; Maguire, *Contact Zones*, 1–5.

25. Frémeaux, *Les colonies*, 15.

26. "P.P.," vol. 2, no. 29, March 16, 1917, 8, WRB 496, CUL. *Pennington Press* renamed itself the "P.P." later in the war.

27. "P.P.," vol. 2, no. 32, April 6, 1917, 3, WRB 496, CUL.

28. *Le mouchoir*, no. 50, October 15, 1917, 41940, HIST. *Le mouchoir* means "the tissue."

29. Garrigues, *Banania*, 32.

30. Pieterse, *White on Black*, 77–78, 88.

31. Pieterse, *White on Black*, 28–29.

32. A. B. W. Fletcher, interview by BBC, 1963, 4102, IWM (source removed).

33. Prud'homme, *Le fusil et le pinceau*, 132.

34. *Les boyaux du 95e*, no. 1, n.d., 2, 49780, HIST.

35. *Le poilu*, no. 85, December 1921, 3, 12494, HIST.

36. See Streets, *Martial Races*.

37. Although tirailleurs sénégalais were typically all represented as Senegalese within trench newspapers, many members were from other parts of French West Africa.

38. Barbusse, *Le feu*, 41.

39. Daughton, "Sketches of Poilu's World," 47.

40. F. B. Turner to his father, June 19, 1918, F. B. Turner Papers, 9588/9, CUL.

41. Barthas, *Les carnets de guerre*, 66.

42. E. D. Ridley diary, entry for December 18, 1914, E. D. Ridley Papers, Add 7066, December 1914–March 1915, CUL.

43. *Le ver luisant*, no.9, June 1916, 5, print collection 12, S-192, UPENN. *Le ver luisant* means "the glow worm."

44. Koller, "Representing Otherness," 128.

45. Willcocks, *With Indians in France*, 5.

46. *Le mouchoir*, no. 41, Christmas 1916, 8, print collection 12, S-155, UPENN.

47. *Le dernier bateau*, no. 5, November 15, 1915, 3, A1, N5, BDIC.

48. Audoin-Rouzeau and Becker, *14–18*, 148, 154.

49. *Le poilu*, no. 10, September 30, 1915, 3, print collection 12, S-164, UPENN; *La première ligne*, no.2, n.d., 2, print collection 12, S-163, UPENN; *The Dump*, Christmas 1917, 15, WRB 515, CUL.

50. This chapter does not look at the trench papers of colonial troops or the papers from other fronts, which typically involved more colonial troops.

51. J. Delorme-Jules Simon, "Baratier," *L'horizon*, no.6, n.d., 1, print collection 12, M-095, UPENN.

52. André Warnod, "Gri-Gri," *L'horizon*, no.6, n.d., 2, print collection 12, M-095, UPENN.

53. S. H. Steven to family, July 11, 1915, Papers of S. H. Steven, 5525 96/29/1, IWM.

54. *Lead-Swinger*, no.7, February 3, 1918, 407, WRB 112, CUL.

55. Fogarty, *Race & War in France*, 156.

56. *Le poilu*, no. 35, July 1917, 4, print collection 12, S-106, UPENN.

57. *La première ligne*, no. 2, n.d., 1, print collection 12, S-163, UPENN. *La première ligne* is named after the front line.

58. *La première ligne*, no. 2, n.d., 1, print collection 12, S-163, UPENN.

59. Cooper, *Colonialism in Question*, 4.

60. Barthas, *Les carnets de guerre*, 528.

61. "Boots, Unlimited," *"P.P.,"* vol.1, no.14, December 1, 1916, 7, WRB 496, CUL.

62. Daniel Henderson, "The Road to France," *Le poilu*, no.38, November 1917, supplement, 12414, HIST.

63. Eric Wolton, interview by Peter Hart, 1985, reel 6, 9090, audio, 31:32, IWM.

64. Willcocks, *With Indians in France*, 2.

65. British Topical Committee for War Films, *With the Indians at the Front*.

66. "Memory of Africa," *Le poilu*, no.3, January 1915, 3, 12419, HIST.

67. "Petit Dictionnaire," *Face aux Boches*, no.3, October 1915, 2, A1, N3, BDIC. The title of this newspaper is simply a reference to facing the Germans.

68. Landau and Kaspin, *Images and Empires*, 237.

69. "L'armée noire," *Le crapouillot*, no.4, September 1917, 2, 19830, HIST. *Le crapouillot* is named after a trench mortar.

70. A. Pranauf, "Chanson du Monsieur qui a vu la Revue du 14 Julliet," *L'artilleur déchainé*, August 15, 1916, 3, print collection 12, S-161, UPENN. The title of the trench paper means "the unchained artilleryman." *Unchained* was commonly part of the title of satirical papers and referred to writing or speaking freely.

71. Das, *India, Empire*, 172.

72. "Our Spahis," *Le Poilu*, no.14, September 1915, 1, 12430, HIST.

73. Fogarty, *Race & War in France*, 205.

74. Joseph Murray, interview by Peter Hart, 1984, reel 7, 8201, audio, 29:11, IWM.

75. Frank Lindley, interview by Jon Cooksey, 1985, reel 2, 26873, audio, 35:01, IWM.

76. Lt. Col. H. F. Bateman-Champain to Claude MacDonald, June 20, 1915, Papers of Sir Claude MacDonald, 11141 P265, IWM.

77. André Warnod, "Gri-Gri," *L'horizon*, no. 6, n.d., 2, print collection 12, M-095, UPENN. *L'horizon* was named in reference to the horizon.

78. André Warnod, "Gri-Gri." *L'horizon*, no. 6, n.d., 2, print collection 12, M-095, UPENN.

79. Fogarty, *Race & War in France*, 222.

80. Guoqi, *Strangers on the Western Front*, 146–47.

81. Jarboe, "Propaganda and Empire," 116.

82. Fell, "Nursing the Other," 160.

83. "Idées Noires," *Rigolboche*, no.26, October 20, 1915, 3, 41429, HIST.

84. *Rigolboche*, no. 12, June 1, 1915, 1, 41415, HIST.

85. *Le klaxon*, no.4, June 1916, 1, A1, N4, BDIC.

86. P. J. Poitevin, illustration, *Rigolboche*, no. 55, August 10, 1916, front cover, 41459, HIST.

87. Merewether and Smith, *Indian Corps in France*, 481.

88. Lunn, *Memoirs of Maelstrom*, 59.

89. Chakravorty, *Indian Nationalism*, 283.

90. Strachan, *First World War*, 61.

91. *Dead Horse Corner Gazette*, October 1915, 4, WRB 422, CUL.

92. *Dead Horse Corner Gazette*, October 1915, 4, WRB 422, CUL.

93. Séché, *Les noirs*, 9.

94. "Publications des 'Poilus,'" *Le poilu*, October 1–15, 1919, 4, 12473, HIST.

4. Other Fronts, Other Wars?

1. A more thorough exploration of the campaigns and armies themselves is provided in the chapter "The Great War in Imperial Context."

2. Strachan, *To Arms*, 497.

3. Pradhan, *Indian Army in East Africa*, x, 22.

4. Morton-Jack, *Indian Empire at War*, 12–13.

5. Morrow, *Great War*, 53.

6. Strachan, *To Arms*, 696.

7. *Le Dernier Bateau*, no. 4, November 1, 1915, 2, print collection 12, XS-073, UPENN.

8. Morton-Jack, *Indian Empire at War*, 14.

9. Strozzi [pseud.], Cockney Critic, *The Gasper*, no. 15, March 15, 1916, 3, CUL.

10. Beaver, *"Wipers Times,"* 32.

11. Frankau, "Left Barrel," 67.

12. "The Situation in the Balkans," *Le plus-que-torial*, no. 3, March 15, 1916, 3, print collection 12, S-188, UPENN.

13. *Le canard poilu*, no. 54, March 1, 1916, 1, print collection 12, S-179, UPENN.

14. Rata, Dépêches, *Le poilu St-Émilionnais*, no. 9, December 2, 1915, 11, print collection 12, S-166, UPENN.

15. *Taca tac teuf teuf*, no. 1, January 15, 1917, 10, print collection 12, S-228, UPENN.

16. *Boum! Voilà!*, no. 2, April 4, 1916, 2, print collection 12, S-104, UPENN.

17. *Le paix-père*, no. 40, December 25, 1916, 2, print collection 12, S-095, UPENN.

18. *Stretcher-Bearer*, vol. 1, no. 2, November 1915, 11, general holdings, British Library.

19. Sansom, *Letters from France*, 121–22.

20. *La guerre joviale*, no. 1, August 1915, 1–2, BDIC.

21. *La guerre joviale*, no. 2, September 1915, 2. BDIC.

22. Hart, *Great War*, 284.

23. Hart, *Great War*, 287.

24. Hart, *Great War*, 285, 287.

25. *The Gasper*, no. 18, June 5, 1916, 8, CUL.

26. Beaver, "Wipers Times," 160. The issue of the *Wipers Times* was January 20, 1917.

27. Henry Hampton Rich, interview by BBC, 1976, 766, IWM (source removed).

28. Ralph Garland Hockaday, interview by BBC, 1963, 4123, IWM (source removed).

29. "The Situation in Russia," *Le tord-boyau*, no. 11, July 1917, 3, print collection 12, M-094, UPENN.

30. Beaver, "Wipers Times," 217.

31. *Le crapouillot*, no. 1, June 1917, 3, print collection 12, S-202, UPENN.

32. Cockfield, *With Snow on Their Boots*, 38–39.

33. Strachan, *To Arms*, 373.

34. Cockfield, *With Snow on Their Boots*, ix.

35. Strachan, *To Arms*, 504. The resemblance was apparent in the absence of artillery, the prominence of disease, the difficulties of supply, and the number of local carriers involved.

36. *Le petit echo*, no. 122, March 11, 1917, 1, print collection 12, S-200, UPENN.

37. Morton-Jack, *Indian Empire at War*, 497.

38. Turhan, *Other Empire*, 9.

39. Said, *Orientalism*, 41.

40. Turhan, *Other Empire*, 162.

41. Twopence [pseud.], "Restrictions," *The Gasper*, no. 19, June 26, 1916, 2, CUL.

42. Turhan, *Other Empire*, 3.

43. Other trench authors certainly had and sometimes referenced him by name.

44. Mesopotamian Alphabet, Beaver, "Wipers Times," 160.

45. Indian rupees became currency in Iraq after the Indian Army began to take territory there. Burrows and Cobbin, "Budgetary and Financial Discontinuities," 249; Beaver, "Wipers Times," 160.

46. Beaver, *"Wipers Times,"* 160.

47. Beaver, *"Wipers Times,"* 160.

48. Beaver, *"Wipers Times,"* 160.

49. Beaver, *"Wipers Times,"* 161.

50. Beaver, *"Wipers Times,"* 160.

51. *Bleutinet*, no. 24, October 1, 1916, 2, print collection 12, S-094, UPENN.

52. *La fusée à retards*, no. 4, 4, BDIC.

53. *Le marteau*, no. 1, September 1915, 4, BNF.

54. *La fusée à retards*, no. 2, 1, BDIC.

55. *Le petit echo*, no. 122, March 11, 1917, 1, print collection 12, S-200, UPENN.

56. Said, *Orientalism*, 40.

57. Strachan, *To Arms*, 693; *L'esprit du cor*, no. 3, July 10, 1917, 7, print collection 12, XS-020, UPENN.

58. Ramamurthy, *Imperial Persuaders*, 60.

59. *Bleutinet*, no. 24, October 1, 1916, 2, print collection 12, S-094, UPENN.

60. *Brise d'entonnoirs*, no.18, January 1918, 4, BDIC.

61. *La musette*, no.1, n.d., 2, print collection 12, S-096, UPENN.

62. "Nous avons tort de considerer les Autrichiens comme des adversaires négligeables. Ce sont, au contraire, d'excellents soldats, et les Italiens doivent tous leurs success à ce seul fait qu'ils sont 200,000 contre Trente." *Le poilu sans poil*, no. 15, n.d., 4, print collection 12, S-098, UPENN.

63. *Le bavardar de l'A.O.*, no. 1, August 20, 1917, 2, print collection 12, S-226, UPENN.

64. *The Gnome*, no. 4, May 1917, CUL.

65. *Le clairon*, no. 4, May 26, 1916, 8, BDIC.

66. *Le bavardar de l'A.O.*, no. 2, September 20, 1917, 1, BDIC.

67. Turhan, *Other Empire*, xi.

68. Said, *Orientalism*, 206.

69. *Chronicles of the White Horse*, no. 2, April 1917, 6, CUL.

70. *Chronicles of the White Horse*, no. 2, April 1917, 6, CUL.

71. *Chronicles of the White Horse*, no. 2, April 1917, 6, CUL.

72. *La bourguignotte*, no. 19, 1917, 2, BDIC.

73. *La bourguignotte*, no. 16, 1917, 2, BDIC.

74. *La bourguignotte*, no. 18, 1917, 3, BDIC.

75. J. W. Barnett diary, entry for February 3, 1916, J. W. Barnett Papers, 666 90/37/1, IWM.

76. J. W. Barnett diary, entry for February 8, 1916, J. W. Barnett Papers, 666 90/37/1, IWM.

77. Strachan, *To Arms*, 496.

78. Fawaz, *Land of Aching Hearts*, 2–3.

79. *La bourguignotte*, no. 15, 1917, 1, BDIC.

80. "The Disenchanted Impression of a Poilu of the Orient," *La bourguignotte*, no. 15, 1917, 2, BDIC.

81. "Disenchanted Impression," *La Bourguignotte*, no. 15, 1917, 4, BDIC.

82. "Shattered Illusions," *Chronicles of the White Horse*, no. 3, July 1917, 7, CUL.

83. A strain of anti-Semitism was within a number of British trench newspapers.

84. CFB, "A Sand Grouse," *Chronicles of the White Horse*, no. 3, July 1917, 11, CUL.

85. *The Gnome*, no. 4, May 1917, 14, CUL.

86. *Le bavardar de l'A.O.*, no. 2, September 20, 1917, 2, BDIC.

87. *Le clairon*, no. 4, May 26, 1916, 1, BDIC.

88. It's possible that if the Ottomans had been the chief enemy of the Entente forces, a more coherent system of values to oppose would have appeared in trench newspapers.

89. *Le clairon*, no. 6, June 11, 1916, 3, BDIC.

90. *The Gnome*, no.3, March 1917, 1, CUL.

91. Said, *Orientalism*, 206.

92. Sancho VII [pseud.], "Fantaisie: Sur Guillaume, empereur des Boches," *La bourguignotte*, no. 16, 1917, 3, BDIC. Some of the lines of the poem include "Tu promis de toujours vivre / Ivre; / Et d'avoir bonne et délectable / Table; / De régner sur le monde esclave / Hâve; / Tu lui promis aussi l'Orient / Riant / Et la maitrise sur l'Autriche / Riche."

93. *La bourguignotte*, no. 18, 1917, 5, BDIC.

94. Fawaz, *Land of Aching Hearts*, 203.

95. Singha, *Coolie's Great War*, 21.

96. *The Gnome*, no. 2, January 1917, 1, CUL.

97. *The Gnome*, no. 2, January 1917, 2, CUL.

98. *The Gnome*, no. 2, January 1917, 9. CUL.

99. *The Gnome*, no. 2, January 1917, 9, CUL.

100. *The Gnome*, no. 2, January 1917, 2, CUL.

101. "What He Did in the Great War," *Chronicles of the White Horse*, no. 2, April 1917, 9, CUL.

102. Henry Hampton Rich, interview by David Lance, 1976, pt. 1, 766, audio, 30:01, IWM, https://www.iwm.org.uk/collections/item/object/80022187.

103. Leslie George Pollard, interview by BBC, 1982, 6694, IWM (source removed).

104. *Chronicles of the White Horse*, no. 2, April 1917, 9, CUL.

105. F. B. Turner to his father, October 4, 1918, F. B. Turner Papers, 9588, CUL.

106. *Brise d'entonnoirs*, no. 1, July 1916, 4, BDIC.

107. "The Belgian Nights," *Lead-Swinger*, no. 5, November 27, 1915, 30, CUL.

108. *La bourguignotte*, no. 18, 1917, 2, BDIC.

109. Wohl, *Generation of 1914*, 39.

110. "Gaza and the Crusades," *The Gnome*, no. 4, May 1917, 10, CUL.

111. "Gaza and the Crusades," *The Gnome*, no. 4, May 1917, 10, CUL.

112. *The Egyptian Gazette*, May 11, 1917, quoted in *The Gnome*, no. 4, May 1917, 10, CUL.

113. E. D. Ridley to family, September 7, 1915, E. D. Ridley Papers, 7067, CUL.

114. E. D. Ridley to family, August 17, 1917, E. D. Ridley Papers, 7068, CUL.

115. Morton-Jack, *Indian Empire at War*, 14.

5. Why War?

1. Porter, *Absent-Minded Imperialists*, 98.

2. "The Autobiography of a Biscuit Tin," *Lead-Swinger*, no. 4, October 1915, 22–23, CUL.

3. *79th News*, October 1914, 118, CUL; *79th News*, January 1915, 2, CUL.

4. *The "P.P.,"* vol. 1, no. 16, December 15, 1916, 12, CUL.

5. "Welsh Division Alphabet," *New Year Souvenir of the Welsh Division*, January 1917, 16, CUL.

6. Fussell, *Great War and Modern Memory*, 232.

7. Parliamentary Recruiting Committee, *Surely You Will Fight*.

8. Beaver, *"Wipers Times,"* 250.

9. Beaver, *"Wipers Times,"* 46. The issue was vol. 2, no. 4, March 20, 1916.

10. F. B. Turner to his father, January 23, 1919, F. B. Turner Papers, 9588, CUL.

11. "Mystery of the Manor House," *Lead-Swinger*, Christmas 1915, 1, UPENN.

12. Fuller, *Troop Morale and Popular Culture*, 160.

13. Hobsbawm and Ranger, *Invention of Tradition*, 43–100.

14. Beaver, *"Wipers Times,"* 246.

15. Audoin-Rouzeau and Becker, *14–18*, 97.

16. *La première ligne*, no. 9, December 1, 1916, 1, print collection 12, S-207, UPENN.

17. *Le poilu du 6–9*, no. 8, March 1917, 2, print collection 12, S-100, UPENN.

18. Loubère, *"Pro patria."*

19. Weber, *Peasants into Frenchmen*, 96.

20. Gildea, *Children of the Revolution*, 305.

21. *Nos filleuls*, no. 2, January 1917, 2, print collection 12, S-165, UPENN.

22. Gildea, *Children of the Revolution*, 299–300; C. Ford, *Creating the Nation in Provincial France*, 227, 230.

23. C. Ford, *Creating the Nation in Provincial France*, 195.

24. *La vie poilusienne*, no. 4, April 1916, 4, print collection 12, S-193, UPENN.

25. *L'echo des gourbis*, no. 2, April 12, 1915, 3, print collection 12, S-181, UPENN; *Le filon*, March 1, 1917, 4, BDIC; *Le filon*, March 20, 1917, 4, 5, BDIC.

26. *Le pastis*, no. 1 (June 25, 1916), 1. print collection 12, S-229, UPENN.

27. Barthas, *Les carnets de guerre*, 495.

28. Barthas, *Les carnets de guerre*, 265.

29. Lyons, *Writing Culture of Ordinary People*, 93.

30. Steinlen, *1916: "La Triennale."*

31. Pierre Chapelle, "Printemps," *Le Poilu du 6–9*, no. 8, March 1917, 2, print collection 12, S-100, UPENN.

32. Pierre Chapelle, "Printemps," *Le Poilu du 6–9*, No. 8 (March 1917), 2, print collection 12, S-100, UPENN.

33. Beaver, *"Wipers Times,"* 88.

34. Pioneer [pseud.], "To the P.B.I.," 131. The issue was from December 1, 1916.

35. "1917—The Year of Decision?," *"P.P.,"* vol. 1, no. 18, December 29, 1916, 2, CUL.

36. George Ellis, "Voices of Empire," *Kit-Bag*, vol. 1, no. 2, June 1916, 53–54.

37. George Ellis, "Voices of Empire," *Kit-Bag*, vol. 1, no. 2, June 1916, 55.

38. *Le poilu*, no. 14, September 1915, 1, HIST.

39. *L'artilleur déchainé*, August 15, 1916, 3, print collection 12, S-161, UPENN.

40. Daniel Henderson, "The Road to France," *Le poilu*, no. 38, November 1917, supplement, HIST, 12414.

41. *Pulham Patrol*, vol. 1, no. 5, February 1918, 183, CUL.

42. Evans, *Empire and Culture*, vii. A number of books have explored the relationship between the Third Republic and empire. Works like Stuart Michael Persell's *The French Colonial Lobby, 1889–1938*, and Henri Brunschwig's *French Colonialism 1871–1914* explore the origins of French colonial expansion. Martin Evans's *Empire and Culture*, Edward Berenson's *Heroes of Empire*, and Alice Conklin's *A Mission to Civilize* address the cultural justifications and impact of empire.

43. Porter, *Critics of Empire*, xxix.

44. Matikkala, *Empire and Imperial Ambition*, 4; Claeys, *Imperial Skeptics*, 282.

45. Matikkala, *Empire and Imperial Ambition*, 45.

46. Brunschwig, *French Colonialism*, 97; Persell, *French Colonial Lobby*, 3.

47. Brunschwig, *French Colonialism*, 103.

48. Evans, *Empire and Culture*, 152–53.

49. Colley, *Britons*, 6.

50. Colley, *Britons*, 8.

51. Said, *Culture and Imperialism*, 14.

52. Said, *Culture and Imperialism*, 14.

53. Burton, *At the Heart of Empire*, 8.

54. Berenson, *Heroes of Empire*; Evans "Culture and Empire, 1830–1962"; Garrigues, *Banania*.

55. *Stretcher Bearer*, vol. 1, no. 3, December 1915, 19, general holdings, British Library.

56. Baycroft, "Empire and Nation," 148.

57. Baycroft, "Empire and Nation," 148.

58. Lyons, *Writing Culture of Ordinary People*, 112.

59. *On les aura*, no. 5, April 15, 1917, 2, print collection 12, S-103, UPENN.

60. *The Gasper*, no. 14, February 28, 1916, 2, CUL.

61. Eksteins, *Rites of Spring*, 116.

62. Eksteins, *Rites of Spring*, 67.

63. Eksteins, *Rites of Spring*, 77.

64. Eksteins, *Rites of Spring*, 91, 94.

65. *Le dernier bateau*, no. 12, January-July 1917, 1, BDIC.

66. *La bourguignotte*, no. 8, April 1916, 6, print collection 12, S-162, UPENN. In biblical passages about the "mark of the beast," 606 is interchangeable with 666.

67. M.L.G., "Beyond," *Fifth Glo'ster Gazette*, no. 14, September 1916, 1, CUL.

68. Beaver, "Wipers Times," 178. The issue was vol. 1, no. 4, March 5, 1917, 10. *Narpoo* and *napoo* were English corruptions of the French *il n'y a plus* and were used to indicate there was no more of something or that something was finished.

69. "Le Rêve du Boche," *Bleutinet*, no. 24, October 1, 1916, 1, print collection 12, S-094, UPENN.

70. Smith, *Between Mutiny and Obedience*, 11.

71. Beaver, "Wipers Times," 277. The poem "Profit and Loss" appeared in *Wipers Times* vol. 2, no. 5, January 22, 1918.

72. Hanna, *Mobilization of Intellect*, 104–5.

73. Hanna, *Mobilization of Intellect*, 86.

74. Northcliffe, *At the War*, 180.

75. Thayer, *Germany vs. Civilization*, 37, quoted in Temkin, "Culture vs. Kultur," 161.

76. Temkin, "Culture vs. Kultur," 157–82.

77. For more information, see Conklin, *Mission to Civilize*; Daughton and White, *In God's Empire*.

78. Thomas and Toye, *Arguing about Empire*, 1.

79. Thomas and Toye, *Arguing about Empire*, 80.

80. Beaver, "Wipers Times," 251. The Christmas issue was vol. 2, no. 4, December 25, 1917.

81. Said, *Culture and Imperialism*, 12.

82. "Mort pour la France," 244. "Mort Pour la France" appeared in vol. 2, no. 3, November 1, 1917.

83. Becker, *Great War and French People*, 327.

84. Porter, *Absent-Minded Imperialists*, 18.

85. Porter, *Absent-Minded Imperialists*, xii.

6. The Imperial Enemy?

1. Pound, *Lost Generation*, 13.

2. The Belgian, Dutch, and Italian empires remained.

3. "La rêve du Boche," *Le Bleutinet*, no. 24, October 1, 1916, 1, print collection 12, S-094, UPENN.

4. *Les quat'z'arts du front*, July 25, 1916, 2, print collection 12, S-216, UPENN; *Le cafard muselé*, no. 2, March 1, 1917, 3, BNF.

5. *The Dump*, Christmas 1917, 15, CUL.

6. *Le poilu*, no. 10, September 30, 1915, 8, print collection 12, S-164, UPENN.

7. *La première ligne*, n.d., 4, print collection 12, S-163, UPENN.

8. *Le poilu sans poil*, no. 15, n.d., 1, print collection 12, s-098, UPENN.

9. *Le ver luisant*, no. 9, June 1916, 3, print collection 12, s-192, UPENN.

10. *Bombes et pétards*, March 14, 1917, 1, print collection 12, s-224, UPENN.

11. "An Eye for an Eye," *Le poilu marmité*, no. 33, November 20, 1916, 3, print collection 12, s-186, UPENN.

12. Graves, *Good-Bye to All That*, 67.

13. *The Dump*, vol. 3, 1917, 1, CUL.

14. Beaver, *"Wipers Times,"* 117. The poem appeared in vol. 1, no. 1, July 31, 1916, 5.

15. *Le poilu du 37è*, no. 10, 1916, 2, print collection 12, s-150, UPENN.

16. Dirks, *Scandal of Empire*, 5.

17. Brunschwig, *French Colonialism*, 179.

18. Eksteins, *Rites of Spring*, 116.

19. Berenson, *Heroes of Empire*, 12.

20. Audoin-Rouzeau and Becker, *14–18*, 104.

21. Northcliffe, *At the War*, 4.

22. Northcliffe, *At the War*, 8.

23. Robertson, "Norman Lindsay and 'Asianisation,'" 173.

24. "Aux Jeunes Soldats morts pour la Patrie," *Le Poilu du 6-9*, no. 8, March 1917, 2, print collection 12, s-100, UPENN.

25. "Lieutenant Langdon leaving for active service," *Stretcher Bearer*, vol. 1, no. 3, December 1915, 16–17.

26. Murphy, *Art of Survival*, 1.

27. Said, *Culture and Imperialism*, xxv.

28. Marlantes, *What It Is Like*, 40–41, 55–56.

29. *Le cafard enchaîné*, Christmas 1916, 1, print collection 12, s-158, UPENN.

30. *Bleutinet*, no. 24, October 1, 1914, 2, print collection 12, s-094, UPENN.

31. T. Knox-Shaw to Francis Jenkinson, November 3, 1918, 6444/K/5, Francis Jenkinson Papers, CUL.

32. Prud'homme, *Le fusil et le pinceau*, 106. For more information, see Barthas, *Les carnets de guerre*.

33. Barbusse, *Le feu*, 32.

34. Barbusse, *Lettres à sa femme*, 250.

35. *La musette*, no. 1, n.d., 2, print collection 12, s-096, UPENN.

36. "Song of the Hun-Eagle," *Fifth Glo'ster Gazette*, no. 14, September 1916, 6, CUL.

37. *Le poilu du 37è*, no. 10, 1916, 4, print collection 12, s-150, UPENN.

38. "A Scrap of Paper," *The Gasper*, no. 15, March 15, 1916, 4, CUL.

39. Claeys, *Imperial Sceptics*, 13.

40. *The Gasper*, no. 15, March 15, 1916, 4, CUL.

41. "Father Bernard Vaughan and the Cameron Highlanders," *79th News*, October 1914, 128, CUL.

42. Jones, "German Empire," 69.

43. Jones, "German Empire," 55.

44. Jones, "German Empire," 60.

45. Jones, "German Empire," 70.

46. "To the 'Slackers' at Home," *Lead-Swinger*, no. 4, November 6, 1915, 2, CUL.

47. Strachan, *First World War*, 49.

48. *Poil . . . et plume*, no. 4, October 1916, 1, print collection 12, S-102, UPENN.

49. Salem el Koubi, "Le Lion au Poilu," *L'écho des guitones*, no. 37, February 30, 1918, 1, 41396, HIST.

50. Hochschild, *King Leopold's Ghost*, 2, 186–94.

51. Berenson, *Heroes of Empire*, 197–98, 202.

52. *Le mouchoir*, no. 41, Christmas 1916, 8, print collection 12, S-155, UPENN.

53. *Télé-Mail*, no. 7, March 16, 1916, 4, print collection 12, S-190, UPENN.

54. Images appear in photo supplement (no page numbers) in Hochschild, *King Leopold's Ghost*, between pages 116 and 117.

55. Hanna, *Mobilization of Intellect*, 87.

56. MacLeod, *Blight of Kultur*, ix.

57. The latter was not an unfounded belief; the Germans did help finance some Indian radicals.

58. MacLeod, *Blight of Kultur*, 161.

59. Porter, *Absent-Minded Imperialists*, 8.

60. Porter, *Absent-Minded Imperialists*, 113.

61. Matikkala, *Empire and Imperial Ambition*, 204.

62. Conklin, *Mission to Civilize*, 75, 105.

63. Conklin, *Mission to Civilize*, 16.

64. Thomas and Toye, *Arguing about Empire*, 230.

65. Fogarty, *Race & War in France*, 53.

66. S. Lewis, "England after the War," *Kit-Bag*, vol. 1, no. 2, June 1916, 52, general holdings, British Library.

67. Northcliffe, *At the War*, 8.

68. *La vie poilusienne*, no. 6, 1916, 1, BNF.

69. *L'écho du boqueteau*, no. 32, July 1916, 3, print collection 12, S-205, UPENN.

70. *La bourguignotte*, no. 8, April 1916, 5, print collection 12, S-162, UPENN.

71. *La bourguignotte*, no. 8, April 1916, 5, print collection 12, S-162, UPENN.

72. Capitaine D., "Lettre Rimée," *Le poilu du 37è*, no. 10, 1916, 4, print collection 12, S-150, UPENN.

73. Berenson, *Heroes of Empire*, 88.

74. Porter, *Absent-Minded Imperialists*, 321.

75. *Trot-Talk*, vol.1, no. 2, April 1, 1918, 19, CUL.

Conclusion

1. Baycroft, "Empire and the Nation," 148.

2. Willcocks, *With Indians in France*, 294.

3. Ciarlo, *Advertising Empire*, 75.

4. For example, see Hull, *Absolute Destruction*; Zimmerer and Perraudin, *German Colonialism and National Identity*.

5. Porter, *Critics of Empire*, xxiii.

6. Hemingway, *Letters of Ernest Hemingway*, 1:147–48.

7. Hemingway, *Letters of Ernest Hemingway*, 1:154.

8. Stice, "Contrast and Contact."

9. Winter, *War beyond Words*.

10. Murphy, *Art of Survival*; Watson, *Enduring the Great War*.

11. Cannadine, *Ornamentalism*, xvii.

12. Conklin, *Mission to Civilize*, 166–67.

13. One example is William Kidd's essay "Representation or Recuperation?" in *Promoting the Colonial Idea*.

14. Nora, *Les lieux de mémoire*.

15. N. J. Laski to Francis Jenkinson, August 29, 1917, Add 6444/L/5, Francis Jenkinson Papers, CUL.

16. *Trot-Talk*, vol. 1, no. 2, April 1, 1918, 27, CUL.

17. Thomas and Toye, *Arguing about Empire*, 231.

BIBLIOGRAPHY

Archival Sources

Bibliothèque de Documentation Internationale Contemporaine (BDIC), Nanterre

Brise d'entonnoirs	*La vie poilusienne*
Face à l'est	*Le bavarder de l'A.O.*
Face aux Boches	*Le clairon*
La bourguignotte	*Le dernier bateau*
La femme à barbe	*Le filon*
La fusée à retards	*Le klaxon*
La guerre joviale	*Le zouzou*

Bibliothèque Nationale de France (BNF), Paris

Le cafard muselé
Le marteau

British Library, general holdings, London

The H.C.B. Gazette
Kit-Bag
Stretcher Bearer
Thumbs-Up

Cambridge University Library (CUL), Cambridge

Trench Newspapers

79th News	*Lead-Swinger*
AAC Journal	*New Year Souvenir of the*
Chronicles of the White Horse	*Welsh Division*
Dead Horse Corner Gazette	*Pennington Press*, later *"P.P."*
The Dump	*Pulham Patrol*
Fifth Glo'ster Gazette	*The Salient*
The Gasper	*Trot-Talk*
The Gnome	

Correspondence and Diaries

Francis Jenkinson Papers
E. D. Ridley Papers

Lieutenant F. B. Turner: letters
to his father, F. B. Turner

Historial de la Grande Guerre (HIST), Péronne

La voix du 75
Le 120 court
Le bochofage
L'écho des guitones

Le mouchoir
Le poilu
Les boyaux du 95ème
Rigolboche

Imperial War Museum (IWM), London

Audio Reels

BBC recording, Patrick Beaver
BBC recording, A. B. W. Fletcher
BBC recording, R. G. Hockaday
Interview reels, Colonel Harold
    Essex Lewis
Interview reels, Frank Lindley
Interview reels, Joseph Murray

Interview reels, Leslie George
    Pollard
Interview reels, Thomas
    Reginald
Interview reels, Henry
    Hampton Rich
Interview reels, Eric Wolton

Film Reels

With the Indians at the Front,
    Part I, January 17, 1916

Papers

Private Papers, J. W. Barnett
    Papers
Private Papers, Sir Claude
    MacDonald Papers

Private Papers, S. H. Steven
    Papers
Lt. Col. S. H. C. Woolrych,
    Reflections of WWI

Trench Newspapers

Staff Herald

Library of Congress, Prints & Photographs Division, WWI Posters, Washington DC

LC-USZC4–10915
LC-USZC4–10902
LC-USZC4–10912
LC-USZC2–4016
LC-USZC2–3908

LC-USZC4–10903
LC-USZC4–10880
LC-USZC2–4005
LC-USZC2–4082

University of Pennsylvania Rare Book and Manuscript
Library (UPENN), Philadelphia

Bleutinet

Bombes et pétards

Boum! Voilà!

La bourguignotte

La marmita

La musette

La petite marmite

La première ligne

L'artilleur déchainé

La saucisse

Le anti-cafard

Le bavardar de l'A.O.

Le cafard enchainé

Le canard poilu

L'echo des gourbis

L'écho des guitones

L'echo des Marmites

L'écho du boqueteau

Le crapouillot

Le dernier bateau

Le mouchoir

Le paix-père

Le pastis

Le petit echo

Le plus-que-torial

Le poilu

Le poilu du 37è

Le poilu du 6–9

Le poilu marmité

Le poilu sans poil

Le poilu St.-Émilionnais

Le rire aux eclats

Le schrapnell

L'esprit du cor

Les quat'z'arts du front

Le tord-boyau

Le ver luisant

L'horizon

Nos filleuls

On les aura

Poil . . . et plume

Poilu-Noël, supplement to Poilu
marmité

Taca tac teuf teuf

Télé-Mail

Published Sources

Allen, James Smith. *In the Public Eye: A History of Reading in Modern France, 1800–1940.* Princeton NJ: Princeton University Press, 1991.

Altick, Richard. *The English Common Reader: A Social History of the Mass Reading Public, 1800–1900.* 2nd ed. Columbus: Ohio State University Press, 1998.

Antier-Renaud, Chantal, and Christian Le Corre. *Les soldats des colonies dans la Première Guerre mondiale.* Rennes: Ouest-France, 2008.

Ashplant, T. G. *Fractured Loyalties, Masculinity, Class and Politics in Britain, 1900–30.* Chicago: Rivers Oram Press, 2007.

Audoin-Rouzeau, Stéphane. *Men at War 1914–1918: National Sentiment and Trench Journalism in France during the First World War.* Translated by Helen McPhail. Providence RI: Berg Publishers, 1992.

Audoin-Rouzeau, Stéphane, and Annette Becker. *14–18: Understanding the Great War.* New York: Farrar, Straus and Giroux, 2002.

Barbusse, Henri. *Le feu: Journal d'une escouade.* Paris: Flammarion, 1965.

————. *Lettres à sa femme 1914–1917*. Paris: Buchet/Chastel, 2006.

Barthas, Louis. *Les carnets de guerre de Louis Barthas, tonnelier, 1914–1918*. Paris: La Découverte/Poche, 1997.

Baycroft, Timothy. "The Empire and the Nation: The Place of Colonial Images in the Republican Visions of the French Nation." In Evans, *Empire and Culture*, 148–60.

Beaver, Patrick, ed. *"Wipers Times": A Complete Facsimile of the Famous World War One Trench Newspaper, Incorporating the "New Church Times," the "Kemmel Times," the "Somme Times," the "B.E.F. Times," and the "Better Times."* London: P. Davies, 1973.

Becker, Jean-Jacques. *The Great War and the French People*. Translated by Arnold Pomerans. New York: St. Martin's Press, 1986.

Beegan, Gerry. *The Mass Image: A Social History of Photomechanical Reproduction in Victorian London*. New York: Palgrave MacMillan, 2008.

Berenson, Edward. *Heroes of Empire: Five Charismatic Men and the Conquest of Africa*. Berkeley: University of California Press, 2011.

Bhownaggree, Mancherjee. *The Verdict of India*. New York: Hodder & Stoughton, 1916.

Brewer, Emily. *Tommy, Doughboy, Fritz: Soldier Slang of World War I*. Gloucestershire, UK: Amberley Publishing, 2014.

British Topical Committee for War Films. *With the Indians at the Front, Part I*. January 17, 1916. Filmstrip, 9:08. 202-1, IWM. https://film.iwmcollections.org.uk/record/1955/media_id/10211.

Brown, Lucy. *Victorian News and Newspapers*. Oxford: Clarendon Press, 1985.

Bruce, Anthony. *The Last Crusade: The Palestine Campaign in the First World War*. London: John Murray, 2002.

Brunschwig, Henri. *French Colonialism 1871–1914: Myths and Realities*. London: Pall Mall Press, 1966.

Burrows, Geoff, and Phillip E. Cobbin. "Budgetary and Financial Discontinuities: Iraq 1920–32." *Accounting History Review* 21, no. 3 (2011): 247–62. https://doi.org/10.1080/21552851.2011.616716.

Burton, Antoinette. *At the Heart of Empire: Indians and the Colonial Encounter in Late-Victorian Britain*. Berkeley: University of California Press, 1998.

Busch, Briton, ed. *Canada and the Great War: Western Front Association Papers*. Ithaca NY: McGill-Queen's University Press, 2003.

Cannadine, David. *Ornamentalism: How the British Saw Their Empire*. Oxford: Oxford University Press, 2001.

Carver, Michael. *The National Army Museum Book of the Turkish Front 1914–1918: The Campaigns at Gallipoli, in Mesopotamia, and in Palestine*. London: Sidgwick & Jackson and the National Army Museum, 2003.

Chakrabarty, Dipesh. *Provincializing Europe: Postcolonial Thought and Historical Difference*. Princeton NJ: Princeton University Press, 2000.

Chakravorty, Upendra Narayan. *Indian Nationalism and the First World War, 1914–1918*. Calcutta: Progressive Publishers, 1997.

Chatterton, Eyre. *Ten Days with the Indian Army Corps at the Front*. London: Society for Promoting Christian Knowledge, 1916.

Ciarlo, David. *Advertising Empire: Race and Visual Culture in Imperial Germany*. Cambridge MA: Harvard University Press, 2011.

Claeys, Gregory. *Imperial Sceptics: British Critics of Empire, 1850–1920*. New York: Cambridge University Press, 2010.

Cockfield, Jamie. *With Snow on Their Boots: The Tragic Odyssey of the Russian Expeditionary Force in France during World War I*. New York: St. Martin's Press, 1998.

Colley, Linda. *Britons: Forging the Nation, 1707–1837*. New Haven CT: Yale University Press, 1992.

Conklin, Alice. *A Mission to Civilize: The Republican Idea of Empire in France and West Africa, 1895–1930*. Stanford CA: Stanford University Press, 1997.

Cook, Tim. "Immortalizing the Canadian Soldier." In Busch, *Canada and the Great War*, 46–65.

Cooper, Frederick. *Colonialism in Question: Theory, Knowledge, History*. Berkeley: University of California Press, 2005.

Cooper, Frederick, and Jane Burbank, eds. *Empires in World History: Power and the Politics of Difference*. Princeton NJ: Princeton University Press, 2010.

Cooper, Frederick, and Ann Stoler. *Tensions of Empire: Colonial Cultures in a Bourgeois World*. Berkeley: University of California Press, 1997.

Costello, Ray. *Black Tommies: British Soldiers of African Descent in the First World War*. Liverpool, UK: Liverpool University Press, 2015.

Crouthamel, Jason. *An Intimate History of the Front: Masculinity, Sexuality, and German Soldiers in the First World War*. New York: Palgrave Macmillan, 2014.

Das, Santanu. *India, Empire, and First World War Culture: Writings, Images and Songs*. Cambridge: Cambridge University Press, 2018.

———, ed. *Race, Empire and First World War Writing*. Cambridge: Cambridge University Press, 2011.

Daughton, James. "Sketches of the Poilu's World: Trench Cartoons from the Great War." In *World War I and the Cultures of Modernity*, edited by Douglas Mackaman and Michael Mays, 35–67. Jackson: University Press of Mississippi, 2000.

Daughton, J. P., and Owen White, eds. *In God's Empire: French Missionaries and the Modern World*. Oxford: Oxford University Press, 2012.

Davis, Paul. *Ends and Means: The British Mesopotamian Campaign and Commission*. Rutherford NJ: Fairleigh Dickinson University Press, 1994.

deForest Lord, George. *Heroic Mockery: Variations on Epic Themes from Homer to Joyce*. Newark: University of Delaware Press, 1977.

Denby, David. *Snark: It's Mean, It's Personal, and It's Ruining Our Conversation*. New York: Simon & Schuster, 2009.

Derrick, Jonathan. "The Dissenters: Anti-Colonialism in France, *c.* 1900–1940." In *Promoting the Colonial Idea: Propaganda and Visions of Empire in France*, edited by Tony Chafer and Amanda Sackur, 53–68. New York: Palgrave, 2002.

Diallo, Bakary, and Lamine Senghor. *White War, Black Soldiers: Two African Accounts of World War I*. Translated by Nancy Erber and William Peniston. Indianapolis IN: Hackett, 2021.

Digre, Brian. *Imperialism's New Clothes: The Repartition of Tropical Africa, 1914–1919*. New York: Peter Lang, 1990.

Dirks, Nicholas. *The Scandal of Empire: India and the Creation of Imperial Britain*. Cambridge MA: Harvard University Press, 2006.

Downing, W. H. *Digger Dialects: A Collection of Slang Phrases Used by the Australian Soldiers on Active Service*. Melbourne, Australia: Lothian Book Publishing, 1919.

Douglas, Allen. *War, Memory, and the Politics of Humor: The Canard Enchaîné and World War I*. Berkeley: University of California Press, 2002.

Echenberg, Myron. *Colonial Conscripts: The Tirailleurs Senegalais in French West Africa, 1857–1960*. Portsmouth NH: Heinemann, 1991.

Ecole Militaire de L'Artillerie et du Genie, *Role de l'officier dans la nation armée*. Versailles: Imprimerie Moderne Maréchaux, 1904–1905.

Eksteins, Modris. "All Quiet on the Western Front and the Fate of a War." *Journal of Contemporary History* 15, no. 2 (Apr., 1980): 345–66.

——— . *Rites of Spring: The Great War and the Birth of the Modern Age*. New York: Doubleday, 1990.

Ellinwood, DeWitt, and S. D. Pradhan. *India and World War 1*. Columbia MO: South Asia Books, 1978.

Erasmus, Desiderius. "Letter to Maarten Van Dorp, 1515." In *In Praise of Folly*, 137–72. Translated by Betty Radice. New York: Penguin Books, 1993.

Evans, Martin. "Culture and Empire, 1830–1962: An Overview." In Evans, *Empire and Culture*, 1–26.

——— , ed. *Empire and Culture: The French Experience, 1830–1940*. New York: Palgrave Macmillan, 2004.

Farwell, Byron. *The Great War in Africa, 1914–1918*. New York: W. W. Norton & Company, 1986.

Fawaz, Leila Tarazi. *A Land of Aching Hearts: The Middle East in the Great War*. Cambridge MA: Harvard University Press, 2014.

Fell, Alison. "Nursing the Other: The Representation of Colonial Troops in French and British First World War Nursing Memoirs." In Das, *Race, Empire and First World War Writing*, 158–74.

Fine, Gary Alan. "Dying for a Laugh: Negotiating Risk and Creating Personas in the Humor of Mushroom Collectors." *Western Folklore* 47, no. 3 (July 1988): 177–94.

Fogarty, Richard. *Race & War in France: Colonial Subjects in the French Army, 1914–1918*. Baltimore: Johns Hopkins University Press, 2008.

Fogarty, Richard, and Andrew Jarboe, eds. *Empires in World War I*. New York: I. B. Tauris, 2014.

Ford, Caroline. *Creating the Nation in Provincial France: Religion and Political Identity in Brittany*. Princeton: Princeton University Press, 1993.

Ford, Roger. *Eden to Armageddon: The First World War in the Middle East*. London: Weidenfeld & Nicolson, 2009.

Frankau, Gilbert. "The Left Barrel." In Beaver, *"Wipers Times,"* 67.

Frankl, Victor. *Man's Search for Meaning*. New York: Pocket Books, 1984.

Frémeaux, Jacques. *Les colonies dans la grande guerre: Combats et épreuves des peuples d'outre-mer*. Saint-Cloud, France: 14–18 éditions, 2014.

French, David. "The Strategy of the Entente Powers, 1914–1917." In *World War I: A History*, edited by Hew Strachan, 54–65. Oxford: Oxford University Press, 1998.

Freud, Sigmund. *Jokes and Their Relation to the Unconscious*. New York: W. W. Norton & Company, 1989.

Fritzsche, Peter. *Reading Berlin 1900*. Cambridge MA: Harvard University Press, 1996.

Fuller, J. G. *Troop Morale and Popular Culture in the British and Dominion Armies 1914–1918*. Oxford: Clarendon Press, 1990.

Fussell, Paul. *The Great War and Modern Memory*. Oxford: Oxford University Press, 1975.

Garrigues, Jean. *Banania: Histoire d'une passion française*. Paris: Du May, 1991.

Gildea, Robert. *Children of the Revolution: The French, 1799–1914*. New York: Penguin Books, 2008.

Gleisner, Nichole T. "Soldier-Poet or Écrivain-Combattant: How the French Trenches of World War I Defined Witnessing." *Studies in 20th & 21st Century Literature* 41, no. 2, article 10 (2017): https://doi.org/10.4148/2334-4415.1929.

Government of India. *India's Contribution to the Great War*. Calcutta: Superintendent Government Printing, India, 1923.

Graves, Robert. *Good-Bye to All That*. New York: Random House, 1957, 1998. First published 1929 by Jonathan Cape & Harrison Smith (New York).

Grayzel, Susan. *Women's Identities at War: Gender, Motherhood, and Politics in Britain and France During the First World War*. Chapel Hill: University of North Carolina Press, 1999.

Greenhalgh, Elizabeth. *Victory through Coalition: Britain and France during the First World War*. Cambridge: Cambridge University Press, 2005.

Guoqi, Xu. *Strangers on the Western Front: Chinese Workers in the Great War*. Cambridge MA: Harvard University Press, 2011.

Hale, Dana. "French Images of Race on Product Trademarks During the Third Republic." In Peabody and Stovall, *Color of Liberty*, 131–46.

Hanna, Martha. *The Mobilization of Intellect: French Scholars and Writers during the Great War*. Cambridge MA: Harvard University Press, 1996.

———— . *Your Death Would Be Mine: Paul and Marie Pireaud in the Great War.* Cambridge MA: Harvard University Press, 2006.

Hart, Peter. *The Great War: A Combat History of the First World War.* Oxford: Oxford University Press, 2013.

Hemingway, Ernest. *The Letters of Ernest Hemingway, 1907–1922.* Vol 1, edited by Sandra Spanier and Robert Trogdon. Cambridge: Cambridge University Press, 2011.

Herzog, Rudolph. *Dead Funny: Humor in Hitler's Germany.* Translated by Jefferson Chase. New York: Melville House, 2011.

Hobsbawm, Eric, and Terence Ranger. *The Invention of Tradition.* New York: Cambridge University Press, 1983.

Hochschild, Adam. *King Leopold's Ghost: A Story of Greed, Terror, and Heroism in Colonial Africa.* Boston: Houghton Mifflin, 1998.

Holland, Norman. *Laughing: A Psychology of Humor.* Ithaca NY: Cornell University Press, 1982.

Hull, Isabel. *Absolute Destruction: Military Culture and the Practices of War in Imperial Germany.* Ithaca NY: Cornell University Press, 2005.

Hynes, Samuel. *The Soldiers' Tale, Bearing Witness to Modern War.* New York: Penguin, 1997.

———— . *A War Imagined: The First World War and English Culture.* New York: Atheneum, 1991.

Jarboe, Andrew. *Indian Soldiers in World War I: Race and Representation in an Imperial War.* Lincoln: University of Nebraska Press, 2021.

———— . "Propaganda and Empire in the Heart of Europe: Indian Soldiers in Hospital and Prison, 1914–1918." In *Empires in World War I*, edited by Richard Fogarty and Andrew Jarboe, 107–35. New York: I. B. Tauris, 2014.

Johnson, Harry H. *The Black Man's Part in the War: An Account of the Dark-Skinned Population of the British Empire; How It Is and Will Be Affected by the Great War; and The Share It Has Taken in Waging That War.* London: Simpkin, Marshall, Hamilton, Kent, 1917.

Jones, Heather. "The German Empire." In *Empires at War: 1911–1923*, edited by Robert Gunwarth and Erez Manelar, 52–72. Oxford: Oxford University Press, 2014.

Keshen, Jeff. "The Great War Soldier as Nation Builder in Canada and Australia." In Busch, *Canada and the Great War*, 1–25.

Kidd, William. "Representation or Recuperation? The French Colonies and 1914–1918 War Memorials." In *Promoting the Colonial Idea: Propaganda and Visions of Empire in France*, edited by Tony Chafer and Amanda Sackur, 184–94. New York: Palgrave, 2002.

Klein, Martin. *Slavery and Colonial Rule in French West Africa.* Cambridge: Cambridge University Press, 1998.

Koller, Christian. "Enemy Images: Race and Gender Stereotypes in the Discussion on Colonial Troops. A Franco-German Comparison, 1914–1923."

In *Home/Front, The Military, War and Gender in Twentieth-Century Germany*, edited by Karen Hagemann and Stefanie Schüler-Springorum, 139–57. New York: Berg, 2002.

———. "Representing Otherness: African, Indian and European Soldiers' Letters and Memoirs." In Das, *Race, Empire and First World War Writing*, 127–42.

Koureas, Gabriel. *Memory, Masculinity and National Identity in British Visual Culture, 1914–1930: A Study of 'Unconquerable Manhood.'* Burlington VT: Ashgate, 2007.

Kutzer, M. Daphne. *Empire's Children: Empire & Imperialism in Classic British Children's Books*. New York: Garland Publishing, 2000.

Landau, Paul, and Deborah Kaspin. *Images and Empires: Visuality in Colonial and Postcolonial Africa*. Berkeley: University of California Press, 2002.

Langbehn, Volker, and Mohammad Salama, eds. *German Colonialism: Race, the Holocaust, and Postwar Germany*. New York: Columbia University Press, 2011.

Le Naour, Jean-Yves. *La honte noire: L'allemagne et les troupes coloniales françaises, 1914–1945*. Paris: Hachette littératures, 2003.

Liebau, Heike, Katrin Bromber, Katharina Lange, Dyala Hamzah, and Ravi Ahuja, eds. *The World in World Wars: Experiences, Perceptions and Perspectives from Africa and Asia*. Studies in Global Social History. Leiden, The Netherlands: Koninklijke Brill NV, 2010.

Lipman, Steve. *Laughter in Hell: The Use of Humor during the Holocaust*. Northvale NJ: Jason Aronson, 1991.

Lloyd, David. *Battlefield Tourism: Pilgrimage and Commemoration of the Great War in Britain, Australia and Canada, 1919–1939*. New York: Berg, 1998.

Loubère, P. *"Pro patria": Le bon evêque de Meaux*. 1914. Poster, lithograph, color, 44 x 32 cm. A. Lasnier, Paris. https://www.loc.gov/resource/cph.3f04005/.

Lucas, Charles. *The Empire at War*. Oxford: Oxford University Press, 1921.

Lunn, Joe. *Memoirs of the Maelstrom: A Senegalese Oral History of the First World War*. Portsmouth NH: Heinemann, 1999.

Lyautey, Maréchal. *Le rôle social de l'officier*. Paris: Bartillat, 2003.

Lyons, Martyn. *The Writing Culture of Ordinary People in Europe, c. 1860–1920*. Cambridge: Cambridge University Press, 2013.

Mackaman, Douglas, and Michael Mays. *World War I and the Cultures of Modernity*. Jackson: University Press of Mississippi, 2000.

MacKenzie, John, ed., *Popular Imperialism and the Military, 1850–1950*. Manchester, UK: Manchester University Press, 1992.

MacLeod, G. Hamilton. *The Blight of Kultur*. London and Edinburgh: Sampson Low, Marston, 1918.

Maguire, Anna. *Contact Zones of the First World War: Cultural Encounters across the British Empire*. Cambridge: Cambridge University Press, 2021.

Marlantes, Karl. *What It Is Like to Go to War*. New York: Grove Press, 2011.

Matikkala, Mira. *Empire and Imperial Ambition: Liberty, Englishness and Anti-Imperialism in Late-Victorian Britain*. New York: I. B. Tauris, 2011.

McPhail, Helen. Translator's note to *Men at War 1914–1918: National Sentiment and Trench Journalism in France during the First World War* by Stéphane Audoin-Rouzeau, viii. Translated by Helen McPhail. Providence RI: Berg Publishers, 1992.

McClintock, Anne. *Imperial Leather: Race, Gender and Sexuality in the Colonial Contest*. New York: Routledge, 1995.

Merewether, J. W. B., and Frederick Smith. *The Indian Corps in France*. 2nd ed. London: John Murray, 1919.

Metcalf, Barbara, and Thomas Metcalf. *A Concise History of India*. Cambridge: Cambridge University Press, 2002.

Metcalf, Thomas. *Imperial Connections, India and the Indian Ocean Arena, 1860–1920*. Berkeley: University of California Press, 2007.

Meyer, Jessica. *Men of War: Masculinity and the First World War in Britain*. Genders and Sexualities in History. New York: Palgrave Macmillan, 2009.

Millard, Candice. *Hero of Empire: The Boer War, A Daring Escape and the Making of Winston Churchill*. New York: Doubleday, 2016.

Morrow, John. *The Great War: An Imperial History*. New York: Routledge, 2004.

Morton-Jack, George. *The Indian Empire at War: From Jihad to Victory, the Untold Story of the Indian Army in the First World War*. London: Little, Brown, 2018.

"Mort pour la France." In Beaver, *"Wipers Times,"* 244.

Murphy, Libby. *The Art of Survival: France and the Great War Picaresque*. New Haven CT: Yale University Press, 2016.

Nasson, Bill. *Springboks on the Somme: South Africa in the Great War, 1914–1918*. New York: Penguin Books, 2007.

Nelson, Robert L. "German Comrades—Slavic Whores, Gender Images in the German Soldier Newspapers of the First World War." In *Home/Front, the Military, War and Gender in Twentieth-Century Germany*, edited by Karen Hagemann and Stefanie Schüler-Springorum, 69–85. New York: Berg, 2002.

——— . *German Soldier Newspapers of the First World War*. New York: Cambridge University Press, 2011.

Nora, Pierre, ed. *Les lieux de mémoire*. 3 vols. Paris: Gallimard, 1984.

Northcliffe, Lord. *At the War*. London: Hodder & Stoughton, 1916.

Nunn, Wilfred. *Tigris Gunboats: The Forgotten War in Iraq 1914–1917*. London: Chatham Publishing, 2007.

Obrdlik, Antonin. "'Gallows Humor'—A Sociological Phenomenon," *American Journal of Sociology* 47, no. 5 (March 1942): 709–16.

Omissi, David. *Indian Voices of the Great War: Soldier's Letters, 1914–1918*. New York: St. Martin's Press, 1999.

Osborn, E. B. "Trench Journals." *Times Literary Supplement*, October 12, 1916, 482.

Parliamentary Recruiting Committee. *Surely You Will Fight for Your [Portrait of King George V] and [Map of Great Britain]. Come Along, Boys, before It Is Too Late*. 1915. Poster, lithograph with halftone color, 74 x 50 cm. Jas. Truscott & Son, London. https://www.loc.gov/item/2003663086/.

Peabody, Sue, and Tyler Stovall. *The Color of Liberty: Histories of Race in France.* Durham NC: Duke University Press, 2003.

Pegler, Martin. *Soldiers' Songs and Slang of the Great War.* Oxford: Osprey Publishing, 2014.

Persell, Stuart Michael. *The French Colonial Lobby 1889–1938.* Stanford CA: Hoover Institution Press, 1983.

Peterson, Derek. *Creative Writing: Translation, Bookkeeping, and the Work of Imagination in Colonial Kenya.* Portsmouth NH: Heinemann, 2004.

Pieterse, Jan Nederveen. *White on Black: Images of Africa and Blacks in Western Popular Culture.* New Haven CT: Yale University Press, 1992.

Pioneer [pseud.]. "To the P.B.I.: An Appreciation." In Beaver, *"Wipers Times,"* 131.

Porte, Rémy. *Du Caire à Damas, Français et Anglais au Proche-Orient (1914–1919).* Paris: Soteca, 2008.

Porter, Bernard. *The Absent-Minded Imperialists: Empire, Society, and Culture in Britain.* Oxford: Oxford University Press, 2004.

——— . *Critics of Empire: British Radicals and the Imperial Challenge.* New York: I. B. Tauris, 2008.

Pound, Reginald. *The Lost Generation.* London: Constable, 1964.

Pradhan, S. D. *Indian Army in East Africa, 1914–1918.* New Dehli: National Book Organisation, 1991.

Prud'homme, René. *Le fusil et le pinceau: Souvenirs du Poilu René Prud'homme 124e ri.* Saint-Cyr-sur-Loire, France: A. Sutton, 2007.

Ramamurthy, Anandi. *Imperial Persuaders: Images of Africa and Asia in British Advertising.* New York: Manchester University Press, 2003.

Reboux, Paul, and Charles Muller. *A la Manière de . . .* Paris: Bernard Grasset, 1913.

Richards, Jeffrey. *Imperialism and Juvenile Literature.* New York: Manchester University Press, 1989.

RME. "The Disc Identity." In *Another Garland from the Front,* edited by F. B. Bagshaw and R. M. Eassie, 107. London: George Pullman & Sons, 1916. https://www.canadiana.ca/view/oocihm.9_09548/109.

Robertson, Emily. "Norman Linsday and the 'Asianisation' of the German Soldier in Australia during the First World War." In *The British Empire and the First World War,* edited by Ashley Jackson, 172–92. New York: Routledge, 2016.

Roper, Michael. *The Secret Battle: Emotional Survival in the Great War.* New York: Manchester University Press, 2009.

Said, Edward. *Culture and Imperialism.* New York: Alfred A. Knopf, 1993.

——— . *Orientalism.* New York: Pantheon Books, 1978.

Sainéan, Lazare. *L'argot des tranchées.* Paris: Éditions de Boccard, 1915.

Sansom, A. J. *Letters from France, Written between June 1915–July 1917.* Edited by Ivy Sansom. London: Andrew Melrose, 1921.

Schneer, Jonathan. *London 1900: The Imperial Metropolis.* New Haven: Yale University Press, 1999.

Schneider, William. *An Empire for the Masses: The French Popular Image of Africa, 1870–1900*. Westport CT: Greenwood Press, 1982.

Scott, James C. *Domination and the Arts of Resistance: Hidden Transcripts*. New Haven CT: Yale University Press, 1990.

———. *Weapons of the Weak: Everyday Forms of Peasant Resistance*. New Haven CT: Yale University Press, 1985.

Seal, Graham. *The Soldiers' Press: Trench Journals in the First World War*. New York: Palgrave Macmillan, 2013.

Séché, Alphonse. *Les noirs: D'après des documents officiels*. Paris: Payot, 1919.

Shurtleff, Len. Foreword to *Canada and the Great War: Western Front Association Papers*. Edited by Briton Busch, x–xi. Ithaca NY: McGill-Queen's University Press, 2003.

Singha, Radhika. *The Coolie's Great War: Indian Labour in a Global Conflict, 1914–1921*. Oxford: Oxford University Press, 2020.

Sinha, Mrinalini. *Colonial Masculinity: The 'Manly Englishman' and the 'Effeminate Bengali' in the Late Nineteenth Century*. Studies in Imperialism. New York: Manchester University Press, 1995.

———. *Specters of Mother India*. Radical Perspectives. Durham NC: Duke University Press, 2006.

Smith, Leonard. *Between Mutiny and Obedience: The Case of the French Fifth Infantry Division during World War I*. Princeton NJ: Princeton University Press, 1994.

Stice, Elizabeth. "Contrast and Contact: Civilians in French Trench Newspapers of the Great War." *French History* 34, no. 1 (March 2020): https://doi.org/10.1093/fh/crz109.

Stocking, George. *Victorian Anthropology*. New York: Free Press, 1987.

Stoler, Ann. *Carnal Knowledge and Imperial Power: Race and the Intimate in Colonial Rule*. Berkeley: University of California Press, 2002.

Stovall, Tyler. "The Color Line behind the Lines: Racial Violence in France during the Great War." *American Historical Review* 103, no. 3 (Jun., 1998): 737–69.

Strachan, Hew. *The First World War*. New York: Penguin, 2003.

———. *The First World War in Africa*. Oxford: Oxford University Press, 2004.

———. *The First World War: To Arms*. Oxford: Oxford University Press, 2001.

Streets, Heather. *Martial Races: The Military, Race and Masculinity in British Imperial Culture, 1857–1914*. New York: Manchester University Press, 2004.

Temkin, Moshik. "Culture vs. Kultur, or a Clash of Civilizations: Public Intellectuals in the United States and the Great War, 1917–1918." *Historical Journal* 58, no. 1 (2015): 157–82. https://doi.org/10.1017/S0018246X14000594.

Terdiman, Richard. *Discourse/Counter-Discourse: The Theory and Practice of Symbolic Resistance in Nineteenth-Century France*. Ithaca NY: Cornell University Press, 1985.

Thayer, William Roscoe. *Germany vs. Civilization: Notes on the Atrocious War*. Boston: Houghton Mifflin, 1916.

Thomas, Martin, and Richard Toye. *Arguing about Empire: Imperial Rhetoric in Britain and France, 1882–1956*. Oxford: Oxford University Press, 2017.

Thompson, Andrew. *The Empire Strikes Back? The Impact of Imperialism on Britain from the Mid-Nineteenth Century*. London: Pearson, 2005.

Todman, Dan. *The Great War: Myth and Memory*. New York: Hambledon and London, 2005.

Turhan, Filiz. *The Other Empire: British Romantic Writings about the Ottoman Empire*. New York: Routledge, 2003.

Van Emden, Richard. *The Trench: Experiencing Life on the Front Line, 1916*. New York: Bantam Press, 2002.

Watson, Alexander. *Enduring the Great War: Combat, Morale and Collapse in the German and British Armies, 1914–1918*. Cambridge: Cambridge University Press, 2008.

Weber, Eugen. *Peasants into Frenchmen: The Modernization of Rural France, 1870–1914*. Stanford CA: Stanford University Press, 1976.

Wilder, Gary. "Panafricanism and the Republican Political Sphere." In Peabody and Stovall, *Color of Liberty*, 237–58.

Willcocks, James. *With the Indians in France*. London: Constable and Company, 1920.

Williams, John. *ANZACS, the Media, and the Great War*. Sydney: University of New South Wales Press, 1999.

Williamson, Henry. Foreword to *"Wipers Times," A Complete Facsimile of the Famous World War One Trench Newspaper, Incorporating the "New Church Times," the "Kemmel Times," the "Somme Times," the "B.E.F. Times," and the "Better Times,"* edited by Patrick Beaver, ix–x. London: P. Davies, 1973.

Winter, Jay. *Sites of Memory, Sites of Mourning: The Great War in European Cultural History*. Cambridge: Cambridge University Press, 1995.

——— . *War beyond Words: Languages of Remembrance from the Great War to the Present*. Cambridge: Cambridge University Press, 2017.

Winter, Jay, and Jean-Louis Robert. *Capital Cities at War: Paris, London, Berlin 1914–1919*. Studies in the Social and Cultural History of Modern Warfare. Cambridge: Cambridge University Press, 1997.

Wohl, Robert. *The Generation of 1914*. Cambridge MA: Harvard University Press, 1979.

Wolff, Larry. *Inventing Eastern Europe: The Map of Civilization on the Mind of the Enlightenment*. Stanford: Stanford University Press, 1994.

Zimmerer, Jürgen, and Michael Perraudin. *German Colonialism and National Identity*. New York: Routledge, 2011.

INDEX

Studies in War, Society, and the Military

Civilians in the Path of War
Edited by Mark Grimsley and
Clifford J. Rogers

A Scientific Way of War: Antebellum
Military Science, West Point, and the
Origins of American Military Thought
Ian C. Hope

Picture This: World War I
Posters and Visual Culture
Edited and with an introduction by
Pearl James

Indian Soldiers in World War I: Race
and Representation in an Imperial War
Andrew T. Jarboe

Death Zones and Darling Spies: Seven
Years of Vietnam War Reporting
Beverly Deepe Keever

For Home and Country: World War
I Propaganda on the Home Front
Celia Malone Kingsbury

I Die with My Country: Perspectives
on the Paraguayan War, 1864–1870
Edited by Hendrik Kraay and
Thomas L. Whigham

North American Indians
in the Great War
Susan Applegate Krouse
Photographs and original documentation by Joseph K. Dixon

Remembering World War I in America
Kimberly J. Lamay Licursi

Citizens More than Soldiers:
The Kentucky Militia and
Society in the Early Republic
Harry S. Laver

Soldiers as Citizens: Former
Wehrmacht Officers in the Federal
Republic of Germany, 1945–1955
Jay Lockenour

Deterrence through Strength:
British Naval Power and Foreign
Policy under Pax Britannica
Rebecca Berens Matzke

Army and Empire: British Soldiers
on the American Frontier, 1758–1775
Michael N. McConnell

Of Duty Well and Faithfully
Done: A History of the Regular
Army in the Civil War
Clayton R. Newell and
Charles R. Shrader
With a foreword by
Edward M. Coffman

The Militarization of Culture in
the Dominican Republic, from the
Captains General to General Trujillo
Valentina Peguero

A Religious History of the
American GI in World War II
G. Kurt Piehler

Arabs at War: Military
Effectiveness, 1948–1991
Kenneth M. Pollack

The Politics of Air Power: From
Confrontation to Cooperation in Army
Aviation Civil-Military Relations
Rondall R. Rice

Andean Tragedy: Fighting the
War of the Pacific, 1879–1884
William F. Sater

The Grand Illusion: The
Prussianization of the Chilean Army
William F. Sater and Holger H. Herwig

Sex Crimes under the Wehrmacht
David Raub Snyder

In the School of War
Roger J. Spiller
Foreword by John W. Shy